S0-BEA-830

POWER AND POVERTY

POWER AND POVERTY

DEVELOPMENT AND DEVELOPMENT PROJECTS IN THE THIRD WORLD

EDITED BY
DONALD W. ATTWOOD,
THOMAS C. BRUNEAU,
AND JOHN G. GALATY

WESTVIEW PRESS / BOULDER AND LONDON

ROBERT MANNING

. OZIER LIBRARY,

DEC 14 1988

Soc
HC
59.72
E44
P68
1988

..Ilahassee, Florida

This book results from a series of seminars held at the Centre for Developing-Area Studies
of McGill University and supported by a grant from the Canadian International Development
Agency. Editing and typing were supported by a grant from the Social Sciences Research
Grants Sub-committee of McGill University. We thank these organizations as well as Linda
Anderson for administering the grants and typing the final manuscript.

Westview Special Studies in Social, Political, and Economic Development

This Westview softcover edition is printed on acid-free paper and bound in softcovers that carry the
highest rating of the National Association of State Textbook Administrators, in consultation with the
Association of American Publishers and the Book Manufacturers' Institute.

All rights reserved. No part of this publication may be reproduced or transmitted in any form or by
any means, electronic or mechanical, including photocopy, recording, or any information storage and
retrieval system, without permission in writing from the publisher.

Copyright © 1988 by Westview Press, Inc.

Published in 1988 in the United States of America by Westview Press, Inc.; Frederick A. Praeger,
Publisher; 5500 Central Avenue, Boulder, Colorado 80301

Library of Congress Cataloging-in-Publication Data
Power and poverty.
  (Westview special studies in social, political, and
economic development)
  Includes index.
  1. Economic development projects—Developing
countries. 2. Economic development projects—
Developing countries—Case studies. 3. Developing
countries—Economic conditions. I. Attwood, Donald W.
II. Bruneau, Thomas C. III. Galaty, John G.
IV. Series.
HC59.72.E44P68 1988   338.9'009172'4   86-32578
ISBN 0-8133-7351-4

Composition for this book originated with conversion of the editors' computer tape.
This book was produced without formal editing by the publisher.

Printed and bound in the United States of America

The paper used in this publication meets the requirements of the American National
Standard for Permanence of Paper for Printed Library Materials Z39.48-1984.

6   5   4   3   2   1

CONTENTS

INTRODUCTION

Donald W. Attwood, Thomas C. Bruneau,
and John G. Galaty

The case studies in this book concern the impact of development projects on societies at various levels of affluence and modernization. They demonstrate the variety of such projects, and the ecological, economic, political and social contexts within which development is attempted but seldom achieved. Indeed, results depend on whether projects are in conflict with these contexts or with other societal goals.

One long-standing question on goals is whether efforts to achieve economic growth can be made compatible with social justice. Some per capita growth is necessary if objectives such as reducing poverty, increasing life expectancies, etc., are to be achieved; but growth in and of itself does not guarantee better livings for the poor. To illustrate these larger issues and to better understand the impact of development projects in widely varying contexts, we commissioned these chapters. Here we shall review the themes which link the chapters together.

State Involvement and International Intervention

In all chapters the predominant role of the state in development is evident. This is true for colonial states in India and Kenya as well as independent nations such as Brazil, Sri Lanka and Upper Volta. Through development schemes, irrigation projects, seed and credit programs, etc., the current role of the state is obvious and paramount. This is in contrast to states which were less interventionist during the earlier industrialization of the West. Today Third World states are active in all aspects of the development process, not only as regulators but also as instigators. This is due to at least three factors:

1. The industrial bourgeoisie, which was crucial for economic development in the West, is missing or weak in many Third World countries

1

today. Due to their precolonial and colonial histories, they are more likely to have 'linked' or 'dependent' bourgeoisies. Thus, if development is to take place, it may fall to the central institution of power, the state, to promote it. States do indeed seek development, some out of genuine concern for their citizens and all to become stronger vis-à-vis neighboring and potentially hostile countries.

2. Third World countries are today seeking to develop when the first and second worlds are already industrialized; they are latecomers. Technology is already elaborated, financial systems are fully defined and markets are in place. It is both easier and more difficult to break into the development process today than it was a century ago: easier in that technology and financing are available and international institutions in place; more difficult in that these systems are already 'tied up' and Third World countries must enter on adverse terms. Consequently, it seems that the entity with the greatest degree of coherence and control—the state—must deal with the external environment in seeking to promote development.

3. One of the defining characteristics of the modern world is the formation and growth of bureaucracies. This is the case whether a society is rich or poor. In fact, relative to other institutions, state bureaucracies are probably larger in Third World nations than in the West. This is due to a number of factors including the residue of colonial institutions and the class interests of elites who led their countries to independence. The state machinery provides employment and power for these elites and their political allies; and bureaucracies acquire their own momentum of growth, which may or may not benefit the publics they claim to serve.

For at least these three reasons, the case studies all reflect the predominant role of the state, whether in irrigation schemes in India, parastatals such as the Autorité des Aménagements des Vallées des Volta in Upper Volta, the Mahaveli project in Sri Lanka or the Bank of Amazonas in Brazil.

The case studies concern development projects at the local level. However, a second obvious theme is the linkage between local, national and international contexts. This is illustrated through the use of foreign experts in Africa, foreign financing in Brazil, Sri Lanka, and Upper Volta, Rockefeller Foundation contributions to the green revolution in India, the involvement of USAID and Harvard University in Sudan, and the need for export markets in most cases. Development is an international process which is both constrained and facilitated by foreign linkages. Most chapters focus on the local level, but they also call attention to the international context. This is highlighted, for example, in Sudan, where foreign experts and funds are obvious at all points in the project, and is implicit in the Brazilian Amazon, where World Bank financing and the stress laid on exports are necessitated by a foreign debt of more than $100 billion.

The predominant role of the state and the international context of development create tension in the legitimation of policies. To citizens of the Third World, development is largely a foreign experience and has been justified as a national goal by results attained elsewhere. Despite attempts at creating indigenous models, such as Ujamaa villages in Tanzania, development remains a Western concept, and as such it is open to question by revitalization movements such as fundamentalist Islam. There is a problem of legitimation because the promise of development has been much greater than the payoff and because goals and means may well clash with indigenous values and habits.

The case studies present a number of counter movements outside official development programs. One is the Sarvodaya movement, which has deep roots in the cultural and religious traditions of Sri Lanka and is consequently less susceptible to the sort of disillusionment endemic to official programs and ideologies. Another example is the Catholic church in the Amazon which, through the Basic Christian Communities, has questioned the development ideology of the state (Bruneau 1982, 1986).

Heavy state involvement means that development is often more a political than an economic process. Development everywhere and at all times involves some people gaining and others losing. The fate of the poor depends on variations in local and regional power relations between classes. The benefits of development are distributed more or less inequitably, depending on the nature and strength, alliances and conflicts, of different pressure groups. In the Amazon, for instance, Schmink's chapter shows the high degree of conflict between *latifundia* and smallholders, in which the state supports the former and church groups work with the latter. Worby's chapter shows how the Tribal Grazing Land Policy has been used by one stratum to increase its land claims. In Sudan, Huntington demonstrates how development projects necessarily involve political conflicts not only between local inhabitants and outsiders, but also within villages, tribes and government agencies. Development is not, then, a straightforward process of introducing new technology or capital and waiting for improvement. Rather, different groups and classes struggle over inputs and benefits, and the results are largely determined by their political strength. The predominant role of the state and the involvement of foreign institutions ensure that the political stakes are high in most development projects.

The View from the Countryside

Development projects look very different through the eyes of the small peasant. From the local level, contact with the state is mainly through government projects and the market. The state is seen as the urban locus of power. Programs and schemes emanate from legislatures and ministerial offices and assume specific form through officials who are posted in small towns or villages but whose loyalty is back to the urban centers that dispatched them. Development projects look very different through the eyes of the small peasant.

From the state's point of view, development requires increased agricultural production and increased appropriation of 'surplus' from the countryside (Hart 1982). Put succinctly, development requires the 'capturing of the peasantry' by the state (Hyden 1980). However, large-scale, state-generated projects often bring little improvement to the small-holding peasants who constitute the bulk of Third World people. The 'blueprint' approach to development (Hyden 1987) is sharply criticized from two angles: that it has not worked at all; or that it has worked to benefit the wrong people, i.e., urbanites, bureaucrats and rural elites. These indictments emerge in most of the case studies.

Development projects often fail precisely because they have not benefitted rural producers. A 'bottom-up' approach might succeed both in raising output and bettering living standards where the 'top-down' approach has failed, but successful models are few and the chances of their widespread replication seem limited.

Goulet presents an account of a "people's alternative," the Sarvodaya Movement in Sri Lanka, which would awaken both spiritual and material potentials through village-level mobilization. Its philosophy presents an integrated ideal of development, which is conceived not simply as an economic process but as one with moral, cultural, spiritual, social, political, and economic goals. But can these ideals be implemented? It seems that Sarvodaya requires some closing of society to the corruption of outside forces. However, the earlier experiences of Burma, China, and Tanzania do not bode well for the practical implications of withdrawal or delinkage from the world economic system.

In Sudan, the Abyei Rural Development Project among the Dinka was supported by USAID, with the aim of relying on local participation within a framework of "integrated rural development," which would link economic advancement with greater equality and concern for the poor. However, the system of participation envisaged by project planners was unworkable in the local context, and the project achieved none of its goals.

Rural dwellers are shrewd in identifying their own interests and discerning who benefits from a particular scheme or innovation. In parts of the Third World, they have often eluded state control simply through forms of passive resistance. When they have embraced initiatives, villagers try to manipulate them for their own ends rather than for the imagined ends of government or international planners. It is mandatory to understand the perspectives of the countryside: first, in order to see why projects are often resisted, and second, to recognize and encourage local innovations—to foster a 'greenhouse' approach in place of the 'blueprint' (Hyden 1987).

Trade and the Market

It is difficult to measure the short-term impact of investment or new technology on rural productivity, so the expansion of trade often serves as an indicator of development. Whether government policies lean toward greater or lesser involvement in the production and distribution of goods, it is necessary for any state to encourage and extract surplus production from the countryside. The state attempts to finance itself directly through taxation and parastatal enterprises and indirectly through international trade. Thus, much of what passes for "development policy" amounts to promoting export crops in order to repay foreign debts, as several of the case studies indicate.

However, this emphasis may have detrimental effects on the peasants, as they are lured away from subsistence to cash crop production. Reyna describes some of the negative effects of large-scale cotton production in Upper Volta, where land was appropriated by the state and reallocated to tenant farmers—the latter suffering from lack of control over their own production, low cotton prices and inadequate supply of subsistence crops. While the production of cash crops may be imperative for the state, the returns to peasants may be inadequate to guarantee subsistence. Rural living standards may decline both because governments force down crop prices (to lower urban costs of living and to raise the profits of state marketing boards) and because of fluctuations in international commodity prices. One of the few options for peasants in these circumstances is withdrawal from the commercial system, as seen in the uprooting of coffee plants in Tanzania and Uganda.

Restrained market involvement is often viewed by governments—of whatever ideological stripe—as indicative of the peasants' 'conservative' character. Advocates of the free market accuse peasants of not being 'price-responsive,' while advocates of a planned economy accuse them of not being adequately responsive to national needs and the imperative to build socialism. Peasants are perceived as offering only as much produce for external distribution as is necessary to supply their own domestic cash and commodity needs, which are thought to be inelastic. The rest of their produce, so the argument goes, is withheld from the market, or else their productive capacity is underutilized. Both Worby and Bennett review this argument with respect to African pastoralists, whose production of livestock is appropriate for non-market accumulation as 'capital on the hoof.' Indeed, the assumed resistance of pastoralists to selling their livestock has led them to be characterized as quintessential conservatives who refuse to act to their own economic advantage.

The argument is partially correct in its observation that peasants and pastoralists often see marketing processes not as a set of opportunities to maximize their returns, but rather as one among several ways to ensure their survival. Particularly in Africa, it is risky to become more assimilated to market systems which are often too weak to ensure consistent supplies of food when local shortages occur. In short, 'market rationality' is often not rational for the peasant.

Rural producers are, however reluctantly, much involved with markets and are integrated into local, regional, national and international exchange systems. The Botswana economy, in Worby's account, depends heavily on the export of livestock, largely to South Africa, for its balance of payments. Masai pastoralists in Kenya and Tanzania sell thousands of animals each year. Most areas of rural Africa experience a proliferation of periodic markets where local produce and crafts are sold, primarily for local consumption. Indeed, in cases such as Uganda and Ghana, where national market networks have collapsed due to lack of transport, low crop prices and official corruption, local markets and subsistence production have flourished, often using barter rather than cash. The dismal decline in food production in Africa over the last decade results partly from such problems, since low crop prices discourage innovation and increases in productivity.

Where higher crop prices are allowed to encourage production, however, planners sometimes assume that privatization of land claims will also increase production for the market. Worby discusses the historical roots and current implementation of the Tribal Grazing Land Policy (TGLP) in Botswana, a policy which rests on a theory of development and a British historical precedent—the idea that privatization and enclosure of rural areas are necessary for the development of commercial livestock production. The same theory underlies several programs for livestock development reviewed by Bennett, including the Kenyan commercial and group ranch programs. In both Botswana and Kenya, privatization and commercialization are buffered by land rights secured for smaller subsistence-oriented stock-holders in 'communal' and 'group' areas. It is clear, however, that long-run planning in both cases envisions the gradual incorporation of these areas into more intensive production, with probable transformation of their tenure systems to individual and private holdings.

Poverty and Development

A crucial dilemma faced by all developing nations is whether to follow a development strategy emphasizing economic growth, or social justice, or (ideally) some combination of growth with equity. Some emphasis on economic growth is required in order to raise living standards and compensate for rapid population expansion. However, even limited gains in per capita agricultural output have proven very difficult to achieve in many countries. Before the late 1970s, agricultural output in China and India barely kept pace with population growth. Meanwhile, many nations in sub-Saharan Africa, unlike those in Asia and Latin America, have experienced declining per capita agricultural output (World Bank 1986:190).

Even where growth has been achieved, however, there are frequent doubts about its effects on the poor. As Worby's chapter suggests, development planners are often caught in a dilemma between promoting commercial expansion by relatively wealthy farmers and herders, which may increase inequality, or redistributing resources in favor of the poor, which may retard economic growth. Although the problem is a general one, the specific processes linking growth and income distribution are highly variable from one region to another.

Several chapters (those by Worby, Reyna, and Schmink) describe situations in Africa and Latin America where greater inequality and even, perhaps, greater poverty result from commercial expansion in the agricultural sector. On the other hand, Attwood's chapter shows that the green revolution in India has not led to widespread displacement of small farmers or to greater unemployment for landless laborers and that the rural poor have even derived a number of new opportunities from this process of technological and commercial expansion. India's experience, similar to that of other Asian countries, is quite different from Africa's and Latin America's. Much of the Asian countryside has been densely occupied by peasant family holdings for centuries, making large-scale commercial land appropriations politically and economically unfeasible. Consequently, where cash-cropping flourishes in Asia, it involves many small and middle farmers, as well as larger ones.

The chapters by Worby and Schmink document the opposite situation, where thinly settled land is opened for commercial exploitation. In Brazil's northeastern and Amazonian regions, there is little political power in the hands of small farmers, so they are easily displaced by

'development' projects in the hands of big corporations and state bureaucracies. In Botswana, there is at least an official ideology in favor
of development for small-scale producers; but this ideology, according
to Worby, is in conflict with the government's need to expand livestock
production for export, which seems more attainable through the promotion of large-scale units.

One reason that policies in Botswana are tacitly biased in favor of
large herders is that government officials themselves invest in livestock
production for export. A similar problem is found in Upper Volta,
where, as Reyna points out, government officials have bought up profitable
cash-cropping lands located near the larger towns.

Whether economic growth does or does not harm the poor in those
few regions where it occurs, there is no doubt that it tends to increase
disparities between regions. Attwood's chapter shows that the rural poor
in India have benefitted from commercial expansion in some regions:
laborers have found more employment, and small farmers have made
their holdings more viable through intensive cash-cropping under irrigation. The condition of the poor in these technologically and commercially advanced regions contrasts with the extreme poverty and
inequality found in the regions which are economically stagnant. In-
terregional disparities are due to differential resource endowments and
levels of state investment in infrastructure, and they are also due to
differences in the political power of the peasantry. In northwestern India,
the heartland of the green revolution, small and middle farmers have
considerable political influence, giving them some control over development policies (Brass 1980). This is much less true, however, in
northeastern India, where the class structure is more polarized and the
economy stagnant.

The fate of the poor, then, is strongly influenced by regional power
structures. These chapters show that development is a *political* process,
often controlled by a limited elite or a particular ethnic group. Huntington's chapter describes eloquently how this occurs and the consequences in terms of projects which go nowhere. Some observers claim
that the market economy, allied with new technology, automatically
brings about a concentration of wealth; but the greater danger to the
poor seems to be the concentration of political power, which occurs
even in 'socialist' states.

Changes in the incidence and severity of poverty can only be understood
through comparative case studies, such as those presented here, which
take account of natural resources, droughts, diseases, population dynamics, etc., as well as politics, commercialization and technical change.
For example, Worby's chapter mentions that new opportunities for
commercial production among pastoralists may increase income disparities

and drive smaller herdowners off the land, while Bennett points out that epidemic diseases, droughts and land policies disrupting customary grazing patterns have had similar effects. The sloughing off of small herd-owners from pastoral society is not a new process. Small herders are particularly vulnerable to accidents, epidemics, droughts, theft and warfare, which may reduce their herds below the level needed for self-sustaining production and drive the herdsmen into laboring occupations in settled communities (Barth 1964). Whether increased commercial production accelerates these long-standing processes remains to be determined.

Variations in natural environments and in the populations they can sustain are of fundamental importance in the geographic distribution of poverty. The chapters by Ludden and Attwood emphasize that the impact of commercial agriculture varies greatly in different regions of India, depending first on rainfall patterns and then on investments in irrigation and other essential infrastructure by the state. The different cropping systems, which vary between wet and dry, tend to nurture different patterns of inequality, political power, population pressure and poverty.

Reyna's chapter also discusses population and poverty. Rapid population growth in the Mossi Plateau area of Upper Volta forced small farmers with large families to look elsewhere for employment. Reyna argues that the main cause was rising fertility rates during the colonial period, a trend which he attributes to economic pressure from the colonial state—pressure which forced families to produce more children in order to have more hands to do the work. However, many demographers would stress declining mortality rates as the primary cause of rapid population growth. Certainly since regular census data have become available, the trend in West Africa has been one of stable fertility combined with declining mortality rates (Hart 1982: 131–34; World Bank 1986:230). If we compare this with long-term data from a country such as India, where reliable censuses have been available since 1871, the same trend is found (Visaria and Visaria 1983), suggesting that changes in mortality, in these drought- and disease-ridden countries, are the main causes of increasing population pressure.

Although we may disagree about the causes of rapid population growth, the consequences clearly include the threat of increasing poverty (cf. Attwood 1979). Demographic factors thus combine with political, economic, technical and environmental factors to weave a complex tapestry of rural poverty. Poverty is not the result of any one set of factors, nor is it likely to be cured by any single prescription.

Economic growth, for example, may be essential to reduce poverty, but it does not necessarily benefit the poor. When the poorer countries are compared among themselves, differences in output per capita do not always correlate with differences in living standards for the poor. For example, the countries of South Asia are about as poor (in terms of GNP per capita) as those of sub-Saharan Africa; yet their average life expectancy and literacy rates were higher (Morris and McAlpin 1982:36). This indicates that some poor countries have been more efficient than others at delivering primary health care, education and other basic services.

If economic output does not predict social performance, neither does type of regime. One revealing comparison is that between China and India, two giant nations with similar problems. China has emphasized mass literacy and health care more than India, producing higher literacy rates and longer life expectancy (Morris and McAlpin 1982: 24–25). On the other hand, Sri Lanka, which has about the same GNP per capita as China, and which does not have a revolutionary socialist regime, nevertheless has similar literacy rates and life expectancy (World Bank 1986:232, 236). In fact, Sri Lanka's rates are above average even for middle-income countries.

These comparisons indicate that we cannot predict poverty reduction from economic output, nor from a superficial labelling of policies and regimes. We need to understand why some regions and countries have made progress against poverty with limited resources, and whether their example can be replicated elsewhere. Comparative case studies, such as those presented here, are essential to sort out these problems.

The theme of this book is that poverty reduction depends more on the distribution of political power than it does on the impact of capital, technology or markets. Where peasants have some access to political influence, or some local autonomy, they are more likely to contribute the information, motivation and local organization which are essential for development projects that really work.

References

Attwood, Donald W. 1979 "Why Some of the Poor Get Richer: Economic Change and Mobility in Rural Western India," *Current Anthropology*, Vol. 20, pp. 495–508, 657–58 (with *CA* comment, pp. 508–16).

Barth, Fredrik 1964 "Capital, Investment and the Social Structure of a Pastoral Nomad Group in South Persia," in Raymond Firth and B.S. Yamey (eds.), *Capital Saving and Credit in Peasant Societies.* Chicago: Aldine.

Brass, Paul R. 1980 "The Politicization of the Peasantry in a North Indian State," *Journal of Peasant Studies*, Vol. 7, pp. 395–426; Vol. 8, pp. 3–36.

Bruneau, Thomas 1982 *The Church in Brazil: The Politics of Religion.* Austin: University of Texas Press.

1986 "Brazil: the Catholic Church and Basic Christian Communities," in Daniel H. Levine (ed.), *Religion and Political Conflict in Latin America*. Chapel Hill: University of North Carolina Press.

Hart, Keith 1982 *The Political Economy of West African Agriculture*. Cambridge: Cambridge University Press.

Hyden, Goran 1980 *Beyond Ujamaa in Tanzania*. Berkeley: University of California Press.

1987 "Approaches to Cooperative Development: Blueprint versus Greenhouse," in D.W. Attwood and B.S. Baviskar (eds.), *Who Shares? Cooperatives in Rural Development*. Delhi: Oxford University Press.

Morris, Morris David and Michelle B. McAlpin 1982 *Measuring the Condition of India's Poor: The Physical Quality of Life Index*. New Delhi: Promilla.

Visaria, Leela and Pravin Visaria 1983 "Population (1757–1947)," in Dharma Kumar (ed.), *The Cambridge Economic History of India*. Vol. 2. Cambridge: Cambridge University Press.

World Bank 1986 *World Development Report 1986*. New York: Oxford University Press.

1

POVERTY, INEQUALITY, AND ECONOMIC GROWTH IN RURAL INDIA

Donald W. Attwood

I

What are the effects of cash cropping on subsistence cultivators? When peasants grow commercial crops, do they endanger their subsistence base, become impoverished, lose their lands? And do agricultural laborers lose their jobs? Such questions have been debated furiously for more than a century. The answers obviously depend on whether we are considering, for example, New World peasants overwhelmed by giant plantations, or Asian peasants selling rice and vegetables in a local market.

This long debate became particularly heated in the late 1960s, when the governments of India and other Asian countries began to promote the spread of new agricultural inputs: high-yielding varieties of seeds, chemical fertilizers, pesticides, better irrigation and new methods of cultivation. The spread of these new inputs unleashed a "green revolution"—a rapid increase in grain production in certain regions, along with a storm of debate about the social impacts of the new technology. Critics of the green revolution argued that the new technology, and the commercialization of production which accompanied it, would impoverish small peasants and agricultural laborers in various ways. For example, small peasants would be unable to afford the new inputs, or would be crushed by debts in efforts to pay for them; in either case, they would be forced to sell off their lands to more competitive large farmers, armed with the new technology. Moreover, agricultural laborers would lose their jobs as a result of mechanization.

The object of this paper is to compare local case studies from various regions in India in order to show whether these pessimistic predictions have been confirmed by experience. In particular, I will summarize my own research in western India, where the social impacts of new technology and commercialization have been traced back over the last hundred years. Several points will be argued here. The first is that the impact of technological change and commercialization varies from region to region. The second is that economic growth in agriculture has occurred primarily in dry regions favored with the establishment of an "irrigation frontier." The third point is that pessimistic predictions are not borne out by the experience of these favored regions: small farmers and landless laborers gain more economic opportunities than they lose. The fourth point is that regions with the worst poverty are those where natural conditions, social structure and lack of infrastructure have inhibited the spread of new technology and cash cropping.

While these are favorable conclusions regarding the social impact of cash cropping and economic growth in rural India, they should not be interpreted to mean that "development" for the poor is an automatic result of such changes. Other factors, which are to some extent independent of economic growth, can also improve the living standards of the poor.

II

It is now two decades since the start of the green revolution in India, and the debate has cooled somewhat. Biplab Dasgupta, a vigorous critic, concedes that the new technology has been adopted by most small farmers wherever the inputs are available and appropriate for local conditions (Dasgupta 1980: 229–32). He also agrees that small farmers have not lost their lands, and agricultural laborers have not been faced with increasing unemployment. A balanced assessment of the changes wrought by the green revolution is given by Sarma (1982). He notes that the new technology widens income disparities but does not generally impoverish small farmers and laborers. On the contrary, more intensive cultivation increases the demand for labor and makes small holdings more viable (ibid. 37–43). Two acres cultivated intensively (with irrigation and double cropping) can support a family better than ten acres cultivated non-intensively. The main problem arising from the green revolution, as emphasized by Sarma and others, is the increase in disparities between regions: between those regions with good soil, irrigation and access to markets, where the new inputs have been adopted successfully, and other regions where agricultural production is stagnant (cf. Lipton 1978).

It should be noted that such regional (and local) disparities are highly intractable, regardless of policy priorities: that is, whether they emphasize economic growth over social equity, or vice versa. Those regions which are more prosperous today have benefitted from very long-term, and expensive, public investments in roads, irrigation and other infrastructure. The more backward regions, consequently, require much more than a supply of new seeds and chemical fertilizers: they need the same heavy investments in infrastructure.

David Ludden's chapter in this volume outlines the historical ecology of Indian agriculture as a basis for understanding the divergent paths of economic change in different regions. Along with other writers (e.g., Stein 1980; Béteille 1974; Beals 1974) he has emphasized the great social, historical and economic differences between "wet" regions of assured rainfall and the drier regions. Most of India gets its rain during just a few months of the year, and half the sub-continent receives less than thirty inches annually (Lewis 1970:18). Consequently, water is supremely important: its abundance or scarcity shapes the techniques of production, the dynamics of population, and the hierarchy of social classes. This chapter, like Ludden's, emphasizes the contrasting changes occurring in wet and dry regions.

Of course, wet zones are not all alike, and there are many transitional regions between the really wet and the really dry. Nevertheless, it is possible to generalize about the contrasts. The wet zones have long had higher population densities with a secure subsistence base; large populations of low-caste, landless laborers; numerically small, high-caste elites of non-cultivating landlords; and rigid, polarized stratification systems. Historically, the main subsistence crop has been rice. The wet-rice regions include the eastern portion of the Gangetic plains, along with the coastal plains and deltas of eastern and southern India.

The dry regions, on the other hand, have long had lower population densities with an insecure subsistence base; smaller populations of low-caste, landless laborers; fewer non-cultivating landlords; and thus more flexible stratification systems dominated by "yeoman peasants" from the middle or upper-middle levels of the caste hierarchy. Before the advent of modern, large-scale irrigation systems, the main subsistence crops were sorghum and millet. These dry regions include the western portion of the Indo-Gangetic plain, along with most of the inland plains and plateaus of western, central and southern India. The dry regions comprise some of the most impoverished, insecure and stagnant portions of the country.

Ecologically and economically, the most favored agricultural areas today are those portions of the dry regions which have received large-scale irrigation systems during the last century or so. These areas include much of the northwest (heartland of the green revolution) and scattered areas in western and southern India. The advantages of these areas are manifold. Irrigation reduces the risk of subsistence crises and multiplies the returns which farmers can obtain from their land. Irrigated land can support a much denser population and small farms become more viable. At the same time, these regions start with lower population densities, so there is less pressure to expand production of traditional subsistence crops; instead, the farmers have room to switch to high-value cash crops like cotton, wheat and sugarcane. In addition, the prevailing stratification systems are flexible, open to economic mobility, and as a result, there are fewer social barriers to innovation and enterprise (Attwood 1984). These favorable conditions can be summed up as the opening of an "irrigation frontier" (Attwood 1985). As in other frontier societies, entrepreneurs are less inhibited by established class relations from gaining access to land, labor, irrigation and capital. The potential wealth expands beyond the control of old elites and is grabbed up by new entrepreneurs (cf. Stone 1984).

The rest of this chapter examines, first, the social impact of commercial agriculture in dry regions favored with irrigation, followed by a look at the rather different problems of the wet regions. Then it discusses in detail the long-term effects of commercial agriculture in western India.

III

Critics of the green revolution rarely make systematic comparisons between what is happening to the poor in regions with high economic growth and what is happening in more backward regions. We are fortunate, however, to have at least one set of case studies covering both types. The Swiss economist, Gilbert Etienne, visited several regions in the mid-1960s before the green revolution and revisited them in 1979 (Etienne 1968; 1982). He was thus able to make comparisons not only between regions but also between conditions before and after the green revolution. What Etienne found is very simple: in the regions of high growth in agricultural production the rural poor are much better off than they were fifteen years ago. They are also much better off (in wage and consumption levels) than their counterparts in the low-growth regions. Etienne makes no precise comparisons between relative inequalities in the high- and low-growth areas, but this question is of secondary importance. What is significant is that the poor have improved their absolute levels of living in the high-growth regions. This pattern holds true particularly for dry regions with irrigation, but it also applies to wet-rice regions with good irrigation where agricultural production has also risen. In these latter areas, employment opportunities and wages have increased, just as in the wheat-growing heartland of the green revolution (ibid. 137). Let us consider the dry regions in more detail.

The rise in agricultural production has been most successful in the northwestern wheat-growing region consisting of Punjab, Haryana, and western Uttar Pradesh states. The prime example of an "irrigation frontier" is in this region, which began to benefit from large-scale canal systems in the mid-nineteenth century (Whitcombe 1972; Stone 1984). After a century of massive and expensive investment in infrastructure, this region was particularly suited for adoption of the new high-yielding varieties of dwarf wheat which were introduced in the mid-1960s. The result has been an 8 percent annual increase in food grain production in Punjab (1960–61 to 1978–79) compared with 2.8 percent for India as a whole (Sarma 1982:27). The dynamic effects of this agricultural boom have also been felt in other sectors of the Punjab economy, giving this state the highest per capita product in the country (ibid.50).

The green revolution in the wheat-growing areas has been extensively discussed and criticized: good summaries of the issues may be found in Sarma (1982) and Sen (1974). Here we shall briefly review the findings of one of the best-informed critics, Biplab Dasgupta (1980). Dasgupta marshalls data from a number of case studies and surveys to demonstrate the failings of the green revolution, but the results are not all negative. Though small farmers are slower to adopt the new technology, most of them do so within a few years (ibid. 229; Sarma 1982:40). Moreover, these small farmers tend to use the new inputs with greater intensity than the larger farmers (ibid.; Dasgupta 1980:232).

On the question of greater inequality resulting from the green revolution, Dasgupta finds several cases in which operated landholdings (but *not* owned lands) have become slightly more concentrated in recent years (ibid. 254–60). However, he makes no systematic comparisons between changes in areas of higher and lower economic growth. (Quite possibly, the ratios of concentration are higher or are increasing more rapidly in the more backward areas?) Data on changes in income or consumption inequality in the green revolution areas are scant and uncertain (ibid. 264–85), though Ahluwalia (1978:36) has found a significant decline in consumption inequality in Punjab and Haryana. Bhalla (1974) also found decreasing income inequalities among farmers who adopted the new technology. However, even if relative inequalities were increasing, they could result from "upward divergence," to borrow a phrase from my colleague, Donald Von Eschen. Upward divergence means the small farmers are moving upward out of poverty, but at a slower rate than the larger ones. While it is not clear whether relative inequalities are increasing in the green revolution areas, the results are probably no worse than suggested by the image of upward divergence.

There is uncertainty about trends in real wages for agricultural laborers, though Dasgupta (1980:330–31) finds that the green revolution has had a favorable impact on real wages, especially in those districts where the new technology has been most heavily adopted. In addition, the total demand for labor in agriculture and ancillary trades and services has been rising very rapidly in these areas, providing more jobs, more diversified employment and much steadier work for laborers and small farmers (Aggarwal 1973). The green revolution, which means raising yields through the use of high-yielding seeds, fertilizer, pesticides and better irrigation, can proceed with or without much mechanization. Moreover, some forms of machinery (such as irrigation pumps) actually increase the demand for labor, and most farms are too small to resort to heavy, labor-displacing mechanization. On balance, more intensive crop production usually means relatively limited mechanization and a higher total demand for labor (Sarma 1982:41–42; cf. Attwood 1987b).

A study of long-term change in one Punjabi village points out that, "with substantially increased crops to be harvested, greater demands for laborers for their transportation, and the development of a variety of off-season occupations for semi-skilled and general labor," more low-caste agricultural laborers "are fully employed at better rates of pay than ever before" (Kessinger 1974:124). Consequently, these laborers are the only local people with no nostalgia for the past. Etienne (1982:134) has also observed that employment expanded and wages rose in many parts of the northwest, where low-caste laborers have found jobs in local industries stimulated by the agricultural boom.

This rising demand for labor has attracted a huge influx of migrants from low-growth regions, such as Bihar and eastern U.P. The result of this migration is that the incidence of absolute poverty may not have declined in Punjab and Haryana (Ahluwalia 1978:34–35). However, this is not an indication of the failure of the green revolution, but rather its success in absorbing and thus mitigating some of the poverty in other regions.

Another example of the impact of irrigated cash cropping in a dry region is found in the south, in Mandya District, Karnataka, where Epstein (1962, 1973) has made comparative and longitudinal case studies. Her results show that cash cropping (sugarcane and rice) in a canal-irrigated village generates more jobs and year-round employment for laborers than in a nearby dry village (ibid. 125–41). (Even in the dry village, jobs have increased due to economic diversification stimulated by the canal.) Real wages in the irrigated village have, as in the northwest, been limited by an influx of migrant laborers from unirrigated regions (ibid. 138–39). So long as sharp inter-regional disparities continue, labor migration will ensure that new job opportunities are inevitably spread very thin.

The impact of the green revolution has been studied in another relatively dry area, North Arcot District in Tamilnadu, by a group from the Center of South Asian Studies at Cambridge (Farmer 1977). New technology has been adopted by a minority of farmers in this area. Given the moderate rainfall, the major constraint on adoption is the need for reliable sources of irrigation. Large farmers have invested in pumpsets, but these are still beyond the means of many small farmers (ibid. 117–118). Nevertheless, some small farmers have achieved high rates of adoption, high intensities of input utilization, and large increases in income (ibid. 112–113).

In this district, the green revolution has had no perceptible impact on land distribution: in a comparison among twelve villages, there was no correlation found between intensive, market-oriented production (which is quite strong in a few villages) and higher concentration of landholdings (ibid. 320). Considering the limited scale of intensified production in the district, the employment effects have been good, leading to a higher total demand for labor, higher wages and lower seasonal fluctuations in employment, especially in those few villages which have adopted modern inputs. The benefits of even limited economic growth have been good, and the main constraint on more rapid growth seems to be the relatively low level of public and private investment in irrigation.

IV

The spread of hybrid seeds and other new inputs has been much slower in the wet-rice regions of eastern and southern India, leading to two kinds of dire prediction: either the new technology will not spread widely due to distortions in the class structure; or if it does, it will further impoverish the rural poor. The case study evidence to be reviewed here, however, tends to suggest that the barriers to adoption are primarily due to shortages of new inputs and infrastructure, and that the poor are suffering not from too much commercialization and new technology but rather from too little. For example, Etienne (1982:136–37) has found coastal areas with good irrigation in Tamilnadu and Andhra Pradesh, where the growth in total rice production has been quite substantial. Real wages and employment opportunities have also grown in these areas.

It has frequently been suggested that the detrimental effects of the green revolution are most pronounced in the humid coastal deltas of southern India. For example, some authors have argued that greater inequality and political tension in Tanjore district, Tamilnadu, have resulted from the new technology (e.g. Frankel 1971). However, as Béteille (1974:142–70) has pointed out, there was considerable inequality and unrest among agricultural laborers in this district even before the start of the green revolution. He also notes that unrest was concentrated

in that part of the district (the "Old Delta") which has been irrigated
for centuries, and where class and caste inequalities were, as a consequence,
particularly extreme. In another part of the district (the "New Delta")
canal irrigation began only in 1934. Social inequalities in the New Delta
are much less extreme, and the green revolution in this area seems not
to have generated much political tension. It appears that negative social
effects of new technology are mainly the result of pre-existing ecological
and social conditions and that their prevalence has been exaggerated.
As Harriss (1977:35) has noted, a single violent clash between landlords
and laborers "has been made the basis for optimistic predictions about
the likelihood of the 'Green Revolution turning red' by a kind of
'rapportage overkill' which has used one incident many times over as
evidence of the imminence of revolution."

Turning to another wet-rice zone in West Bengal near the Bihar border,
this area has been intensively studied by Bandyopadhyay and Von Eschen
(1982, 1987). In designing their research, they set out to verify the
prediction that those rural areas which are more intensively tied to the
urban-oriented market economy will experience impoverishment and class
polarization. What they found, in fact, was exactly the opposite. They
compared two sets of villages: one set connected by roads to market
towns, and the other not connected. These latter villages experienced
much greater poverty and inequality, and the impoverishment seems to
have accelerated over the last generation or so due to population pressure.
On the other hand, in the connected villages the rates of downward
mobility were lower; job opportunities for laborers and small farmers
were more numerous and diversified; and small farmers could invest
savings from their wages in agricultural production, thus increasing the
viability of very small holdings whose produce found a ready market in
town. In these and other ways, the rural poor benefitted from greater
access to urban markets. And once again, if wages did not rise substantially,
it was because the relatively prosperous villages were flooded with migrant
laborers from the stagnant villages.

Adoption of green revolution inputs was not high in this area as a
whole, but the reason was simply that adequate supplies were not available.
Moreover, because inputs were scarce, their distribution was heavily
skewed toward the big landowners. It was the *scarcity* of the new
technology (and the complementary infrastructure, like roads and irrigation works) which was most harmful to the poor. Whatever the levels
of inequality *within* the villages which had good connections to urban
markets, these were overshadowed by the much greater disparities *between*
this set of villages and those which had no connections. It was the
state's failure to provide infrastructure and new technology which in-

tensified the impoverishment of these latter villages and generated greater levels of inequality in the region.

V

The preceding sections have summarized case studies comparing the social impact of economic change and stagnation. Basic contrasts between wet and dry regions have been pointed out, and the advantages gained by dry ones when favored with irrigation have been noted. These can be examined in more detail through my own research on a dry region of western India.

The stark contrasts between growth and stagnation which characterize Indian agriculture as a whole can be seen in miniature in western Maharashtra state. Areas of rapid growth are found in several river valleys which have been provided with large-scale canal irrigation systems over the last century. Sugarcane, the principal cash crop, has brought prosperity to these canal areas. On the other hand, in the hilly plateau regions between these valleys, where rainfall is sparse and uncertain, the rate of growth has been very low and subsistence is frequently precarious (Attwood 1987c).

The first major canal system in this region was completed by the British government in 1874, followed by a series of six others phased in through the mid-1930s. For geographic reasons, these canals were smaller and more expensive than those built in the northwest. Consequently, by 1976 only 11 percent of the cultivated area in Maharashtra was under irrigation, as compared with 81 percent in Punjab (Sarma 1982:46). Although the irrigated area in this region was relatively small, the innovations and transformations in the canal villages were as intensive as in the northwest (Attwood 1984, 1985).

The canals were first built for the sake of famine protection, but the local cultivators, for good technical reasons, chose not to use the canal water on subsistence crops (Attwood 1987b). Canal water was only put to regular use after a caste of innovative market gardeners, the Saswad Malis, migrated to the new canal tracts, rented land and began growing sugarcane. Cane was soon adopted by most of the local cultivators and became the premier commercial crop along the canals. Some village families grew rich on this crop, while many small and middle farmers relied on it as their main source of cash income.

These former dry villages were not densely populated, so there was initially a shortage of labor for growing cane, particularly at harvest time. As a result, real wages rose until the great depression of the 1930s, and the cultivators meanwhile adopted labor-saving equipment and methods (Attwood 1984). Much of the labor for harvesting and crushing cane, boiling the juice and making crude sugar was supplied by seasonal migrants from the dry villages. These migrants were usually dry farmers with their own bullock carts, who had little else to occupy them at home during the slack season. Permanent migrants also settled in the new canal tracts, fleeing precarious conditions in the dry villages to meet the demand for construction workers and year-round laborers. They also came for opportunities to rent or buy land and grow sugarcane themselves.

The most successful cane growers became big commercial farmers and entrepreneurs: some organized cooperative credit and market societies; some grew cane for the new sugar factories which sprang up after 1932; and some started their own sugar factories. The Saswad Malis, as a minority immigrant group, cooperated well among themselves and established a sugar factory in 1934. This pattern was later imitated, after 1950, when cooperative factories were established by cane growers of other castes all along the canals. By 1980 there were sixty large-scale cooperative sugar factories in operation in Maharashtra. In 1950, the region had produced just 10 percent of the total white sugar in India, mostly from private factories established by Bombay industrialists in the 1930s. By 1980, Maharashtra produced 32 percent of Indian white sugar, with 90 percent of that coming from cooperative factories.

Most of the members of these cooperatives are small growers, with an acre or less under sugarcane. Along the canals, nearly all the cane growers, whether small or large, have now been incorporated into the cooperatives. Fully 75 percent of the sugarcane grown in this region is processed into pure industrial white sugar, compared with a national average of just 34 percent (Cooperative Sugar 1980:491). While the leaders and organizers of these cooperatives have mostly been large growers, the benefits of membership have spread to more than 200,000 growers of all sizes (Baviskar 1980; Attwood and Baviskar 1987).

At least half the cooperative factories operate with good technical and economic efficiency, and some are outstanding by any standard (ibid.). They all provide integrated credit systems along with centrally organized labor teams for harvesting cane and transporting it to the mills. In addition, these factories provide organizational support for other cooperatives, and for schools, colleges, medical clinics, etc. These factories are a striking success among development projects in India, *and* they were initiated, organized and managed by the cane growers themselves. They are the culmination of a long series of innovations "from below" (Baviskar and Attwood 1984; Attwood 1985, 1987a).

Bringing irrigation to a dry land multiplies the effective land area. Land which could only be cropped once a year, or once every two years, now yields two or three crops annually—and more valuable crops with higher yields. This means that the same land under irrigation can support more farmers and laborers than it could when dry. Consequently, instead of driving small farmers off the land, the commercial economy of this region has actually sustained them in the face of ever-increasing demographic pressure. A detailed study of changes from 1920 to 1970 in one canal village found no increase in the concentration of lands owned by big farmers (Attwood 1979). In fact, all holdings, large and small, diminished rapidly due to partitioning among multiple heirs. At the same time, the small farmers, unlike the big ones, actually bought more land than they sold. The small farmers survived economic competition and population pressure because irrigation and intensive cash cropping expanded the effective land area available for all.

The overall rate of population growth rose rapidly in Maharashtra (as in the rest of India) after 1920, and this pressure was intensified in the canal villages by a massive influx of migrants from the surrounding dry areas. In fact, the source of at least 70 percent of the landless laborers now living in the canal tracts derives from this process of migration, *not* from small farmers being driven off the soil (ibid.). In past decades, migrant laborers even found opportunities to rent and purchase land, and in some cases their descendents are big cane growers and political leaders today. Economic growth in the canal tracts enabled them to absorb large numbers of poor people from the dry areas, offering opportunities for employment and even land ownership.

In 1970–71, I took a sample survey in one of the canal villages, followed by a resurvey of the same 132 families in 1978–79. The results provide a detailed record of changes in living standards during the 1970s. These changes were measured in terms of levels of consumption (especially food consumption) and levels of saving and investment. Families were considered to be better off in 1979, as compared with 1970, if food consumption had increased or if savings or investments rose while food consumption remained adequate (at two full meals a day throughout the year).

The results are quite striking: no less than 57 percent of the small farmers (those with less than 2.5 acres of irrigated land) and 35 percent of the landless laborers were significantly better off at the time of the second survey. (This resurvey occurred not during one of the periodic booms in the local sugar economy, but rather in a long period of low sugar prices, so the improvements were not simply the result of a short-term cycle.) On the other hand, 24 percent of the landless laborers were definitely worse off by 1979. In some cases, these unfortunates were elderly or infirm persons separated from their adult children (if any). The rather limited gains for the landless laborers as a whole can be explained in part by the downturn of the sugar economy during this period, as well as by the continued immigration of laborers from the dry areas nearby, which held down wages.

Nevertheless, the poor in general and the small farmers in particular have made impressive gains. A strategy which many small farmers and laborers followed was to diversify jobs held and investments made by each family. The success of this strategy depends on employment growth and diversification, which the laborers and small farmers themselves help to bring about, by investing in a range of production and service activities. Employment and incomes outside agriculture, both in the formal and informal sectors, were available to small farmers, landless laborers and members of the lowest castes. As a result, in the 1970's, no less than 43 percent of the landless laborers made productive investments of Rs. 500 or more in such things as cows, buffaloes, bullocks, sewing machines, shops, land, etc. (Note that the category of "landless laborers" specifically excludes the better-off landless families, such as teachers and shopkeepers, who did not engage in menial labor.) Partly as a result of these investments, 25 percent of landless families who were engaged in agricultural labor in 1970 were able to give up this low-paying and low-status work by 1978. Indeed, 14 percent of the landless laborers bought small plots of crop land, thereby leaving the lowest stratum. Also, 34 percent of the small farmers expanded their landholdings in this decade. Taking account of all transactions (including purchases, sales, partitions, added irrigation, land reforms, etc.), the small farmers and landless laborers gained more land per family than the middle or large farmers. (Middle farmers were those holding between 2.5 and 15 irrigated acres in 1970, large farmers those with more.) Among the 65 families who were small farmers or landless laborers in 1970, total landholdings doubled to 62 irrigated acres in 1979. This was not a large improvement, but the trend was in the right direction, contrary to the predictions of those who view commercialization as a disaster for the rural poor.

Small farmers were in a position to invest more than landless laborers: they had more savings and more credit. The average landless laborer invested only about Rs. 1,800 during this decade, while the average small farmer invested about Rs. 5,800, compared to about Rs. 14,000 for the middle farmer and Rs. 66,000 for the large. This confirms the general impression that one type of advantage (in the amount of land owned) leads to the cumulation of others (in the amounts of money saved, borrowed and invested). However, this impression is often exaggerated to the point where investment capital is assumed to be monopolized by the rich. This impression is emphatically contradicted by the data. If investments per acre (that is, in proportion to previous assets) are examined, we find that the disparity runs in the opposite direction: small farmers invested about Rs. 5,800 per acre, while middle and large farmers invested only about Rs. 2,000 per acre. The same holds true for access to institutional sources of credit (that is, banks, cooperatives and government offices): the small farmers obtained Rs. 1,700 per acre from these sources, as compared with less than Rs. 500 per acre for the middle and large farmers.

These findings suggest two interesting points. First, it is commonly believed that small farmers obtain higher yields per acre because they put more of their own labor and supervision into their crops (which they do); but these figures also suggest that, under favorable circumstances, small farmers may invest more capital per acre than the larger ones. Second, it is also commonly believed that banks and cooperative societies discriminate against small borrowers; but these figures indicate that greater equity is possible, though perhaps only in a high-growth region where the total credit supply is reasonably plentiful.

To summarize, then: in this locality of high agricultural production, the poor (especially the small farmers) have benefited from the growth of diversified opportunities for employment and investment—even despite saturation with immigrant labor from low-growth areas nearby. The demand for labor has increased and the employment structure has diversified due to a combination of private and public investments. First came the irrigation canals, followed by sugar factories. The number of cooperative factories rose sharply in the 1970s, along with ancillary private investments, creating a much higher demand for labor. The results have included unionization of migrant harvest workers, accompanied by occasional strikes; tripartite negotiations among factories, unions and government; and a series of higher wage agreements in recent years. However, migration and demographic pressure limit the jobs and wages available for individual workers, even though laborers as a whole have gained many new opportunities.

Continued poverty and insecurity in the dry villages necessitate a more vigorous distribution of public investment outside the old canal tracts. Indeed, the Government of Maharashtra, assisted by loans from the World Bank, has undertaken a huge program of new canal construction, and it may also invest in much-needed improvements in irrigation management. These efforts help to alleviate the basic source of poverty and inequality in the region, which is the scarcity of water.

VI

The case studies reviewed here suggest the prospects for growth in Indian agriculture vary from one ecozone to another. The social impact of economic growth, where it does occur, is often favorable in terms of employment and other opportunities for small farmers and landless laborers. While growth may increase relative inequalities through a process of upward divergence, the problems of absolute poverty are far more severe in the stagnant regions.

This does not mean, however, that economic growth is the only means of achieving "development" in a broader sense. Comparisons among Indian states show, for example, that the standard of living of the majority (as measured in terms of life expectancy, literacy and infant mortality rates) is higher in Kerala than in Punjab, even though the former is only average in terms of production per capita, while the latter is at the top (Sarma 1982:50; Morris and McAlpin 1982:58–59). International comparisons also point to the same conclusion: some poor nations (such as Sri Lanka) have achieved much more than others in terms of raising living standards of the majority (ibid. 84–85; World Bank 1986:180). The political, cultural and historical reasons for these different levels of social performance have not received the serious attention they deserve, but such issues go beyond the scope of this paper.

Irrigation, drainage and flood control works, along with other basic infrastructure such as roads and schools, are the primary requirements for stabilizing and enhancing agricultural production in the backward regions of India. Those regions which are prosperous today are those which have benefited from prolonged investment in irrigation. The same investments are needed in other areas, although it may be true for India, as for China, that "all of the easier and cheaper sources have been tapped" (Murphey 1982:62). What is immediately apparent in western Maharashtra is true for much of India: long-term investments in irrigation have made some areas prosperous, while the remaining dry areas are stagnant and insecure.

The problems of the high-rainfall regions are somewhat different, but they too need better coverage from, and better management of, irrigation, drainage and flood control works. Because of high population densities combined with rigid and polarized stratification, farmers in wet-rice regions may have greater difficulty in making efficient use of new irrigation and technology (though this has apparently not been a problem in the New Delta of Tanjore district). Consequently, the wet-rice regions may require more effective land reforms and redistribution of political power than they have had up to now. However, the case studies reviewed here suggest that irrigation and new technology will not by themselves increase poverty in these regions, even in the absence of vigorous redistributive measures. Consequently, the provision of improved infrastructure should not be made to wait on better land reforms, which may never come. In any case, land reforms are certainly no substitute for infrastructure and technology. The experience of China is instructive in this regard.

Despite massive redistribution and reorganization in the 1950s, per capita agricultural production did not increase until the late 1970s when policies were redirected; and sharp inter-regional disparities have probably still not been reduced (Lardy 1982; Vermeer 1982; Parish 1981; Parish and Whyte 1978; Nolan and White 1979).

In the absence of large-scale mechanization, technical change and commercialization in agriculture usually provide new opportunities for employment and investment to the rural poor, at least in Asia. This is demonstrably true in those regions of India already experiencing rapid growth; moreover, it seems likely to be true even in the more stagnant areas, provided that sufficient investments in infrastructure and new technology are made. The rural poor are not required to choose between a slow "trickle down" of benefits from urban industrial growth or an even slower wait for more radical land reforms. Employment-oriented investments in agricultural production can provide a mix of both growth and equity (Mellor 1976), as shown, for example, in the irrigated areas of Maharashtra.

One result of regional disparities deriving in part from past investment patterns is that poverty tends to migrate from low to high-growth areas. This sometimes gives the impression that economic growth causes poverty to multiply, whereas the opposite is the case. The dynamic regions are able to absorb, and thus mitigate, some of the poverty from the stagnant ones. What poor people need in these latter areas is more new infrastructure and technology, not less. It is the failure to provide these resources which perpetuates poverty and increases inequality between regions.

References

Aggarwal, Partap C. 1973 *The Green Revolution and Rural Labour.* New Delhi: Shri Ram Centre for Industrial Relations and Human Resources.

Ahluwalia, Montek S. 1978 "Rural Poverty in India: 1956–67 to 1973–74." *World Bank Staff Working Paper* No. 279, pp. 1–42.

Attwood, Donald W. 1979 "Why Some of the Poor Get Richer: Economic Change and Mobility in Rural Western India," *Current Anthropology.* Vol. 20, pp. 495–516, 657–58.

1984 "Capital and the Transformation of Agrarian Class Systems: Sugar Production in India," in M. Desai, S.H. Rudolph, and A. Rudra (eds.), *Agrarian Power and Agricultural Productivity in South Asia.* Delhi: Oxford University Press and Berkeley: University of California Press.

1985 "Peasants versus Capitalists in the Indian Sugar Industry: Impact of the Irrigation Frontier" *Journal of Asian Studies* 45:59–80.

1987a "Social and Political Preconditions for Successful Cooperatives: The Cooperative Sugar Factories of Western India," in D.W. Attwood and B.S.

Baviskar (eds.) *Who Shares? Cooperatives in Rural Development*. Delhi: Oxford University Press.

1987b "Irrigation and Imperialism: The Causes and Consequences of a Shift from Subsistence to Cash Cropping," *Journal of Development Studies* Vol. 23, pp. 341–66.

1987c "Risk, Mobility and Cooperation in Maharashtrian Villages," in D.W. Attwood, M. Israel and N.K. Wagle (eds.) *City, Countryside and Society in Maharashtra*. Toronto: Centre for South Asian Studies, University of Toronto.

Attwood, D.W. and B.S. Baviskar 1987. "Why Do Some Cooperatives Work But Not Others? A Comparative Analysis of Sugar Cooperatives in India," *Economic and Political Weekly*. Vol. 22, No. 26, pp. A38–A56.

Bandyopadhyay, Suraj and Donald Von Eschen 1982 *The Conditions of Rural Progress in India: A Case Study of Bengal*. Report to the Canadian International Development Agency, Ottawa.

1987 "Villager Failure to Cooperate: Does It Matter? What Accounts for It? Some Evidence from West Bengal, India," in D.W. Attwood and B.S. Baviskar (eds.) *Who Shares: Cooperatives in Rural Development*. Delhi: Oxford University Press.

Baviskar, B.S. 1980 *The Politics of Development: Sugar Cooperatives in Rural Maharashtra*. Delhi: Oxford University Press.

Baviskar, B.S. and D.W. Attwood 1984 "Rural Cooperatives in India: A Comparative Analysis of their Economic Survival and Social Impact," *Contributions to Indian Sociology*. Vol. 18, No. 1. pp. 85–107.

Beals, Alan R. 1974 *Village Life in South India*. Chicago: Aldine.

Béteille, André 1974 *Studies in Agrarian Social Structure*. Delhi: Oxford University Press.

Bhalla, G.S. 1974 *Changing Agrarian Structure in India: A Study of the Green Revolution in Haryana*. Meerut: Meenakshi Prakashan.

Cooperative Sugar 1980 *Cooperative Sugar Directory and Yearbook*. New Delhi: National Federation of Cooperative Sugar Factories.

Dasgupta, Biplab 1980 *The New Agrarian Technology and India*. Delhi: Macmillan.

Epstein, T.S. 1962 *Economic Development and Social Change in South India*. Bombay: Oxford University Press.

1973 *South India: Yesterday, Today and Tomorrow*. New York: Holmes and Meier.

Etienne, Gilbert 1968 *Studies in Indian Agriculture*. Berkeley: University of California Press.

1982 *India's Changing Rural Scene*. Delhi: Oxford University Press.

Farmer, B.H. (ed.) 1977 *Green Revolution? Technology and Change in Rice-Growing Areas of Tamil Nadu and Sri Lanka*. London: Macmillan.

Frankel, Francine 1971 *India's Green Revolution: Economic Gains and Political Costs*. Bombay: Oxford University Press.

Harriss, John 1977 "Bias in Perception of Agrarian Change in India," in B.H. Farmer (ed.), *Green Revolution? Technology and Change in Rice-Growing Areas of Tamil Nadu and Sri Lanka*. London: Macmillan.

Kessinger, Tom G. 1974 *Vilyatpur 1848–1968: Social and Economic Change in a North Indian Village*. Berkeley: University of California Press.

Lardy, Nicholas R. 1982 "Food Consumption in the People's Republic of China," in Randolph Barker and Radha Sinha (eds.), *The Chinese Agricultural Economy*. Boulder: Westview Press.

Lewis, W. Arthur (ed.) 1970 *Tropical Development 1880–1913*. London: Allen and Unwin.

Lipton, Michael 1978 "Inter-Farm, Inter-Regional and Farm–Non-Farm Income Distribution: The Impact of the New Cereal Varieties," *World Development* Vol. 6, pp. 319–37.

Mellor, John W. 1976 *The New Economics of Growth*. Ithaca: Cornell University Press.

Morris, Morris D. and Michelle B. McAlpin 1982 *Measuring the Condition of India's Poor: The Physical Quality of Life Index*. New Delhi: Promilla.

Murphey, Rhoads 1982 "Natural Resources and Factor Endowments," in Randolph Barker and Radha Sinha (eds.), *The Chinese Agricultural Economy*. Boulder: Westview Press.

Nolan, Peter and Gordon White 1979 "Socialist Development and Rural Inequality: The Chinese Countryside in the 1970s," *Journal of Peasant Studies*. Vol. 7, pp. 3–48.

Parish, William L. 1981 "Egalitarianism in Chinese Society," *Problems of Communism*. January-February, pp. 37–53.

Parish, William L. and Martin King Whyte 1978 *Village and Family in Contemporary China*. Chicago: University of Chicago Press.

Sarma, J.S. 1982 *Agricultural Policy in India: Growth with Equity*. Ottawa: International Development Research Centre.

Sen, Bandhudas 1974 *The Green Revolution in India: A Perspective*. New Delhi: Wiley Eastern.

Stein, Burton 1980 *Peasant State and Society in Medieval South India*. Delhi: Oxford University Press.

Stone, Ian 1984 *Canal Irrigation in British India*. Cambridge: Cambridge University Press.

Vermeer, E.B. 1982 "Income Differentials in Rural China," *China Quarterly*. No. 89, pp. 1–33.

Whitcombe, Elizabeth 1972 *Agrarian Conditions in Northern India 1860–1900*. Berkeley: University of California Press.

World Bank 1986 *World Development Report*. New York: Oxford University Press.

2

THE POLITICAL ECOLOGY AND ECONOMIC DEVELOPMENT OF MIGRATORY PASTORALIST SOCIETIES IN EASTERN AFRICA

John W. Bennett

"Eastern Africa," for the purposes of this paper, consists of the following countries: Sudan, Ethiopia, Somalia, Kenya and Tanzania. However, Kenya and Tanzania—"East Africa"—will be featured in this version of a longer monograph (Bennett 1984). Significant numbers of migratory pastoralist people live in all five countries, and attempts at inducing these populations to relinquish their migratory way of life, and to shift their distinctive mode of livestock production to one approximating sedentary ranching, have been made repeatedly from the late nineteenth century to the present. Such efforts at production intensification, and the associated requirement of nucleated settlement, are not unique to eastern Africa, but occur in other parts of Africa, the Middle East and Central Asia, wherever substantial numbers of people raise livestock on transient pasturage. Such people represent the last substantial body of Old World humans following a pattern of social and economic life differing from the village-city sedentarism originating in the Bronze Age. The fact that the pastoralist style of life has proved to be remarkably resistant to change is partly due to the relative geographic isolation of people exploiting marginal lands (i.e., lands not easily or profitably cultivated for crops), and partly because this mode of existence has remarkable resources for self-subsistence.

By the 1880s, the migratory utilization of pasturage was viewed as politically incompatible with the expectations of African colonial governments interested in preventing tribal disputes over land occupancy. After independence was achieved, the institutions of the new African

31

nations required citizens to reside in one place, receive social services and intensively utilize resources in order to maximally contribute to the productivity and income of the country. Thus the fate of migratory pastoralists is intrinsically tied to the political systems of the new nations in which they are now enclaved: the 'political ecology' of pastoralists becomes the process of adjusting resources, the modes of production and patterns of social life to these demands.

This process of change and adaptation is an ecological one insofar as a new relationship between humans, animals and the arid-semi-arid grass- and range-lands must be worked out if the social disruption and environmental degradation so frequently associated with the 'development' of pastoralist economies is to be avoided. Such disturbance of socionatural systems, which had existed in a state of relative balance earlier in the nineteenth century, has not ceased in the contemporary era of independent nations. From this perspective, 'development' is really a matter of achieving a new set of relationships between pastoralism and physical resources, and between pastoralists, their agriculturalist neighbors and government agencies. This cannot be achieved overnight, nor exclusively by means of development projects, but will emerge as part of the adaptive evolution of populations and institutions in nation-states.

This chapter will begin with a definition of migratory pastoralism, plus a review of basic issues in the development process. This is followed by a summary of the demography of pastoralist peoples in the countries of eastern Africa and a discussion of eastern Africa as a socionatural system and the way attempts to modify migratory pastoralism contributed to destabilization of tribal systems of resource use. The penultimate section deals with the policies of colonial governments pertaining to pastoralists and early attempts at developmental change. The chapter concludes with a review of the principal themes and problems associated with contemporary development projects affecting pastoralists.

Pastoralism: An Introductory Description and a Definition of the Development Process

Pastoralism and Nomadism

In this chapter, we shall attempt to avoid the use of the terms 'nomadism' and 'nomads' since there is no simple association between the migratory way of life and livestock raised in the pastoralist manner. Table 2.1 illustrates the relationships between the relevant terms and concepts as developed by ethnologists.

In popular usage, the term 'pastoralism' refers to the relatively mobile adaptations concerning pasture use in cell 6. Technically speaking, the

Table 2.1. Pastoral and Nomadic Economies

Settlement Types	Food-Collecting Bands and Tribes	Crop Farming Village Dwellers	Livestock Raising Peoples
Sedentary, nucleated settlement	(1) Rare or extinct tribes (e.g., Northwest Pacific Coast Indians)	(2) Crop raising often combined with livestock	(3) Ranching, dairying, etc.
Mobile, transient settlement	(4) Hunter-gatherer bands (e.g., Bushmen of the Kalahari)	(5) Combinations of seasonal cropping plus livestock, with wet-dry seasonal movement	(6) Regular, frequent movement for pasture use: nomadic pastoralists

term should apply as well to the modes in cell 5. 'Nomadism' refers to a mode of production which requires a population to move regularly, and often, in search of food or resources, and to permit their livestock to breed while moving, so to speak. Thus, 'nomadic pastoralism' would refer to those groups in cell 6 who move often or continually. Livestock raised by people in cells 2 and 3 are usually of different breeds or varieties that those produced by people in cells 5 and 6. In this chapter, the people in cells 5 and 6 are called *migratory pastoralists,* but obviously they need not be continuously nomadic. 'Transhumant' is the term most often applied to people who live in more or less permanent villages but go out on grazing expeditions in the local dry season (cell 5). These people operate livestock regimes based on permanent agricultural settlements.

In the earlier literature on migratory pastoralism, the problem of settlement versus nomadism was generally handled via the concept of sedentarization. This implies that to become sedentary, i.e., to accept fixed settlement of some kind, usually the village, is a major evolutionary change from one mode of life to another. This concept was based on nineteenth century theories of social and economic evolution among subsistence tribal peoples. In fact, most pastoralist tribes have both sedentary and migratory sections or groups, and changing from one mode to another has been more common than believed. The migratory habits of pastoralist groups have been carried on in the context of economic necessity by peoples with full awareness of the circumstances of settled life, who have repeatedly demonstrated their capacity to adapt to this form of settlement when the occasion or necessity arises.[1]

Still, if a group which has been moving frequently begins to accept a degree of settled life, there will be consequences for the social organization and daily routines. P.T.W. Baxter has described some of these changes for the Ethiopian Boran people: "sedentarization tends to narrow the range and alter the texture of social relationships" (1975:224). This occurs with acceptance of crop agriculture, in which close relationships tend to develop among a small number of neighboring farmers. On the other hand, in the migratory mode, kinship relationships, 'herd-partnerships,' and other institutions tend to become geographically wide-ranging. However, it should be remembered that such changes are reversible: pastoralists are remarkably flexible and can modify social relations as they alter their mode of production.

The main institutional differences between a transient adaptation and a nucleated one pertain to land tenure, inheritance and other customs concerning property ownership and transmittal, and general economic activity patterns. These institutions are intimately adapted to the transient mode of life and production, although they are not completely resistive to change. Of the set, land tenure is perhaps the most crucial, since the 'communal' use of range means that the notion of freehold ownership of defined tracts does not exist. In its place, the herding group will have rights to use particular tracts at certain times; others will have rights to use the same pasture land at other times of the year. There is no simple way to harmonize this system of overlapping customary usufruct tenure with Western institutions of legal freehold tenure. And in any event, once the nation-state comes into existence, land tenure becomes a matter of constitutional control and guarantee. The flexible and fluctuating usufruct systems, continually altered as herding groups interact, become impossible to maintain or tolerate. Similar difficulties pertain to the taxation of land or animals (since, for example, animals can be detached from herds, and 'lent' to associates in more fortunate pasture areas).

Since pastoralists generally inhabit marginal lands, they are familiar with fluctuating climate and variable soil and pasturage and with the uncertainties these introduce into the production process. A variety of defensive social and economic strategies have evolved through the years to cope with these conditions. Migratory life itself permits adjustment through moving to a more fortunate locale. Some adaptations are technical, including ways to minimize bovine disease (to be described later); others include ways of husbanding water. Significant strategies also exist in the social system and, as previously noted, involve exchange relationships with friends and relatives, as well as diversity of production and income. A herd owner facing severe drought in his customary territories can lend all or some of his livestock to a partner in a more favored region for the duration, taking them back when the drought period is over.[2]

Economic Systems and Change in Migratory Pastoralism

Knowledge of pastoralism as a way of life has a foundation in tribal studies made by ethnologists during the past forty years. In this work, migratory pastoralists were viewed originally as a detached segment of mankind: an autonomous society deriving from remote historical origins and representing the classic stereotype of the isolated, culturally-integral tribal entity (for a discussion, see Galaty 1981b). The focus of interest in these earlier researches was on spatial movement, and the way this movement affected social organization and subsistence patterns.[3] Later studies shifted to a more specialized ecological approach, being concerned with how a balance was maintained, under presumably undisturbed conditions, between the human population, animals, and pasture resources.[4]

Following independence, the new governments of East Africa endeavored to modify the production regimes of pastoralists toward sedentary livestock production, or simply to reduce the amount of land available as pasture to migratory groups in order to encourage more intensive use and management of resources. Such projects were in the main continuations of colonial experiments. The schemes rarely fulfilled expectations, and in many instances disrupted pastoralist systems and the relationships between pastoralists and their cultivator neighbors and associates.

These experiences led country governments and the international development assistance agencies to promote research designed to determine the reasons for failure of the schemes. In addition to these research projects, the development agencies sponsored a series of conferences to permit an exchange of data and views. These efforts by anthropologists and livestock and range specialists during the last decade contributed to the literature of pastoralism as an econo-ecological type. They also supplied a fresh view of pastoralists as people required to cope with greatly altered geographic, economic and political conditions.[5]

The relative failure of development schemes and projects was viewed as a matter of importance for two reasons: first, in many African countries, pastoralists were an important source of animal products and nutrition; hence, their activities deserved strengthening and encouragement, not inhibition. Second, the persistent failure of development schemes was a matter of concern to ministries and technical assistance agencies because of their cost, and because the schemes were believed to have been carefully conceived and planned. Success in agricultural development never comes easily; however, it was harder to achieve in the livestock programs involving pastoralists than for other modes of production. Clearly, reasons had to be sought.

In many respects, development schemes attempted in eastern Africa became a testing ground for pastoralist development everywhere; likewise, much of the new research took place in this region, along with the two most recent large international conferences.[6] However, research carried out by anthropologists and livestock and range specialists in West Africa, North Africa and the Middle East has also made significant contributions to the enlarged understanding of modern migratory pastoralism.

Much of the work of the past decade has focussed on the difficulty of encouraging pastoralists to increase the offtake of animals for commercial sales, and the way this problem has led to excessive size of herds and consequent overgrazing: seemingly a classic case of "tragedy of the commons" (Hardin 1968; Brokenshaw, Horowitz, and Scudder 1977). That is, development schemes designed to reduce herd size and increase offtake, and thereby permit a more adaptive response to the restriction of grazing opportunities resulting from permitting rangeland to pass into other uses, appeared to have the opposite effect: increase in herds, and a static or reduced offtake. Another factor related to this was the alleged tendency for pastoralists to fail to respond rationally to increased prices: the so-called "negative price response" (Low 1980). Recent research on this process shows that pastoralists have distrusted development initiatives which promise financial rewards or enchanced resources but, for many reasons, fail to deliver. Moreover, intermittent droughts lead pastoralists to maintain large herds in order to ensure some animals in case of large losses. These and other factors have persuaded pastoralists to "rationally preserve a measure of traditional production strategies, geared to subsistence rather than markets" (Livingstone 1977). Under conditions of increased pressure from all quarters, individual herd owners tend to keep as many animals as possible in order to protect the continuity of the breeding herd. This can lead to resource degradation. The situation has led many analysts to define the overall problem as caused by the *combination of communal pasturage and individual herd ownership*—a combination that worked well under indigenous systems, when range was virtually unlimited, but became destructive when the system was constrained or disturbed under development.

A second major theme in the work of the 1970s has been an attempt to view migratory pastoralism as a system larger in scope than a tribal entity or a group of herd owners speaking a common language. This came about as a result of the growing realization that one major reason for the disappointing results of so many projects was their concentration on particular segments of an interconnected whole. By intervening in one segment, key processes of linkage and dependence were interrupted, leading to system breakdown. The most typical evidence was the abuse of pasturelands and the failure of programs for reducing the number of livestock to correct this abuse. Much of the later development-inspired research and the conferences were devoted to defining the dimensions of pastoralism and its key interdependencies.[7]

Eastern Africa has a transitional economy in the sense that the indigenous population is required to use cash as the major medium of exchange, even though a varying fraction of production continues to be used for subsistence. The pastoralist population (like all agriculturalists in the developing countries) thus finds itself in the middle: its successful subsistence economy, plus its long-term barter exchange with townsmen and cultivators, has been greatly modified by developing commercial relations. While pastoralists have always sold a proportion of their stock, recent economic change, plus insistent development programs of the country governments, now requires them to sell more in order to obtain the money they need to live and to retain a place in the regional and national networks. This means that the governments need to find a niche in the economy for pastoralists to permit them to develop a substitute for food obtained from animals. Equally important is some means for them to invest their cash income from animals in productive enterprise. Investments in real estate, gold and houses are typical of some groups, such as Baggara pastoralists in Sudan, but not of others, particularly the Masai, who have clung to conservative tribal economics. Unfortunately, investments in herds alone do not yield the leverage needed in a modernizing economy.

Involvement of pastoralists in the emerging commercial systems have the effect of increasing income disparity among the herd owners. The larger owners find it easier to enter the modern economy and many are amassing wealth, control over property, land and labor. Smaller herd owners lose ground and turn to wage labor in the towns and cities. Many of these part-time or proletarian pastoralists receive the backing of relatives who continue to raise livestock; thus, as Anders Hjort concludes, pastoralism in some regions supports the modern economic sector by providing partial subsistence for the families of wage laborers (1981:141).

Others turn to farming as a way into the new economic system. Crop raising was never foreign to pastoralist tribes, nearly all of whom have had cultivator sections or have resorted to farming during periods of drought or other disturbance of the livestock regime (for a study, see Haaland 1972). Again, the wealthy herd-owning kin groups can invest in farmland and even subsidize village cultivators in other tribes to produce forage for their herds. The poor pastoralists, on the other hand,

tend to become transformed into small-holder peasants who exist as
marginal producers or who are caught up in agrarian development
programs or agribusiness schemes. No statistics exist to tell us how
common this is or what its effect on livestock production over time
may be. Again, pastoralism is caught up in a transitional era in East
African economic development, and it is difficult to predict the final
outcome. However, increasing wealth for the few and the creation of
extensive patron-client systems among the wealthy and the poor seem
to be the order of the day.

Some development programs are designed to integrate pastoralists
into dryland crop farming communities as livestock producers, users of
farm-raised forage and as mixed farmers. The best known of these schemes
is the ASAL (arid-semi-arid-land) approach in Kenya (Ngutter 1979).
Where pastoralists (like some Masai in Kenya and northern Tanzania)
are moving into crop-raising as an important adjunct to livestock, the
ASAL programs would permit the Kenya groups to receive seed for
drought-resistant crops, loans for development of difficult soils and
facilities for developing exchange relationships with local marginal farmer-
settlers in the region. (In the 1970s in both Kenya and Tanzania there
were hostilities between the Masai and such newcomers). Aside from
the ASAL program in Kenya, the Sudanese have experimented with
integrated pastoralist-farmer programs in western Sudan and the El Obeid
and Abyei regions for a number of years, and a similar project was
recently inaugurated in the upper Blue Nile, where pastoralist refugees
from Ethiopia have congregated and are interacting with local farmers.
These integrated programs have their difficulties, but they offer the first
approach to pastoralist development which appears to take account of
the changing realities of resource distribution and modes of production
in eastern Africa.

For some time to come, most livestock production in East Africa
will be divided among pastoralists, farmers, and the commercial ranches
and parastatals—although the parastatals have experienced considerable
difficulty in maintaining efficient or profitable operations. In any case,
a move toward entrepreneurial emphases in production and extensive
social and economic supports must accompany the emergence of a true
stratified production system on regional or national bases. Pastoralists,
even though they may sell increasing numbers of animals, still find it
necessary to maintain the subsistence phase of the production system,
which includes all facets of livestock breeding and finishing.

As pastoralists become part of more complex modern systems of
exchange, the issues of concern extend beyond the classical topics of
social organization, herds, ecological ratios or range and water management. Pastoralist peoples must find a place in the emerging national

social systems; hence, they need to be considered in the contexts of employment, income levels, standard of living, socioeconomic class and power positions, job training and skills, and education. As J. Nkinyangi (1981) shows for Kenya, education has become a major factor in social and occupational advancement, and pastoralists are increasingly disadvantaged since their mobility and lack of incentive to take advantage of facilities available in rural settlements makes it difficult for them to send children to school. The government has tried a number of experiments to assist them: waiving tuition in the boarding schools; providing mobile schools in automotive trailers; and special fellowships. None of these work very well, partly because the government is unwilling or unable to provide funds for the extra costs associated with special or unusual facilities. The Kenya Masai do not use the facilities mainly, Nkinyangi feels, because of the inadequate instruction, relatively high fees, poor food and unreliable transportation. Cultural conflicts between cultivator and pastoralist children were also serious. However, these may be transitional phenomena; there are signs of the Masai moving toward education and other participative involvements.

In an emerging national system, political power is needed to guarantee the expensive programs needed to promote transition, and this requires leadership. Although the Kenya government has appointed a number of Masai to ministerial positions, these people have not exerted leadership and political mobilization skills among their own people. In the long run, political organization and representation for pastoralists, along with forms of entrepreneurship, will be the essential instruments for economic development, if this remains a significant objective.

A Note on Pastoralist Demography

Table 2.2 gives data assembled by Stephen Sandford (1976a, 1976b) on the populations of various pastoralist groups in Africa south of the Sahara. These figures contain some implications for policy. Pastoralists constitute an unevenly distributed population and mode of production in the countries of East Africa, ranging from 70 percent of the Somalian population to 1 percent or less for Tanzania. This by itself suggests that there can be no single solution to the pastoralist issue; it must be handled by the respective countries in their own ways, with concern for demographic significance or the lack of same.

However, the number of pastoralists in any country will not necessarily correlate with the degree of concern or attention paid them. Botswana, in southern Africa, with only about 2 percent of the national population classifiable as migratory pastoralists, has apparently had more success with its cooperative ranching schemes than other countries; this is due

Table 2.2.   Eastern African Pastoralist Populations

Country	Pastoralist Populations	Percent of Total Country Population
Angola	500,000	8%
Ethiopia	1,600,000	4%
Kenya	1,500,000	12%
Somalia	1,700,000	70%
Sudan	3,900,000	22%
Tanzanian Masai	100,000	1% or less

Sources: Angola: Sandford's estimate based on Carvalho 1974;
Ethiopia: Sandford's estimate based on unpublished Ethiopian
data; Kenya: FAO Expert Consultation 1972; Somalia: FAO
Group Fellowship Study 1972; Sudan: FAO Group Fellowship Study
n.d.; Tanzania: FAO Expert Consultation 1972.

in large part to the fact that important members of the national government come from the pastoralist minority, and to the fact that the majority of farmers are also cattle raisers (Steven Lawry, personal communication). This has encouraged more intensive planning and experimentation with circumscribed grazing regimes, with careful attention to the needs and interests of the tribal groups themselves. Since the majority of peasant agriculturalists in Botswana also raise livestock, pastoralist traditions and interests pervade the general culture even though only a small minority are continually transient. (For a study of a typical Botswana mixed farming-pastoralist development scheme, see Gulbrandsen 1980).

Kenya, with 12 percent of its population classifiable as migratory pastoralists (mainly Masai, Samburu, Turkana, Somali, Rendille, Borana and Gabbra tribal entities), has experimented with a variety of livestock, grazing and cooperative production schemes, but most of its national development investment has gone into intensive cultivation, commercial and private ranching, and export crop production. Pastoralists in Kenya account for a small proportion of national income, whereas in an agrarian society like Botswana, the livestock output of the minority nomads, plus the majority farmer-pastoralists, account for as much as 30–35 percent.

In Sudan, pastoralists constitute 22 percent of the national total, but this fraction represents nearly 100 percent of the population of the western half of the country. The government has done relatively little with its pastoralists from the standpoint of sedentarization or ranching schemes. Most agrarian development programs in Sudan have concentrated upon large districts in the central and southern portions of the country, where crop-livestock farmers can benefit from irrigation, improved roads, marketing schemes and other inputs. Many of these projects involve pastoralists since the affected tracts cut into traditional dry-wet season grazing migration routes. The projects—as, for example, those in the vicinity of El Obeid—have attempted to organize symbiotic relationships among pastoralists and farmers, with limited success.

Tanzania's development work with its Masai groups in the northern part of the country has attracted more attention than the relatively small numbers of pastoralists might warrant, as compared with other countries. This is because the region west of Arusha in the Tanzanian Masai heartland has been the site of many technical livestock projects, villagization experiments and regional development programs. These projects have received careful scrutiny by a large number of livestock, anthropological and rural development specialists over a period of fifteen years, and have been influential in the general literature on pastoralist development.

East Africa as a Socionatural System

Academic historians of East Africa have customarily interpreted the principal movements and events in political and social terms. Among these, the slave trade, colonial repression and colonization are viewed as the major forces affecting indigenous populations and shaping their reactions. A focus on the distinctive problems of indigenous production systems, especially pastoralism, calls attention to a different set of factors which, while brought into being by the political and social, may have been of more direct influence. Helge Kjekshus (1977) has referred to these as the collapse of a "man-controlled ecological system." Whether cause or effect, there is no doubt that the European investiture of East Africa was followed by a series of changes in the physical environment and animal and human populations of wide scope, and from which the socionatural systems of the region have not yet recovered. In this sense, development programs might be redefined as a continuation of the attempt to recover a reasonable balance in human-natural relationships, instead of ways to increase income.

One general consequence of all these ecological and physiological disturbances was famine, beginning in the 1890s and continuing at intervals well into the early 1900s. This was the famine that the colonialists viewed as cyclical or normal in the indigenous socionatural system. It is perhaps understandable that colonial authorities and scholars were unwilling or unable to acknowledge the extent to which European intervention and its policies contributed to the disruption of the ecological system. In any case, as the twentieth century wore on, colonial wars, rebellions, persecutions, population resettlements, agricultural development schemes and other measures introduced by colonial governments had their effects.

There seems little doubt that the interpretations of East African ecological history contributed by Kjekshus, Ford and others contain elements of truth. However, it is a matter of various levels of causation: while Europeans may or may not have directly caused all animal and human disease vectors, their activities in disrupting delicate balances of human and animal populations and resources were responsible for a general reorientation of ecological relations. The slave trade, used by many historians as a primary factor in breakdown, can be viewed as having less significance: population reduction, or disruption of local production systems do not appear, in the analysis of available accounts, to have been of sufficient magnitude to account for the disasters beginning in 1890. Also significant is the fact that the slave trade had diminished to a trickle by 1890 and was stopped shortly after. The major ecological breakdown was subsequent to this.

The ecological history of East Africa provides one background theme for the interpretation of pastoralist development: attempts at changing livestock regimes among indigenous populations must contend with a heritage of fear and distrust based on the feeling that European intervention produces disasters. Since the country governments have, on the whole, continued to follow development policies with roots in the past, the reluctance of pastoralists and cultivators to accept such methods with enthusiasm is understandable—even when they understand and want improvements such as animal health measures, tractors, marketing facilities and the like.

Note should be made of the curious episode of the concept of the "cattle complex" worked out by Melville Herskovits (1926) and other anthropologists in the 1920s and 1930s. This notion was based on the distinctive attitude known as the "ethnographic present." This refers to a need to reconstruct the patterns of native life previous to substantial European or American contact, and then to present the resulting depiction as contemporary. This appears to be precisely what Herskovits did in his early writings on Africa. Obviously, aspects of the traditional system were operative, as already noted. However, a number of vital elements of the nineteenth century and the later reconstituted and revised systems were ignored: in particular, the agronomic sophistication of the native regimes, or their intricate cultural ecology of livestock and pasture use and management; their familiarity with markets and the commercial value of their animals (aside from or in addition to their insistence on the wealth factor of herds); and their skill with trading and symbiotic relations with cultivators and townsmen.

Thus, it would appear that foreign attempts at understanding these complex socionatural systems have distorted their meaning and complexity, for good as well as questionable intentions. These distortions have accompanied, and in many instances created, havoc in these systems; this appears to have been a continuous process, not a recent episode.

Policies of Pastoral Development from the Colonial Era to the Present

Perceptions of Pastoralism

A number of observers of the eastern African scene attribute some of the difficulties encountered by pastoralist developers to attitudes forged in the elites of the sedentary indigenous societies, combined with Western concepts of the culture and evolutionary status of nomadic societies. One source of Western concepts has already been mentioned: the 1920s idea of the "East African cattle complex." This conception held that migratory pastoralists lived in a world apart from other producers of agricultural commodities, insofar as they raised livestock for wealth, prestige and subsistence, rather than for monetary gain. In the course of research associated with development programs, this conception has been greatly modified and largely replaced by a more sophisticated notion of pastoralism as a complex system involving many economic activities and involved in markets and commercial relationships in varying ways and degrees.

Peter Rigby developed an interesting sidelight on the issue, by noting that up to the time of his writing, the principal conception of pastoralism held by many writers, government officials and Western livestock specialists related to their 'conservatism': meaning their stiff resistance to efforts to commercialize their livestock regimes (for an example, see Shorter 1974). In reviewing accounts of pastoralism dating from the 1960s, Rigby noted that these accounts attributed the conservatism to socio-cultural phenomena: ". . . it could be generalized that the conservatism attributed to predominantly pastoral societies is thought to derive from intrinsic features of their social systems: their economic and social organization and their systems of value. External factors are recognized as contributing to conservatism, but are assigned a secondary place" (1969: 43–44). He continues, "These generalizations compete with an equally popular but contradictory one. Lurking behind all but the most sophisticated theories of social change at the macro-historical level is the idea that there is some kind of natural evolution from one kind of economy to another."

In other words, Rigby feels that resistance to innovation among pastoralists was attributed to culture or social organization, and that this idea in turn was probably based on the nineteenth century evolutionary theory of cultural and economic change which held that pastoralism was a residue from an earlier stage, or that it was possibly an offshoot of indigenous development, representing an end-product of one line of evolution and therefore not amenable to modification. This theory was elaborated by anthropologists in different ways, with considerable disagreement; for example, C.D. Forde in 1934 argued that pastoralism was inherently unstable since pastoralists concentrated on only one mode of production, which could, therefore, easily make its transition to combined farming-livestock modes (1934: 403). Others reversed the sequence, holding that pastoralism was a late, specialized offshoot of crop agriculture (see Johnson 1973, for a summary of this view).

Randall Baker carries the evolutionary ideas down into the present, attributing them to planners and administrators in the country governments and development agencies: "Initially, early administrators and travellers framed their account of the pastoral peoples in terms of noble-savage imagery, thus establishing a trail of false mysticism which bedevils interpretations of pastoral behaviour to the present day" (1974:3). He continues by noting that the idea is akin to that of the gypsy who lives a romantic, free life, refusing to put down roots in settled civilization. We should add that such romantic images always have a counter-image: people who refuse to accept the norms of civilized life can be seen as untrustworthy, thieving, petty criminals. Such attitudes prevented an understanding of the complex land tenure and ecological systems of pastoralists. By the post-World War II period, Baker notes, this romantic mystique had changed to the conceptions of irrational production and resource management and resistance to innovation we have already mentioned.

T. Monod developed the criminality theme in the Introduction to his 1975 symposium volume. He noted that Europeans were particularly concerned with this, due to their awareness of frequent cattle raiding and tribal feuding by pastoralists. He suggests that these fears may have psychological origins in European peasant fears of predatory nomads, as well as more specific and recent experiences by settlers in East Africa. (Perhaps the attitudes might even go back to the Middle Ages and the Mongol invasions!)

C. Widstrand (1973) in a paper on the Kenya Special Rural Development Program and its involvement with pastoralists describes still another facet of the interpretations of pastoralism made by sedentary peoples: paternalism. A paternalistic attitude, like the earlier romantic images, is two-edged: a feeling that pastoral peoples are a special charge, a burden, and that one must do his best for them, coupled with a fear of their unpredictable or childish behavior. This is translated into action in the form of apparently benevolent development programs which limit the mobility of pastoralists but fail to compensate for the resource deprivation such schemes have usually caused. "Native reserves," "block grazing schemes" and "group ranches" are seen by Widstrand as implementations of a subjectively-determined policy to contain pastoralists, remove their dangers, avoid open repression and seem to help them make an accommodation to modernity—but without really doing so.

Clare Oxby provides additional details. She describes the main arguments used by governments—colonial and post-colonial—to justify interventions with pastoralists as follows (1975:4):

1. to 'raise their standard of living';
2. to integrate them into the national society;
3. to make them easier to administer;
4. to prevent them from posing a military threat to their national governments;
5. to make them economically self-sufficient;
6. to make them contribute to the national economy;
7. to make pastoral nomadism a 'viable' form of livelihood;
8. to promote better diplomatic relations with the governments administering pastoral nomads.

This list includes just about everything: paternalism; economics; fears and need for containment and pacification; needs for settlement of boundary problems and other political aspects. Pastoralists need to be assisted, but they have responsibilities as members of new nations. Such objectives are not figments, but rather judgments based on historical experiences, and like all such judgments are colored by values and prejudices as well as rationalizations and guilt from the colonial era, or resentments of barbarous tribals on the part of villagers and city elites. The economic-assistance theme received substantial reinforcement from World Bank and USAID sources in the mid-1970s, with their emphases on alleviation of poverty and guarantees of 'basic needs.' Pastoralists were viewed as 'poor' because they lacked possessions; however, from the point of view of peasant smallholders, pastoralists were the rich, since they possessed a store of capital: animals. If they were indigent in some localities, it was because of temporary drought, or development programs, not some intrinsic defect in the mode of production. If they had been dangerous and unruly in the past, or the present, it was because they needed land to permit expansion of herds—itself a source of misunderstandings, since with communal land tenure no one was supposed to 'own' or 'appropriate' land. The attitudinal dynamics of the situation closely resemble the situation of American settlers and military on the American Western frontier in the latter half of the nineteenth century; perhaps these are inevitable formations in frontier situations characterized by disparity of economic scales and modes.

The ease-of-administration argument set forth by colonial and independent governments is an especially common one and lies beneath, in particular, the elaborate programs followed by Tanzania with regard to the Masai. Generally this argument is spelled out as a matter of providing social services and agricultural inputs to pastoralists, who must undergo sedentarization or at least some intermittent nuclear settlement. Such arguments are based in part on evolutionary dicta: that by sedentarizing pastoralists, one turns them into agriculturalists, from which they pass to the third stage: townsmen or industrial workers. The "villagization" attempts (as they were known in northern Tanzania) were thus viewed as historically necessary and inevitable, not simply as a beneficial exercise designed for some short-term objective. Such conceptions have ignored the fact that pastoralists in the Middle East and Africa have become familiar with such occupations as manual labor, taxi-driving, oil-well-rigging, industrial labor and so on, without requiring the transitional stages of settlement mandated by the evolutionary theorists.

The responsibility and obligation theme must be taken seriously, and not equated with attitudes deriving more from ignorance and prejudice. In this context, the anthropological commentators and the pro-pastoralist spokesmen have not always shown an awareness of the basic imperatives of the nation-state framework. A note of ethnic preservationism has been present in some of the anthropological defenses of migratory pastoralism as a way of life, and this perspective has generated considerable controversy, both within anthropology and between anthropologists and development specialists. Modern nations do require their citizens to be incorporated into productive activities which have some relationship to the needs of the whole population: such demands will be made and must be met in some degree. The alternative would seem to be a tribal reserve system in which the ethnic group is kept in a kind of living museum status, which creates persistent social and political difficulties for everyone concerned.

A History of Development Initiatives

England, Germany, and France competed for domination of eastern Africa during the latter half of the nineteenth century, the issue reaching a stage of resolution in the late 1880s and 1890s with the assignment of Tanganyika to Germany; Kenya and Sudan to Britain; and Madagascar to France. World War I saw a shift of control in Tanganyika from Germany to England; France remained in control of the island until World War II, and its subsequent independence. The countries of the Horn had a brief Italian period.

British policies with respect to pastoral tribes have been documented by various writers. Representative examples of the part of this literature dealing with Kenya can be summarized. J. Lamphear (1976) has examined the relations of the Turkana to the British in the period around 1900, when the various bovine diseases became epidemic and the tribes resorted to raiding in order to replace depleted herds. The British responded with punitive expeditions which stopped much of the raiding, but also disrupted Turkana movements for pasturage, aggravating their difficulties. British policies with respect to the Masai in the same period are detailed by, among others, R. Waller (1976). As a result of the rinderpest epidemics, many Masai turned to agriculture, both in the southern semi-arid range areas and also in more suitable lands farmed by Kikuyu and Kamba. The latter movements were based on familiarity with the region due to the Masai custom of permitting their young men to seek farm labor employment among these tribes in the past. However, the farming episode had some aspects of an invasion and was occasionally resisted by the agricultural tribes. As herds increased, the mutual hostilities did likewise, requiring British intervention. The upshot was a curious alliance between the British and the Masai, in which the latter served as a kind of mercenary army, raiding other tribal groups with a history of depredation. These activities served to create an enmity for the Masai which persists today.

E.R. Turton (1972) details the history of groups of Somali tribesmen in Kenya in the period 1893 to the 1960s. By 1919, British punitive expeditions had succeeded in pacifying these people and pushing them into the far northeast region where they would presumably constitute less danger to Turkana and other indigenous Kenya peoples. However, Somali never accepted pacification and continued to follow their historical pasturage routes down to and into the period of independence. British attempts at corralling Somali into block grazing schemes were also resisted, and the persistent hostility of the Somali to the British culminated in 1960 in a serious secession movement of these people, echoes of which continue to be heard in northern Kenya.

The evolution of colonial policies toward pastoralists and pastoralism can be sketched, using Kenya (for which the best data exists: see Mighot-Adholla and Little 1981) as the example: the pattern of pacification, alienation of pastoral grazing lands and treatment of migratory pastoralists as savage or barbarous tribes continued down to World War II. During the period, the British engaged in a number of attempts to develop superior grazing facilities and water resources, but most of the measures emphasized conservation and less intensive use of pasturelands which they perceived as undergoing progressive deterioration. Occasionally, the British admitted that this deterioration was largely caused by colonial disruption of land use patterns evolved during the nineteenth century by indigenous pastoralist and cultivator peoples. However, on the whole, the traditional system was faulted as the cause of the environmental problems. Pastoralist livestock was ignored as unsuitable for commercial production, and due to the bovine diseases, was rigorously quarantined so as to shield European cattle from infestation (a policy which had little effect on the whole). This also meant that no attempt was made to develop markets for pastoralist livestock; indeed, in many districts, efforts were made to prevent them from entering sales programs. The period of World War II marked a change in policy to the extent that the British embarked on a campaign to encourage African agriculturalists, including pastoralists, to intensify commercial food production for war preparation. However, this had little effect in the pastoralist areas due to restrictions on pasture and to lack of interest on the part of pastoralists in increased commercial sales, since they had less need for the available urban or cultivator-oriented tools and consumer goods.

Continued deterioration of rangeland led the British to inaugurate their first coordinated development program aimed at pastoralism, and the lineal ancestor of all subsequent development plans down into the contemporary period. This was the "Ten Year Plan: 1946–55," which was based on a resettlement scheme for the semi-arid regions of Kenya and Tanganyika. The activities included nearly all of the specific targets of later plans: rinderpest control; locust control; tsetse eradication; borehole development; irrigation; erosion control; reforestation; rural road construction; and some marketing boards and programs. Pastoralist and semi-cultivator groups were moved into new areas to eliminate overuse. The Plan conceived of the problems of pastoralism and range areas as essentially those of conservation of physical resources, caused by overpopulation, overconcentration and overproduction. This basic philosophy guided development projects in East Africa for a long time. The pastoralist population was considered as the vehicle of deterioration and abuse, and secondarily as a body of people deserving education or assistance in overcoming the disruption of their livelihood induced by colonial intervention.

In the mid-1950s, the Ten Year Plan evolved into a somewhat different approach, based on concepts of resource management and land tenure. It was considered that the pastoralist style of management of communal grazing was inherently defective or non-rational. In 1954, the Ten Year Plan was supplemented by the Swynnerton Plan which aimed at the introduction of private land ownership among pastoralists coupled with encouragement for a shift to cultivation of export crops. Excess pastoralist population was urged to migrate to cities and enter the labor force. Field projects included the earlier types, but also included more emphasis on marketing of livestock, and also the first intensive attempts to reduce herd size and control grazing movements by introducing block territories for particular sets of herd owners and tribal sections. Such attempts to limit migratory pasturage were not entirely new, since the British had tried them in northern Kenya earlier in the century, but more in line with pacification or corralling policies, rather than as attempts to improve grazing resources or adjust herd size to carrying capacity. Most of these schemes had dwindled to inconspicuous efforts by 1960, but the period also saw the beginning of the second major facet of the contemporary development program: the attempt to tackle the central issue of over-stocking and pasture and range management.

While this represented a gain in the sense that attention was finally being directed toward the key components of the pastoral system, there was no coherent theory or model of migratory pastoralism as a system, nor of pastoralists in conjunction with other modes of production and occupation. Basically, the problem was viewed narrowly as one of 'proper' land use, not as a matter of transforming a socionatural system out of adjustment with its physical and socioeconomic environments. Thus, 1960 can be taken as the beginning of the era of frustration among the developers: while they were aware that the direct or obvious sources of trouble were being addressed, the efforts at change were consistently defeated by resistance from pastoralists, or by their seeming inability to learn the correct routines.

East Africa suffered a serious drought in the early 1960s, which resulted in a predictable response: a return to conservation themes in assistance and development programs. In 1963, Kenya established a Range Management Division in its Ministry of Agriculture, and this new agency was put in charge of pasture development and range conservation. A few years later a Livestock Marketing Division was created to facilitate the sales programs for surplus animals, particularly in pastoralist groups. This agency was responsible for a still-continuing program involving the sale of pastoralist animals from the northern ranges to farmers in the south who finish them. This program has some advantages insofar as it assists pastoralists in participating in stratified production systems, but according to some critics (e.g., Mighot-Adholla and Little 1981: 147), this policy has hampered more potentially pro-ductive programs to integrate pastoralist and farmer economies in par-ticular regions built on traditional barter systems.

In 1965, the International Livestock Research Centre inaugurated its East African Livestock Survey with the cooperation of the country governments. This provided the first substantial body of comparative information on production, marketing, and other facets. It resulted in new initiatives and agencies, and an awareness of the importance of animal husbandry—which up to that time had taken a back seat to crop production. Among other things, the Survey underlined the need for positive measures to establish pastoralist production on a commercial basis, and its possible significance as a source of national income in the export livestock markets. For Kenya, the major effect was the Group Representatives Act of 1968 which created the grazing-block system, or at least put the institution of pastoralist grazing reserves—an old idea— on a formal legal tenure basis. Pastoralists were enabled to register for tracts of land which would be assigned to them as their 'group ranch'— the term by which the institution came to be known. The system was implemented mainly in Masai districts, and comparable developments in Tanzania, although based on somewhat different principles, were established about the same time.

The history of the group ranches is complex, and in the earlier literature (i.e., Hess 1976), is mainly a story of failure insofar as the explicit objectives were not met. Restricted pasturage required stock reduction, and quotas were set in order for the herding group to qualify for assistance in the form of veterinary services, borehole drilling and the like. This led to conflict within the herding groups, with the large herd owners seeking quotas proportionate to their holdings, and urging enforcement of the quota system in order to keep small owners from building up their herds. The big owners simply kept increasing their herds regardless of quotas in accordance with the natural momentum of pastoralist livestock production under climatic uncertainty. The restricted pasturage combined with the persisting system of individual herd ownership resulted in social tension and overgrazing, and no device emerged or was created to ensure responsibility for controlling herd sizes or pasture use.

However, the 'failure' of the group ranch is strictly relative to the objectives one expects it to achieve. The more recent literature strikes a different note: Clare Oxby points out (1981), that while group ranches in Kenya may not be capable of serving the goal of commercializing beef production (the commercial ranches are more suitable for this purpose), the group ranch does confer tenure rights to land on pastoralists, and pastoralists have shown some ability to adapt to the more intensive modes of production that such restricted grazing requires, although this process has been a slow one. Moreover, in some districts the group ranch has gradually become a focus of settlement: Masai in Kenya and Tanzania are using the government-created centers of social services as places to house aging relatives and as places of temporary residence for mothers and children of families who take advantage of educational facilities. Whether these movements can be considered as the first steps toward 'sedentarization' is a matter of debate. Finally, the Masai, at least, have developed a sharp sense of property ownership concerning land, and have defended their titles to group ranch territories with tenacity (Galaty 1980).

"Supervised Grazing Blocks" were simply a continuation of the old grazing blocks in the northeast introduced by the British many years previously, but now with greater government intervention and control. Grazing fees were charged, a device expected to provide a negative incentive to pastoralists to control stock population. However, as in the case of the group ranches, pastoralists did not stay within the boundaries of the blocks, and they ignored grazing fees or failed to provide accurate reports on herd sizes. In addition, the pastoralist herds of the northeast are multi-species, and it proved impossible to pasture cattle, camels, sheep and goats in the same restricted areas. Pasture rotation schemes were worked out for cattle by government supervisors, who had inadequate knowledge for the task.

The problems of various restricted-grazing instrumentalities in pastoralist development are many, but are all underlain by drought. None of the schemes—early or late—considered the effect of greatly reduced forage production due to moisture deficiencies on grazing and herd health and survival. Nor were marketing facilities created to deal with emergencies of this kind. The onus was thrust on the pastoralists themselves, who were expected to make quick adjustments. While they are capable of handling drought, their ability to do so is hampered by the changes in grazing facilities introduced by the development projects. The 'conservatism' of pastoralists, as seen by developers, is often little more than the reduced capacity for strategic choice. The ecological consequences have been severe: range development projects have often worsened the conditions they were designed to correct (Talbot 1972).

Pastoralists perceive land—pasture, range—as a place to practice grazing; to raise as many livestock as possible for domestic use and for markets when that is feasible or profitable. They use land for foraging for useful plants, charcoal, honey, occasional wide game. Governments, on the other hand, view land as a multiple-use resource, of significance to the entire nation. Game parks, plantations, farming, commercial livestock production, urban settlement are all potential uses for rangeland—particularly, the better range in semi-arid and sub-humid regions. When rangeland formerly used by pastoralists passes into new uses, pastoralists experience increasing difficulty in doing what is necessary to raise the animals they wish to raise, and to cope with recurrent conditions such as drought which require flexible and mobile responses. The history of development in pastoralist districts shows a consistent neglect of consulting the pastoralists themselves, arbitrary modifications of land tenure and use patterns, and inauguration of assistance programs which are neglected or withdrawn at the first sign of trouble. Pastoralists have been low-priority populations; until some means is found to enhance their contribution to the political economy of East African countries, they will continue to lose ground—both figuratively and in reality.[8]

The Contemporary Development Projects[9]

Since the early 1960s, development initiatives in eastern Africa have been dominated by U.S. funds, administered primarily through the World Bank and USAID, although many projects have enjoyed participation from CIDA and European agencies. No single accounting of all expenditures for livestock development projects has been made, and an accurate figure would be impossible to achieve, given the many different types of funding, currencies, exchange rates and the like, over the twenty-odd years of projects. USAID in 1980 estimated that the agency had spent approximately US$618 million on livestock projects over the 1970–1979 period in all countries of Africa with an AID mission. A strictly unofficial estimate made by the writer for World Bank livestock-related projects in East Africa alone is in the neighborhood of US$100 million (mostly as loan credits). These figures omit, of course, direct expenditures by country governments and supplemental funds provided for projects not directly related to livestock, or to their human raisers, but which would serve the industry; e.g., range conservation; rural roads which might help move animals to market; or village development schemes. Obviously many millions of dollars were spent in the fifteen to twenty years of post-independence livestock-related projects in eastern Africa alone.

Moreover, most projects mainly affected farmer-cattle producers or groups transitional between migratory and village life, not true migratory herders. A preliminary, and as yet very rough calculation by the writer aimed at determining just what proportion of foreign aid funds were directed toward migratory pastoralists in eastern Africa (Ethiopia, Somalia, Kenya, Tanzania), suggests that not more than one-third and not less than one-fifth of all development funding was supposed to benefit these people. However, since many of the projects were poorly conceived and were not designed in a way that could benefit pastoralists, the amount of money that actually assisted pastoralists in their transition to a new and viable ecosystem was probably very small.

One reason for this is to be found in the tendency to conceive of the development task as centered on the construction and improvement of government bureaus or parastatal organizations charged with the responsibility of developing commercial livestock systems. Such organizations may concern range management, land tenure, commercial ranch operation, marketing, road construction, water resource development, abattoirs, hide processing, milk processing and any other relevant aspect of animal industry. While all international development agencies participated in such activity, the World Bank projects seem especially characteristic. The reason for this may lie in the structure of Bank funding operations: funds are not direct grants, but loans, and a responsible agency must exist for guaranteeing repayment. By establishing a company, staffed by government or quasi-government personnel, this responsibility element is presumably secured.

However, on the whole and in the views of the evaluation teams hired by the agencies themselves, none of the USAID or World Bank projects funded between 1960 and 1975 were considered to be a success. Nearly every organization created by the projects was judged to be in or close to bankruptcy, organizational disintegration or operating in a state of gross inefficiency within a few years after inception. A second funding project usually would follow, designed to revive the organization or to render its services more effective. Most of the second-stage livestock projects in eastern African countries were, in whole or part, attempts at recouping losses. However, whatever else they may have accomplished, such projects simply increased the indebtedness of the country governments, especially in the Bank projects.

The reasons for the failure of these government and parastatal organizations charged with the task of commercializing production among pastoralists and farmers are to be found in their ignorance or neglect of the important needs of livestock production in the transitional subsistence-commercial indigenous regimes. The factors include: ecological and economic reasons for herd movement; marketing and pricing policies which discouraged, rather than facilitated, offtake; the failure to deliver promised improvements such as water supplies; the tendency for the project to operate over a short time period, on the assumption that production regimes with generations of indigenous success could be transformed quickly; and others. Underlying the design of most livestock projects was a view derived from Western economic theory: that to induce changes in production strategies among agriculturalists all one has to do is provide market incentives; or more generally, appropriate economic-technological inputs automatically yield expected economic outputs.

Projects designed under the influence of this philosophy contain an element of built-in failure. The larger social environment of pastoralist production is ignored, and the task is focussed sharply on cattle alone. For example, most projects designed to encourage pastoralist offtake

were based on the assumption (rarely stated) that national livestock
prices would provide the necessary incentive for a flow of animals toward
the companies, and hence, the revenue which would permit the organization to function at a profit, returning funds to the government,
which could then repay the loan. However, frequently governments would
fix livestock prices artificially low in order to keep meat and other animal
product prices low for the consumer, thus sabotaging producer incentives
to sell animals. The aid grant could not be made on the condition that
prices would be favorable to the producers, since this would be considered
interference in domestic political and economic policy.

Likewise, attempts at introducing modern marketing systems were
often conceived in a vacuum—as if the traditional social reciprocities
and marketing systems of the villages and rangelands did not exist. An
occasional project paper might mention the inefficiency of these systems
of middlemen and moneylenders, usually in a derogatory sense as
impeding adequate pricing or as manipulating the producers so as to
maintain small monopolies, but the activities of the marketing companies
established by the projects were defined simply as offering 'better' services.
Since in nearly all cases these had only modest success, the traditional
systems persist. In addition, these local livestock buyers in African
countries play roles in the general social wellbeing and financing of small
producers, however inefficient or even exploitative they might be considered from the technical-aid standpoint. However, in some cases, as
in Somalia, the development projects had the effect of increasing the
activities of the traditional middlemen, to the disbenefit of the producers
(Aronson 1982).

While the later projects were conceived under the aegis of 'basic needs'
philosophy of the mid-1970s development milieu, most of the project
designs appear to give only lip service to the goal. The 'beneficiaries'
in these later projects could be formally designated as pastoralists (and/
or farmers), but a careful analysis of the project objectives and budgets
turned up little that could be considered beneficial to the producers.
Most of the financial emphasis was, as already noted, on organizations—
and on various high-technology construction projects such as holding
pens, range improvements, road building, the purchase of bulldozers,
trucks and so on. While in the later projects funds were allocated to
'training,' in most cases these were minuscule compared to the expenditures for organization and construction, and almost always concerned
with the training of technical experts from the companies, ministries
or research institutes, not the producers themselves. In addition, in
Kenya and Tanzania, larger proportions of project money often went
to the commercial ranching sector than to the pastoralist and farmer

producers, suggesting that the underlying government motive was really to develop export beef production.

Summing up, it can be said that the internationally-sponsored livestock development projects aimed at pastoralists in the 1960s and 1970s were concerned mainly with commercial beef production, with government and company organization and with arrangements to repay loans, rather than with the general welfare or even the increase of livestock production among smaller indigenous producers. These objectives reflect familiar constraints in the international development agencies, but there is little doubt that they also mirror objectives of the country governments of eastern Africa as well—objectives which stem from many causes, including the general financial consequences of previous projects. As for migratory pastoralists, there is no doubt they are responding to the pressures on them to settle down and raise wanted products, but the precise direction of change, and its rate, is still unclear. That it will vary for different populations and countries goes without saying.

Notes

1. See Ole Saibull 1974; Ndagala 1982; for a discussion of Masai 'sedentarization.'

2. See D.L. Johnson 1973 for a description of how Sahelian pastoralists coped with drought prior to government intervention.

3. For typical tribal monographs, see Evans-Pritchard 1940; Gulliver 1955; Lewis 1972.

4. For a monograph, see Dahl 1979; early attempts at synthesis or discursive modelling of the main lines of the two stages of ethnological research may be found in Spooner 1971 and Dyson-Hudson 1972. For symposia illustrating the thrust of the earlier work, see Monod 1975; and Irons and Dyson-Hudson 1972.

5. For a symposium volume illustrating this broadened perspective, see Galaty, Aronson and Salzman 1981.

6. Salzman 1980; Galaty, Aronson and Salzman 1981; but for an earlier conference, stimulated mainly by West African work, see Lefebure 1979. For some attempts to construct systemic models of pastoral ecology and production, see the following: Carr 1977; Dahl and Hjort 1976; Picardi 1974.

7. Or what Peter Little 1980 called the "total environment."

8. This historical summary of early development policies was based mainly on the following: Hess 1976; Jahnke 1978; Livingstone 1979; Mighot-Adholla and Little 1981; Nkinyangi 1981. Some detailed accounts of the "group ranch" are: Ayuko 1981; Baker 1976; Galaty 1980, 1981; Hopcraft 1981; Jacobs 1975. Although Kenya was selected as the principal example, more attention will be given Tanzania in other versions of this paper. However, for Tanzania the following items are useful: Hyden 1980; Ole Saibull 1974; Ole Parkipuny 1975; Rigby 1980. The main issue in the Tanzanian Masai situation is the attempt of

the government to promote sedentarization in line with its policies to develop a cooperative-collective village form.

9. This section is a very brief summary of a study of most of the key project documents for World Bank and USAID livestock projects in the following countries: Kenya, Tanzania, Somalia, Ethiopia. These projects were operative in the period 1970–1981, although aspects of some of them are still in effect. The full length analysis of the materials is found in a monograph written by the author for the Land Tenure Center of the University of Wisconsin and USAID, published as a Research Paper by the Center in 1984.

References

Aronson, Dan. R. 1980 "Must Nomads Settle: Some Notes Toward Policy on the Future of Pastoralism," in P. Salzman (ed.), *When Nomads Settle: Processes of Sedentarization as Adaptation and Response*. New York: Praeger.

1982 "Pastoralists: Losing Ground in Somalia," *Anthropology Resource Center Newsletter*. March.

Ayuko, Lucas J. 1981 "Organization, Structures, and Ranches in Kenya," *Pastoral Network Paper 11b*. London: Overseas Development Institute, Agricultural Administration University.

Baker, Randall 1974 *Perceptions of Pastoralism*. Edinburgh: Center for Tropical Veterinary Medicine.

1976 "Innovation Technology Transfer and Nomadic Pastoral Societies," in M. Glanz (ed.), *The Politics of Natural Disaster*. New York: Praeger Publishers.

Baxter, P.T.W. 1975 "Some Consequences of Sedentarization for Social Relationships," in T. Monod (ed.), *Pastoralism in Tropical Africa*. London: International African Institute and Oxford University Press.

Bennett, J.W. 1984 "Political Ecology and Development Projects Affecting Pastoralist Peoples in East Africa." Land Tenure Center, Research Paper No. 80. Madison, Wisconsin.

Boserup, Ester 1965 *The Conditions of Agricultural Growth: The Economics of Agrarian Change under Population Pressure*. Chicago: Aldine Publishing Co.

Brokenshaw, David W., Michael M. Horowitz and Thayer Scudder 1977 *The Anthropology of Rural Development in the Sahel*. Binghampton: Institute for Development Anthropology and USAID.

Campbell, David J. and George H. Axinn 1980 "Pastoralism in Kenya," *Report No. 30: Africa*. Hanover, N.H.: American Universities Field Staff.

Carr, Claudia J. 1977 "Pastoralism in Crisis: The Dasanetch and their Ethiopian Lands," *Research Paper No. 180*. Department of Geography, University of Chicago.

Carvalho, Cruz de. E. 1974 " 'Traditional' and 'Modern' Patterns of Cattle-Raising in SW Angola." *Journal of Developing Areas*. Vol. 8, No. 2, pp. 199–225.

Dahl, Gudrun 1979 "Ecology and Society: The Boran Case," in C. Lefebvre (apparent ed.), *Pastoral Production and Society*. L'Equipe Ecologie et Anthropologie des Sociétiés Pastorales. Cambridge: Cambridge University Press.

Dahl, G. and A. Hjort 1976 "Having Herds: Pastoral Herd Growth and Household Economy," *Studies in Social Anthropology No. 2.* Department of Social Anthropology, University of Stockholm.

Dyson-Hudson, Neville 1972 "The Study of Nomads," in W. Irons and N. Dyson-Hudson (eds.), *Perspectives on Nomadism.* Leiden: Brill & Co.

Evans-Pritchard, E. 1940 *The Nuer.* Oxford: Oxford University Press.

FAO Group Fellowship Study Tour Reports n.d. "Settlement in Agriculture of Nomadic, Semi-nomadic, and Other Pastoral People." FAO-TA 2810. FAO Near East Regional Study.

1972 "Animal Husbandry, Production and Range Management in the Near East."

FAO Expert Consultation 1972 "The Settlement of Nomads in Africa and the Near East." FAO-RP20.

Ferguson, Donald T. 1980 *A Conceptual Framework for the Evaluation of Livestock Production Development Projects and Programs in Sub-Saharan West Africa.* Ann Arbor: Center for Research on Economic Development, University of Michigan.

Ford, J. 1960 "The Influence of Tsetse Flies on the Distribution of African Cattle," in Proceedings of the First Federal Science Congress, Salisbury, Rhodesia.

1971 *The Role of the Trypanosomiases in African Ecology.* Oxford: The Clarendon Press.

Forde, C. Daryll 1934 *Habitat, Economy and Society.* New York: Harcourt Brace.

Fumagalli, Carl T. 1978 "An Evaluation of Development Projects among East African Pastoralists," *African Studies Review: The Social Sciences and African Development Planning.* Vol. 29 Special issue, pp. 49–63.

Galaty, John G. 1980 "The Maasai Group-Ranch: Politics and Development in an African Pastoral Society," in P. Salzman (ed.), *When Nomads Settle: Processes of Sedentarization as Adaptation and Response.* New York: Praeger.

1981a "Organizations for Pastoral Development: Contexts of Causality, Change, and Assessment," in J. Galaty, D. Aronson and P. Salzman (eds.), *The Future of Pastoral Peoples.* Ottawa: International Development Research Centre.

1981b "Introduction: Nomadic Pastoralists and Social Change," in J. Galaty and P. Salzman, (eds.) *Change and Development in Nomadic and Pastoral Societies.* Leiden: Brill & Co.

Galaty, John G., Dan Aronson and Philip C. Salzman 1981 "The Future of Pastoral Peoples." Proceedings of a Conference held in Nairobi, Kenya, 1980. Ottawa: The International Development Research Centre for the Commission on Nomadic Peoples, International Union of Anthropological and Ethnological Sciences.

Gulbrandsen, Ornulf 1980 "Agro-Pastoral Production and Communal Land Use: A Socio-economic Study of the Bangwaketse." Rural Sociology Unit, University of Bergen. Issued by the Ministry of Agriculture, Botswana.

Gulliver, P.H. 1955 *The Family Herds: A Study of Two Pastoral Tribes in East Africa: Jie and Turkana.* London: Routledge & Kegan Paul.

Haaland, Gunnar 1972 "Nomadism as an Economic Career among the Sedentaries of the Sudan Savannah Belt," in I. Cunnison (ed.). *Essays in Sudan Ethnography.* London: C. Hurst.

Hardin, Garrett 1968 "The Tragedy of the Commons," *Science.* Vol. 162, pp. 1243–48.

Herskovits, Melville J. 1926 "The Cattle Complex in East Africa," *American Anthropologist* Vol. 28, pp. 230–72; 361–88; 494–528; 633–44.

Hess, Olean 1976 "The Establishment of Cattle Ranching Associations Among the Masai in Tanzania," *Occasional Paper No. 7.* Ghana: USAID, (Cornell University).

Hjort, Anders 1981 "Herds, Trade and Grain: Pastoralism in a Regional Perspective," in J. Galaty, D. Aronson and P. Salzman (eds.), *The Future of Pastoral Peoples.* Ottawa: International Development Research Centre.

1982 "A Critique of "Ecological" Models of Pastoral Land Use," *Nomadic Peoples.* Vol. 10, pp. 11–27.

Hopcraft, Peter N. 1981 "Economic Institutions and Pastoral Resources Management: Considerations for a Development Strategy," in J. Galaty, D. Aronson and P. Salzman (eds.), *The Future of Pastoral Peoples.* Ottawa: International Development Research Centre.

Hyden, Goran 1980 *Beyond Ujamaa in Tanzania.* Berkeley: University of California Press.

Irons, William and N. Dyson-Hudson (eds.) 1972 *Perspectives on Nomadism.* Leiden, Netherlands: Brill & Co.

Jacobs, Alan H. 1975 "Masai Pastoralism in Historical Pespective," in T. Monod (ed.), *Pastoralism in Tropical Africa.* London: International African Institute and Oxford University Press.

Jahnke, H.E. 1978 "A Historical View of Range Development in Kenya." Nairobi: International Livestock Centre for Africa, Livestock Development Course Note 23, 1.

Johnson, Douglas L. 1973 *The Response of Pastoral Nomads to Drought in the Absence of Outside Intervention.* New York: United Nations Special Sahelian Office.

Kjekshus, Helge 1977 *Ecology Control and Economic Development in East African History.* London and Nairobi: Heinemann.

Konczacki, Z.A. 1978 *The Economics of Pastoralism. A Case Study of Sub-Saharan Africa.* London: Frank Cass.

Lamphear, John 1976 "Aspects of Turkana Leadership During the Era of Primary Resistance," *Journal of African History* Vol. 17, pp. 225–243.

Lefebure, Claude 1979 "Introduction." *Pastoral Production and Society.* Proceedings of the International Meeting on Nomadic Pastoralism, Paris. New York: Cambridge University Press.

Lewis, B.A. 1972 *The Murle.* Oxford: Clarendon Press (British Social Anthropological Study of Southern Sudan Group).

Little, Peter D. 1980 "Pastoralism and Strategies: Socio-economic Change in the Pastoral Sector of Baringo District, Kenya," Working Paper No. 368, Institute of Development Studies, University of Nairobi.

Livingstone, Ian 1977 "Economic Irrationality Among Pastoral Peoples: Myth or Reality?" *Development and Change.* Vol. 8, pp. 209–30.

1979 "Socio-Economics of Ranching in Kenya," in G. Dalton (ed.), *Research in Economic Anthropology,* Vol. 2. Greenwich Connecticut: JAI Press.

Low, Allan 1980 "The Estimation and Interpretation of Pastoralists' Price Responsiveness," Pastoral Network Paper 10c, London: Overseas Development Institute, Agricultural Administration Unit.

Lundgren, Bjorn 1975 *Land Use in Kenya and Tanzania.* Stockholm: Royal College of Forestry, International Rural Development Division.

Mighot-Adholla, S.E. and Peter D. Little 1981 "Evolution of Policy Toward the Development of Pastoral Areas in Kenya," in J. Galaty, D. Aronson and P. Salzman (eds.), *The Future of Pastoral Peoples.* Ottawa: International Development Research Centre.

Monod, Theodore (ed.) 1975 *Pastoralism in Tropical Africa.* London: Oxford University Press.

Ndagala, D.K. 1982 ""Operation Imparnati": The Sedentarization of the Pastoral Masai in Tanzania," *Nomadic Peoples.* Vol. 10, pp. 28–39.

Ngutter, L.G.K. 1979 "Kenya Government Policy in Semi-Arid Areas: Its Evolution." Paper presented at the Workshop on the Development of Kenya's Semi-Arid Areas. Institute of Development Studies, University of Nairobi.

Nkinyangi, John A. 1981 "Education for Nomadic Pastoralists," in J. Galaty, D. Aronson and P. Salzman (eds.), *The Future of Pastoral Peoples.* Ottawa: International Development Research Centre.

Ole Saibull, S.A. 1974 "Social Change Among the Pastoral Masai of Tanzania in Response to the Ujamaa Vijijini Policy." Dar es Salaam, Tanzania: University of Dar es Salaam. Faculty of Arts and Social Sciences.

Oxby, Clare 1975 *Pastoral Nomads and Development.* London: International African Institute.

1981 "Group Ranches in Africa." *Overseas Development Institute Review.* No. 2, pp. 44–56.

Ole Parkipuny, M.L. 1975 "Masai Predicament Beyond Pastoralism: A Case Study in the Socio-Economic Transformation of Pastoralism." Dar es Salaam, Tanzania: University of Dar es Salaam, Institute of Development Studies. (Duplicated report).

Picardi, A.C. 1974 "A Systems Analysis of Pastoralism in the West African Sahel: Evaluating Long-term Strategies for the Development of the Sahel-Sudan Region," *Annex 5.* Centre for Policy Alternatives, Massachusetts Institute of Technology.

Rigby, Peter 1969 "Pastoralism and Prejudice: Ideology and Rural Development in East Africa," in P. Rigby (ed.). *Society and Social Change in Eastern Africa.* Kampala: Makerere Institute of Social Research, Nkanga Editions, No. 4:42–52.

1980 "Pastoralist Production and Socialist Transformation in Tanzania," in A.D. Anacleti (ed.), *Jipemoyo 2/1980.* Dar es Salaam and Helsinki: University of Helsinki for Ministry of National Culture and Youth, Dar es Salaam, and Finnish Academy.

Salzman, Philip C. 1972 "Multi-Resource Nomadism in Iranian Baluchistan," in W. Irons and N. Dyson-Hudson (eds.), *Perspectives on Nomadism*. Leiden: Brill and Co.

1980 (ed.), *When Nomads Settle: Processes of Sedentarization as Adaptation and Response*. New York: Praeger.

Sandford, Stephen 1976a "Size and Importance of Pastoral Populations." London: Overseas Development Institute, Agricultural Administration Unit: Design and Management of Pastoral Development; Pastoral Network Paper 1c (mimeographed).

1976b "Human Pastoral Populations." London: Overseas Development Institute, Agricultural Administration Unit: Design and Management of Pastoral Development; Pastoral Network Paper 2c (mimeographed).

Shorter, Aylward 1974 "Conservative Pastoral Societies," in Shorter (ed.), *East African Societies*. London: Routledge and Kegan Paul.

Spooner, Brian 1971 "Towards a Generative Model of Nomadism," *Anthropological Quarterly*. Vol. 44. pp. 198–210.

Swidler, Nina 1980 "Sedentarization and Modes of Economic Integration in the Middle East," in P. Salzman (ed.), *When Nomads Settle: Processes of Sedentarization as Adaptation and Response*. New York: Praeger.

Talbot, L. 1972 "Ecological Consequences of Rangeland Development in Masailand, East Africa," in M.T. Farvar and J.P. Milton (eds.), *The Careless Technology: Ecology and International Development*. Garden City, New York: Natural History Press.

Turton, D. 1976 "Response to Drought: The Mursi of Southwestern Ethiopia," in J.G. Garlick and R.W. Keay (eds.), *Human Ecology in the Tropics*. New York and Toronto: Halsted Press (Symposia for the Study of Human Biology, Vol. 16).

Turton, E.R. 1972 "Somali Resistance to Colonial Rule and the Development of Somali Political Activity in Kenya 1893–1960," *Journal of African History*. Vol. 13, pp. 117–143.

Waller, Richard 1976 "The Masai and the British 1895–1905: The Origin of an Alliance," *Journal of African History*. Vol. 17, pp. 529–553.

Widstrand, Carl G. 1973 "Pastoral Peoples and Rural Development: A Case Study." Vetenskapssamhallet I; Uppsala. *Annales*. Vol. 17, pp. 35–54.

3

DEVELOPMENT STRATEGY IN SRI LANKA AND A PEOPLE'S ALTERNATIVE

Denis Goulet

Development policy in Sri Lanka since Independence in 1948 represents efforts made by successive freely-elected governments to find an optimal mix of social welfare and economic growth. Earlier governments had already committed themselves to a welfare strategy, providing all citizens with free education from the primary to high school levels, food subsidies and health services. Universal suffrage, established in 1931, created a political channel for the people. And although in 1948 the new nation was poor and its economy depended heavily on three cash crops (tea, rubber, and coconuts), its balance of payments position was strong and government budgets regularly showed a current account surplus. Nevertheless,

> . . . beneath this economic well-being lay the organic weaknesses which were to create the major disequilibria of the fifties and sixties . . . it was only in the mid-fifties and the sixties that the inherent weaknesses in (Sri Lanka's) export structure became increasingly evident as the terms of trade began to move consistently against her (Marga 1979:2–3).

Moreover, explosive social tensions reigned on the island. One conflict involved the English-speaking elite (who ruled the nation until 1956) and those who spoke Sinhala, language of the majority ethnic group (70 percent of total population). A second polarity pitted the Sinhalese against Tamils (accounting for 20 percent of population in two component groups: long-established "Ceylonese" Tamils and imported estate labor, the "Indian" Tamils). These problems greatly hampered successive governments in their attempts to combine welfare and growth. After the

armed insurrection of 1971, a political calculus founded on these polarities
habitually tilted policy scales in one direction or the other in response
not only to needs, but to perceived requirements of national security
as well. At all times, especially after foreign reserves were depleted in
the mid-1950s and budgets began registering current account deficits,
Sri Lankan governments sought a policy which would make what was
economically necessary also politically feasible, in a setting where the
"production capacity of the economy failed to expand fast enough to
fulfill the new aspirations that were generated through the social programmes that were implemented." (Marga 1979:17). When Sri Lanka's
"rational" economists acted on the advice of international aid-givers and
stimulated growth, they did so at the expense of welfare sectors in the
public budget, thus giving rise to outcries of a sellout from the political
opposition.

The purpose of this chapter is not to review the economic history of
Sri Lanka, but to analyze the relationship between a large grassroots
movement and the government's development strategy, described by
President J.R. Jayewardene as a move away from "an era of subsidy to
an era of self-sufficiency." (Ceylon Daily News, 21 July 1980). After
outlining national strategy and highlighting a few sectoral priorities, I
shall summarize the philosophy and practice of the Sarvodaya Movement,
along with its views on government relations. Afterwards, I shall examine
the value choices facing Sarvodaya if it is to survive in an altered social
and economic environment and preserve its authenticity as a non-elite
grassroots movement.

Government Policy

In 1977 the right-of-center United National Party (UNP) returned
to power with an overwhelming majority. It won 143 of 168 seats in
the National Assembly, along with popular approval for shifting from
a parliamentary to a presidential system of rule. Because the UNP staked
its prestige and its bid for re-election in 1983 (postponed by referendum
until 1989) on its development program, that program's specific objectives
are worth examining.

The new government blamed the socialist orientations of its predecessor,
the Sri Lanka Freedom Party, led by Mrs. Bandaranaike for depressing
the national economy, resulting in massive unemployment, slow growth,
low productivity in public sectors, and a welfare program which deprived
producers and investors of incentives. Within two years the new government could already point with pride to its GNP growth record: 8.2
percent in 1978 and 6.2 percent in 1979. According to Planning Minister
Ronnie de Mel, it also offered

. . . a package of economic and financial policies intended to revive and resuscitate the economy, which was at breaking point when we took over. We liberalised the economy, dismantled the maze of administrative controls and encouraged private enterprise. At the same time we undertook a massive program of public sector reconstruction to build-up the run-down infrastructure and stimulate and develop the productive sectors (Ministry 1980:iii).

These measures, the government claims, constitute "a fundamental shift in the approach to economic management, namely, from one of intervention and controls to that of guiding the economy towards a course of rapid and self-sustaining growth."

Although they deliberately seek to promote economic growth, government planners recognize the need for large public expenditures on social services for poor sectors of the population. Even as it continues to provide social subsidies, however, the governments seeks new ways to employ the poor more productively. Three main sectors have been designated to stimulate growth and employment: export-led manufacturing; urban construction; and the Accelerated Mahaveli Project, a vast scheme to bring new areas under irrigation and generate rural employment. Lesser priorities include international tourism and a rural housing scheme. All these programs require foreign resources in the form of investment capital and concessionary financial aid.

To illustrate the strategy more concretely, I shall now describe three macro-sectors (export-led manufacturing, Mahaveli and tourism policy), as well as the government's general stance toward foreign resources. Value conflicts in Sri Lankan society resulting from government initiatives in these domains are crucially relevant to the survival of Sarvodaya as an alternative development strategy.

Export-led Manufacturing

The government seeks "the maximum utilization of domestic resources" because Sri Lanka's "unexploited land, water and power together with the vast pool of the educated unemployed" (Ministry 1980:4) are major assets for accelerating growth. Growth can obviously take many directions, but the country's estate agriculture is heavily committed to cash crops—tea, rubber and coconuts; and the traditional food sector is tied to the production of staples—rice, chilies, onions and vegetables. Sri Lanka lacks industrial capital; therefore, its planners have concentrated not on manufacturing for the domestic market but for export. Planners say that manufacturing for export can simultaneously create employment (in 1977 unemployment in Sri Lanka was 20 percent of the labor force) while yielding rapid foreign exchange earnings. The government launched a drive to attract foreign investors, using as its main inducement a newly-created Investment Promotion Zone (IPZ) located outside the capital and administered by the Greater Colombo Economic Commission (GCEC). Although a foreign Investors' Advisory Council and a Local Investors' Advisory Council to promote investments outside the Colombo area have also been established, the centerpiece of manufacturing strategy is clearly the IPZ. Southern Asia already contains many choice manufacturing sites: Singapore, Hong Kong, Taiwan, and Free Trade Zones in Malaysia. Consequently, Sri Lanka's zone could prove attractive only if it offered foreign investors a generous package of incentives.

Promotional materials distributed by the GCEC praise Sri Lanka's natural beauty, its political stability (obviously compromised in the wake of the communal violence which erupted in July of 1983), the industry of its citizens and invoke its abundant natural resources—not the least of which are precious stones. However, the key attraction for foreign investment is a bundle of economic incentives revolving around attractive tax laws; for example, there is a 100 percent tax exemption on corporate and personal earnings for up to ten years, and no limit on equity holdings of foreign investors.

By 1980 eight thousand new jobs had already been created, with projections for fifty thousand jobs once all approved factories begin operating at full potential (in three to five years). Investors come from twenty-six countries; many are small entrepreneurs from Singapore, Hong Kong, India and Korea. Sri Lanka's rationale for 'competing with Singapore' is twofold. First, says one official, labor-intensive industries are no longer profitable in Singapore; therefore, now is a favorable time to provide other opportunities for investors interested in low-salaried but highly productive workers in Asia. A second reason is that, by offering privileges to manufacturers who will also find their own markets for the goods produced, Sri Lanka can quickly gain a foothold in world marketing arenas. These two justifications form part of a more comprehensive one, namely, that the IPZ is but one component in a 'package' of policies aimed cumulatively at increasing and diversifying production, creating employment, and earning foreign exchange for the nation. Arguing that any sound national development strategy requires that attention be paid to creating urban jobs, apologists conclude that the creation of some industry is indispensable. But the purchasing power of Sri Lanka's domestic market is too low (GNP per capita is $190 annually in a country of 14.5 million inhabitants, of whom 80 percent are rural dwellers) to warrant manufacturing for internal consumption alone. The final argument is that IPZ earnings will be used for development purposes benefitting the nation at large.

Mahaveli

In geographical scope, technical complexity, cost and potential impact on the country, the Mahaveli Dam Project is Sri Lanka's largest developmental undertaking ever. In the words of the *Economic Review* 1978:

> The focus of the Accelerated Mahaveli Development Programme will be the construction of five major reservoirs, which are due to provide both for the regulation of a greater part of the water resources of the Mahaveli Ganga and the base for the development of the balance of irrigable areas in this project.

Within Sri Lanka, the Mahaveli is more than a mere project: it has assumed the status of a great leap forward in civilization, or, as one government publicity release declares: "This is the nation's chosen path to salvation" (Ceylon Daily News, 22 July 1980).

Under pressure from the World Bank and other donors alarmed over this "over-ambitious" program, the government made what Finance Minister de Mel terms "massive cuts" in the program. Even in its "accelerated" form, the Mahaveli Scheme is now confined to three dam projects, with work on Randenigala postponed to 1984 and Moragahakanda indefinitely. In spite of these cuts, the World Bank still complains that Mahaveli "remains highly ambitious and will greatly strain available manpower, material and financial resources." Government planners counter with a litany of expected benefits, chief of which is eventual food self-sufficiency, eliminating the need to import over 25 percent of the nation's rice requirements. The number of families to be settled in newly cultivated lands is variously listed as 140,000 or 225,000. Advocates further claim that the scheme will "provide direct livelihood to a million people when we take into account the families already settled there and those who are drawn by the new economic opportunities." To foreign currency savings realized by food sufficiency are added massive energy benefits: "801,000 kilowatts—a power output that is more than double the totality produced by the extant power-sources of the whole Sri Lanka" (Lanka Guardian, 15 July 1980).

Tourism

Tourism is an important, although secondary, ingredient of national development strategy. The government plans to conduct an in-depth review of policy once 500,000 tourists are registered in a single year. If arrivals continue to increase at present rates, policy revision may become necessary within one or two years. When interviewed by this author, however, President Jayewardene observed that "Then maybe we'll have to go to a million tourists," thereby implying that the ceiling had already been raised. A second government criterion for controlling tourism is that the revenue it generates shall not account for more than 5 percent of annual GNP. A third measure is that tourist revenues should not exceed 10 percent of the country's foreign exchange earnings.

International tourism holds out the prospect both of large gains and of huge losses. Because economies heavily dependent on tourism are vulnerable to catastrophic market shifts, strategies must maximize advantages while minimizing risks. The *Economic Review* complains that Sri Lanka's tourist policy-makers have never given sufficient thought to such optimization. Yet if one may judge on the basis of two seminars held in 1978 on the impact of tourism, the 'hard questions' have been faced by the government.

Incentives to tourist investments in Sri Lanka include the previously mentioned tax incentives, generous capital allowances, investment relief, and income tax exemptions for foreign personnel. More importantly, the government's devaluation of the rupee made Sri Lanka competitive in the scramble for 'package-deal' tourist sites. Far more than the island's historical monuments, 2500 years of culture, or unequalled scenic beauty, it is the new exchange rate which attracts tourists to Sri Lanka.

Critics of government policy charge that tourism increases the country's dependence on foreign economic decision-makers; accelerates domestic inflation; leads to moral decline—prostitution, commercialization of personal values, and increased drug traffic; and promotes 'images of consumption' which harm Sri Lanka's commitment to a Basic Human Needs strategy aimed at providing a decent sufficiency of essential goods to all citizens. Government planners reply that whatever evils flow from their policy are kept within tolerable bounds (by the ministrations of Tourist Policy, legislation against prostitution, nudity and drug traffic, etc.). Compared with the benefits derived from tourism—mainly foreign currency earnings and jobs—the risks are insignificant. Greater risks arise, however, from the perceptions of foreign travelers regarding the political climate of Sri Lanka at any given time. Violence associated with the so-called "Black Week" (25–30 July 1983) greatly damaged the image of tourism in 1983.

Foreign Aid

Sri Lanka's development experts view foreign assistance as "essential to bridge the current account deficits arising from the high levels of investment required for the other objectives to be accomplished" (Ministry 1980:iii). In 1979 external aid—one third in grants, the rest in soft loans—covered 65 percent of public investment; aid flows for 1978 and

Table 3.1. Sri Lanka's Aid Receipts 1978-79

(Millions of Rupees)

	Loans		Grants		Total	
	1978	1979	1978	1979	1978	1979
Project Aid	1,221.7	617.1	241.6	1,067.5	1,463.4	1,684.7
Commodity Aid	1,134.7	1,266.5	272.2	558.5	1,406.9	1,825.0
Food & Other Aid	535.5	274.2	444.9	307.2	980.3	581.4
TOTAL	2,891.9	2,157.8	958.7	1,933.3	3,850.6	4,091.1

Source: External Resources Department, Ministry of Finance and Planning

1979 are shown in Table 3.1. Although financial assistance committed in the first half of 1980 totalled over Rs. 5.1 billion in loans and Rs. 995.1 million in grants, the future was not unequivocally rosy. David Housego, Asia correspondent for *The London Financial Times,* voiced the fear that Sri Lanka's debt servicing burden, already 10 percent of foreign earnings, could easily rise to a crushing 40 percent by 1990 (see Table 3.2). Much supplementary external financing is swallowed up by global and domestic inflation and, notwithstanding Sri Lanka's present good fortune, foreign aid is becoming more difficult to obtain. Although public investment now planned by the Sri Lankan government presupposes yearly increases of 5 percent in resources available, informed observers doubt that tax revenues or external aid can rise at that pace. If, therefore, the government is to avoid cutting back on programs on which it has staked so much, it must either augment its domestic borrowing or resort to international commercial loans. The first course would 'dry up' the money pool which private investors must tap to sustain high rates of investment in the national economy, whereas international commerical borrowing is both expensive and tightly controlled.

The World Bank later urged cuts, not only in Mahaveli, but also in housing and urban development schemes. It likewise counseled further tax reductions to the private sector, and "fixing rigid financial limits on the total amount that will be devoted to unavoidable subsidies, irrespective of erosion by inflation" (Lanka Guardian, 15 July 1980). Were the government to follow this advice, however, it would suffer severe political losses. Consequently, it will probably resort to the risky expedient of increased international commerical borrowing, although at present the nation's leaders are still trying to persuade donors not to reduce aid.

Table 3.2

External Public Debt and Debt Service Ratios

(Sri Lanka)

External public debt outstanding and disbursed				Interest payments on external public debt (millions of dollars)		Debt service as percentage of:			
Millions of dollars		As percentage of GNP				GNP		Exports of goods and services	
1970	1981	1970	1981	1970	1981	1970	1981	1970	1981
317	1,585	16.1	36.6	12	49	2.0	2.1	10.3	5.7

Source: World Development Report 1983, Washington, D.C.: World Bank, Table 16, p. 178.

They know that Sri Lanka, as Housego puts it, has become the "test case of IMF realism."

Sarvodaya's Alternative Strategy

A.T. Ariyaratne, founder of Sarvodaya, states that "A poor country like Sri Lanka would have gone 99 percent on the road to development if development goals were properly defined and understood by the people." Rural people, he adds,

. . . have to understand the language of the people who plan for the whole country or they have to stand up in revolt. Therefore it is very necessary and very important that at the very outset we have to evolve a development theory and philosophy which is intelligible to all the people in the country: the rural as well as the urban; the educated as well as the less educated; the people who manage society as well as those who are subjected to all sorts of management.[1]

Sarvodaya, says its founder, aims to bring about "the total awakening of all, by means of pooling together all those human and material resources that individuals and groups are prepared to share of their own free will." In its first decade (1958 to 1968) Sarvodaya concentrated its efforts on the personality awakening of participants in Shramadana camps (Shramadana is the donation of labor to accomplish some task useful to one's community). A second step, still in progress, stresses village awakening. For the Movement's leader, however,

The awakening of the personality of an individual is closely linked with the family and the social environment in which such persons live and grow up. Similarly, the awakening of a village community is closely linked up with the national environment of which the villages are an integral part. Therefore, as the number of village communities participating in Sarvodaya activities increased, concepts of national development as relevant to village people's traditions, experience and aspirations also developed among them. *Thus Deshodaya or the awakening of the nation also became a Sarvodaya ideal.*

In the present-day world no community or nation can pursue a path to development without influencing and being influenced by what is happening in other countries. . . . As the Movement took national proportions it also had to develop its own concepts on world development. In other words *Vishvodaya or the awakening of the world* community as a whole became a fourth ideal to strive for by the adherents of the Movement.

Thus the Sarvodaya Movement in Sri Lanka works towards the integrated ideal of the development of Man and Society as persons, families, village and urban groups, nations and one world community (Ariyaratne n.d.:2–3).

Sarvodaya's answer to the question "Awakening to what?" is incomprehensible without reference to classical doctrines of Theravada Buddhism, which counsels a middle way between all extremes: indulgence and abnegation, absorption in the world and total flight, atomistic salvation and collective deliverance.

For Theravada Buddhism, which is the value base of Sarvodaya's village action, the goal of true development is that all individuals progress toward full enlightenment. The task of social policy, therefore, is to create conditions favoring such progress. Progress requires that the basic needs of all people be satisfied and that society at large obey the rules of *dharma* or righteousness. Sarvodaya draws its definition of development from dialogue with villagers who identify six intertwined elements in what modern thinkers call 'development': a moral element (right action and righteous livelihood), a cultural one (accumulated beneficial experiences along with customs, beliefs, art, music, song, dance and drama, which help maintain community spirit), a spiritual one (awakening of one's mind), a social one (access of all to physical and mental health, knowledge, culture, etc.), a political one (the enjoyment of fundamental rights by all and freedom to shape one's political environment), and an economic one (meeting human needs). Over five hundred families surveyed identified ten basic needs: a clean and beautiful environment, an adequate supply of safe water, minimum clothing, a balanced diet, simple housing, health (optimum spiritual and social as well as physical well being of the individual), communication, fuel, education and cultural and educational development.[2]

Sarvodaya refuses to consider as absolute the 'goods' held out by standard capitalist and socialist models of development and the manner in which these goods are to be sought. Benefits are not to be pursued in violent ways, nor in a mode which confirms men and women in craving after illusory satisfactions, but in a manner which substitutes the political participation of the masses for decisions made by any despot—royal, presidential, bureaucratic or a collective party.

Development should start from the grass-roots, from the village up. People should fully participate in planning for development and in the implementation of such plans. The technological knowledge prevailing at the people's level and the available local resources should be used initially. Progressively and appropriately it could be upgraded with advanced knowledge. National development plans should be based, not partially but totally on this broad-based people's participation. It should first strive to satisfy the basic needs of the people and not artificially created wants that are a blind imitation from materialistic cultures. . . . The ideal of Sir Lanka being a 'Dharma Dveepa' (Land of Righteousness) and 'Danyagara' (Land of Plenty) is always foremost in the minds of the Sarvodaya workers. (Ariyaratne n.d.:134).

Such is Sarvodaya's image of development; but what form do its practical activities take in villages?

Action in the Village

After experimenting with Shramadana camps for ten years, Sarvodaya undertook more comprehensive development programs in one hundred villages. The scheme rapidly expanded to cover one, two, and later five thousand villages, although, obviously, not all activities have been launched in each village. Usually a school for preschool children is opened, with young village women recruited to serve as teachers. The curriculum emphasizes moral values, work in a common garden, and initiation to basic health and hygiene. Where possible, specific groups in villages are organized around their work interests: there are farmers' groups, others for young adults, mothers, children, and so on. Other programs center on creating new opportunities for a "right livelihood": batik and sewing shops, mechanical repair and carpentry, farming on new plots, technology innovation units, and printing presses. Social and community service activities, in turn, range from health care centers, to community kitchens, trust funds for local credit, and libraries.

The key activity, however, is training of village leaders in development education institutes, some local, others regional or national in scope. Sarvodaya favors a model of the learning society—a lifelong process of awakening ever more deeply to reality, to one's place in shaping that reality, and to the meaning of one's action in any arena of work.

Considerable energies are spent coordinating local activities with Sarvodaya groups in neighboring villages and districts. The goal is to link villages one to another, to the nation, and eventually to the world itself. Not only has Sarvodaya encouraged international student exchange, it has also begun to promote International Sarvodaya Seminars. One recent document describes its practical activities as follows:

During the past eighteen years the Movement has in varying degrees developed programmes that embrace every aspect of human life. What was initially a Social Service Project on the part of students and teachers in the form of Shramadana Camps in backward villages, designed primarily to give them an educational experience, gradually developed itself over the years into a national as well as an international movement having concomitant elements of what are generally known as welfare as well as development programmes including not only increased productivity and economic growth, but a broad range of social services as well.[3]

The World Bank praises Sarvodaya's success in promoting village activites inexpensively. To the question "How much has all this cost?" one official Bank document replies:

> The Sarvodaya budget for 1979–80 was $2.3 million, an average of less than $1,000 per village assisted. Voluntary labor and other payments in kind contributed many times that amount. Of the cash budget, some 80 percent came from international assistance (both private and official), 10 percent from Sri Lankan donations and 10 percent from the sale of commodities produced in Sarvodaya's training farms and schools.

What impresses the Bank most favorably, however, is the way Sarvodaya "has involved the people in development" (World Bank 1980:75).

Relations to Power

In its struggle to survive and expand since 1958, the Movement has clearly defined its attitude toward government and other elite groups. Sarvodaya has two reasons, one philosophical and the other practical, for selectively cooperating with the national government. Its philosophical basis is the Buddhist notion of a dharmic or righteous society, which requires citizens and even the Sangha (order of monks) to stimulate rulers to practice justice. Hence, no absolute chasm divides the moral quest for enlightenment from economic and political activities: Sarvodaya does not fear compromise by acting politically. Its practical reason for cooperating selectively with the present government, without however allying itself to the ruling UNP party, is simple. From its beginnings the Movement has condemned all elite models of development brought from the West, whether capitalist or socialist, and rejected any top-down bureaucratic or political imposition of solutions to problems. Sarvodaya has always approached the rural masses for practical alternatives to development. Therefore, now that government leaders endorse Sarvodaya's ideology and approve its emphasis on village programs, the Movement will not abstain from playing a normative role in Sri Lanka's national life. If it backs away from today's development challenges, Sarvodaya risks becoming a counter cultural sanctuary for disillusioned anti-modernists. To quote a German sociologist, Sarvodaya believes that the history of mankind need not necessarily founder on "the insanities of private capitalism and the hypocrisies of totalitarian Communism" (Kantowsky 1980:292).

Will collaboration with present rulers compromise the Movement's freedom or its purity? Ariyaratne replies confidently that Sarvodaya is navigating its own course when dealing with the government. He reminds critics that limited cooperation was also extended to earlier governments and that, notwithstanding fears of a 'sell-out' voiced by policitians and intellectuals, villagers approve his course of action.

Such involvement with the government does, however, pose alternative choices to the Movement as it faces the future.

Sarvodaya's Future: Two Possibilities

Sarvodaya has no master plan to avoid becoming the ideological arm of the ruling party, but relies instead on its pragmatic judgment to counter the danger. Because this experimental attitude has served it well since 1958, Ariyaratne predicts that Sarvodaya will neither collapse nor become corrupt. In 1978 he wrote "The Sarvodaya Shramadana Movement has completed twenty years of its existence. The Movement hopes to survive for many more decades to come. The Movement's survival will make human civilization richer, even in a small way" (Ariyaratne 1978:3).

Sarvodaya faces difficult value conflicts whether the government's development strategy succeeds or fails.

If Government Strategy Succeeds

Sarvodaya is now a national force and the symbol of an alternative form of development for Sri Lanka. Its two objectives are: to work effectively as a non-elite, rural-based development strategy around values of non-violence, self-denial, equality and a general attitude of "sharing and caring" for all; and to convert national leaders to Sarvodaya's methodology and practice as they design and carry out national macro-development policies. This ambition is doubly difficult as Sarvodaya lacks prior experience in handling macro-development issues, and the institutional procedures and vested interests of national developers are directly opposed to Sarvodaya's approach: planning by the people and subordinating economic goals to broader spiritual-cultural ends.

The Movement believes, nonetheless, that it can achieve the two goals. Its optimism is founded on past experience: Sarvodaya has often learned new modes of acting simply by acting. It is evident, nevertheless, that Sarvodaya will face special problems of survival with integrity if government policies prove successful. Three difficulties merit special attention. The first is the tension existing between tradition and the government's promotion of Western values in several important domains. The conventional wisdom about aggregate economic growth seems to be endorsed by official planners; so too are mainstream notions as to the merits of large scale projects. Generous "incentives" offered to producers (in the manufacturing sector) and to consumers (in the tourist industry) tend to legitimize a two-tiered model for Sri Lankan society. One tier makes life comfortable for a rich minority, while the other tier keeps rural and urban masses satisfied with low wages and austere consumption levels. But why should it be good for tourists to spend money on superfluous objects, and bad for ordinary Sri Lankan citizens to do so? What justification exists for giving wealthy industrialists air conditioned houses, imported luxury cars and domestic servants, while subjecting poor workers to power cuts, water rationing, and low wages? Does the government truly believe that maximizing growth through greater market incentives will result in a 'trickle down' of benefits to the masses? Trickling down is precisely what growth-oriented strategies elsewhere in the world have not achieved.

Conventional modernization theorists claim that dynamic performance follows upon the displacement of traditional motivational systems in favor of aspirations after wealth by upwardly mobile entrepreneurs. Sarvodaya, in contrast, preaches cooperation amongst all members of a community, not exceptional reward for a few outstanding 'achievers.' What Albert Hirschman calls ego-focused and group-focused images of change need to coexist harmoniously[4] if socially acceptable change is to occur. Sarvodaya is concerned lest individualistic incentive systems adopted by Sri Lankan government policy gain wide sway in the land. Can the Shramadana ethic of "sharing and caring" survive in a society which rewards competition for money? Will not the 'cash mentality' undermine Sarvodaya's appeal to young people to contribute their energies to a life of service?

The second difficulty centers on the urban/rural polarity. Although the government seeks greater welfare for rural people, its priorities risk widening the gap in living conditions between city and countryside. Most tourist installations are located in or around the nation's cities, and jobs generated by tourism are going mainly to urban workers. Similarly, industries attracted by tax incentives concentrate around the cities. Construction and housing schemes are heavily weighted to favor cities, with lesser benefits going to villages. Even the Mahaveli Program, designed to benefit rural people, is so capital intensive and high-technology oriented that, for many years to come, it will probably benefit mainly the bureaucrats, engineers, and foreign experts working on it. If successful, the program will doubtless bring great blessings to the countryside, but will new lands and irrigation waters be allocated by city-based officials possessing little sensitivity to the needs of rural people?

Throughout the third world a strong bias privileges cities over rural areas in the siting of investments, social services, amenities, bureaucratic attention and general infrastructure (Lipton 1977). Although some years ago Sarvodaya launched modest development activities in Colombo, its main force still resides in its rural membership. If amenities accumulate in urban areas, will the Sarvodaya model of simple living in poor villages retain its appeal to talented young villagers?

The third pitfall concerns traditional values. Will market-oriented lines of development in the nation at large relegate Sarvodaya to the role of fighting a rear guard defense of traditional values? If government strategy succeeds, Sri Lanka could be well on the way to becoming a consumer society like Singapore, Taiwan and South Korea. If this happens, would not Sarvodaya's Basic Human Needs approach to development be interpreted as a past-oriented, nostalgic vision? This risk is related to the danger that successful modernization will dilute Sri Lankans' attachment to their own values.

Moreover, there is the possibility that as Sri Lankan society moves toward conventional consumerism Sarvodaya will assume for Sri Lankans the image which Shakers and Amish have long had for mainstream Americans. Can the Movement be germane enough to the nation's current social evolution to avoid taking on the aura of a vestigial link to a glorious past of noble but obsolete values?

To overcome these dangers Sarvodaya must devise a pedagogy of simple living which is persuasive to people living in a 'modern,' and not solely in a 'traditional,' context. Gamini Iriyagolle, a critic of the Mahaveli scheme, asks whether Sarvodaya can have any role to play in a society once general well-being has replaced widespread poverty.[5] He suggests that if Sri Lanka turns its back on its traditions while avidly pursuing affluence, it may fail to keep sight of Sarvodaya's emphasis on basic needs and its call for awakening to the deeper spiritual values in human life. This is why Sarvodaya must create an antidote to current values even as it contributes to their spread; it must discover equivalent benefits in modern life to complement the traditional wisdom rooted in Sri Lanka's past.

If Government Policy Fails

Sri Lanka's development strategy entails many risks: foreign assistance may dry up, world inflation may overwhelm efforts to build up national productive capacities, the Mahaveli Program may remain only half finished and prove prohibitively expensive, the Investment Promotion Zone may yield insufficient benefits to justify expenditures on infrastructure and generous incentives, and tourism may prove both unprofitable and culturally destructive. In short, the UNP's development gamble could fail. And even if the UNP were to win the elections, its government might still be saddled with an expensive development program which would continue to drain resources while producing few benefits. Such an outcome would result in an array of problems.

Rising political unrest would ensue, and a new revolutionary movement capable of overthrowing the government and setting the nation on a course similar to that planned by the abortive April 1971 insurrection of the Janatha Vimukthi Peramuna (People's Liberation Front) might emerge. If the government's program fails, disaffection with democratic procedures might embolden a new generation of unemployed youth to conduct armed struggle with a view to altering radically the ground rules governing political, social and economic life in Sri Lanka. The Armed Forces are no doubt better armed in 1980 than they were in 1971. But under the hypothesis of failed development, their loyalty to a regime which had linked the country's destinies to world financial institutions might well erode.

A second danger is the escalation of communal strife between Tamils and Singhalese. If the government cannot "deliver the goods"—jobs, services, and opportunities for fuller political participation at district and local levels—its vulnerability to attacks by radical Tamil separatists will increase. The most serious concern at present is reestablishing Sri Lanka's credibility as a viable, multi-cultural nation. An arduous and delicate process of reconciliation must occur if there is to be any hope of a political solution to communal discord. Moreover, great material damage was caused by the violent incidents of July and August, 1983. President J.R. Jayewardene (Address to the Nation, 22 August 1983) listed the cost: "Hundreds of people lost their lives, thousands lost their jobs, houses were burnt, factories destroyed." Many Sri Lankan observers think that unless mutual confidence between Tamils and Singhalese can be restored, the tenuous social bond holding the nation together will have been shattered. Separatists already accuse the government of tampering, through its settlement policies, with the demographic balance between Tamils and Singhalese in border districts. And 'moderate' Tamil politicans, out of touch with younger, more radical constituents, may be compromising themselves by making public utterances at variance with their private pronouncements. In public they endorse the creation of a separate Tamil nation (*Eelam*), while privately they reassure their Singhalese colleagues that they really support a single Sri Lankan nation, respectful of minority rights. The history of communal tensions since Independence is not reassuring. High unemployment, runaway inflation, humiliating dependency on outside financial bodies and rising criticism of government policies could easily engender greater repression.

Generalized economic depression is another by-product of failed development policy. Notwithstanding the high GNP growth rates recorded in recent years, domestic agricultural production which is vital to the nation's economic health grew only marginally in 1979 (at a rate of 0.7 percent over the previous year). If paddy production is excluded the remainder of domestic agriculture failed to record any growth at all in 1979. More generally, growth in recent years "appears somewhat 'unbalanced' in that it is heavily biased towards trade, construction, commerce, transport, etc., while agriculture and industry have lagged behind. A growth process of this nature must necessarily generate substantial inflationary pressures in the domestic economy" (Economic Review 1980:4). Inflation results when incremental resources pumped into the economy are not matched by additional production. More dangerously, even such growth as is achieved may condition Sri Lankans to consume more than their country can produce.

More alarmingly, the increase in income inequalities has grown. Rising income disparities are perhaps "inevitable in the context of the particular economic policies pursued in the past two years. But the continuation of these trends over the long term could have serious social repercussions, for economic growth by itself will not be meaningful to the masses unless it is accompanied by an equitable sharing of fruits" (ibid.) Recent studies by the American economist Irma Adelman (1977) conclude that the benefits of growth cannot reach the poorest sectors of the population unless access to productive assets is opened up to them before technologies for increasing productivity are introduced. The democratization of access to the means of production—land, finance capital, and organizational networks—must precede the 'big push' for greater production and higher productivity. Sri Lanka's national planners seem to have made the contrary assumption, namely: that growth will generate incremental goods which can be 'filtered down' to needy masses through public welfare expenditures. The weakness of this approach is that global inflation and increased dependence on outside resource partners pressure the government to minimize subsidies to the poor while maximizing incentives to producers. This strategy is politically explosive unless it can quickly offer tangible economic benefits which dampen the criticism of those disadvantaged by national priorities. The poor are doubly deprived when they suffer relative as well as absolute deprivations. It is intolerable for them to go hungry if they see well-fed tourists and foreign managers. As noted earlier, success in the strategy adopted by the government depends on rapid growth in export earnings. Singapore and South Korea, the 'success stories' in this domain, achieved phenomenal leaps in export earnings within four to five years after launching their strategies. It is admittedly too early to judge Sri Lanka's chances of repeating the success of these two nations. Nevertheless, the island's sluggish performance in 1979 augurs ill for a quick takeoff into the promised land of reduced balance of payments deficits.

What posture should Sarvodaya contemplate if Sri Lanka's strategy fails? In order to retain its authenticity as a non-elite people's development movement, Sarvodaya must avoid an intimate association with any government. Such an embrace would invalidate Sarvodaya's claim of being the repository of indigenous values which it will defend in the face of pressures to modernize. It would likewise invalidate its promise of offering a realistic alternative to development models shaped by imperatives lying outside the value system of Sri Lanka's rural masses. Two opposing dangers face Sarvodaya should the government's development gamble fail: a loss of authenticity or the destruction of the Movement. Were the nation's development efforts to falter, revolutionary agitation might well prevail or, conversely, the government might become a repressive dictatorship. Given its commitment to non-violent revolution, Sarvodaya could attract those seduced by the violent option only if it had a successful development policy of its own. Moreover, if it is to serve as a foil to repressive rule, Sarvodaya must have maintained a safe distance from any regime adopting such rule. Under the scenario of failed development, Sarvodaya's best hope for survival with integrity lies in serving as a 'plank of salvation' to a foundering nation. It cannot play this role if it endorses the pattern of development promoted by national rulers, or if it fails to produce visible results in the domain of its own value-based alternative mode of development. If national development falters, financial independence for Sarvodaya assumes great importance. The Movement must not remain too reliant on foreign inputs; otherwise it could be paralyzed by a hostile government through the simple expendient of cutting off its outside revenues. Apart from this extrinsic danger, however, and on more intrinsic grounds, Sarvodaya should wish to become relatively less dependent on foreign financing. Financial independence is desirable for Sarvodaya if only to demonstrate that it can make good its promise to offer a "right livelihood" to large numbers of people. Clearly, Sarvodaya's vocation consists of something greater than serving as an efficient channel of untied aid from developed countries to the poor of the third world. To urge greater financial autonomy upon Sarvodaya, however, in no way invalidates the Movement's rejection of Western standards of financial self-reliance. As Ariyaratne correctly argues, financial self-reliance in individual projects is often impossible until wider patterns of economic dependence inherited from a colonial past have been altered, thus removing structural obstacles to self-reliance.

Sarvodaya has now taken the lead to promote national reconciliation in the aftermath of the destructive violence which ravaged the country in July and August of 1983. Ariyaratne pleaded for "non-party democracy" which elevates "the office of the President above party affiliations. It is conceivable that a form of Presidency—Chief Executiveship—predicated on the obtaining of national consensus could be created . . . for at least a period sufficiently long to heal the wounds and bind the nation once again" (Ariyaratne 1983:25). The Movement has organized public campaigns for dialogue and amity, fund raising and refugee assistance to aid victims of violence, and public walks to dramatize the need for communal solidarity.

Conclusion: Is Grassroots Development Viable?

Sarvodaya now faces a new challenge: can its development approach, rejecting elitism, urban bias and the assumptions of modern economics, survive and preserve its integrity once it begins to interact with macro-policy arenas? Even hardened realists concede that 'bottom-up' approaches can only succeed on a small scale basis and at the community level. What has not yet been tested, however, is whether development from the bottom upwards can become effectively normative for the strategy of a nation operating in a global context wherein modernity remains associated with market values, monetary rewards to elicit social effort, and the desirability of abundant consumer objects. Even Mao's China, at the height of communes and backyard steel furnaces, exhibited a different specimen of development: it was a case of a government promoting local economic autonomy from the top downwards. Sarvodaya's experience, however, and the choices it now faces are qualitatively different. The Movement stands at a development crossroad: the issue is whether or not it will survive with integrity in the coming years.

By the standards of most development professionals, Sarvodaya's ambition is presumptuous folly. Here precisely lies the central point: Sarvodaya declares that it is the professionals who ignore what true development is. They distort its meaning and ally themselves to vested interests which propagate destructive illusions under the banner of "development." Consequently, no category of people more than professionals themselves needs to reconsider the true nature of development. Thus Sarvodaya reiterates Ivan Illich's assertion of the "paradoxical counter-developmental nature of what is generally called development." As it is currently promoted development is illusory in its assumptions, its nature, and the benefits it promises. "Enlightenment" consists of understanding that genuine development is the arousal of all individuals, local communities, nations, and the human race itself to the central importance of *metta* (loving kindness towards all living beings), *karuna* (compassionate action which attacks the causes of suffering), *mudita* (which leads people to find their joy in altruistic service, not in selfish gratification), and *upekka* (that lasting serenity which frees one from the thraldom of prestige and fame or, conversely, of criticism and hostility). If Sarvodaya deserves to be taken seriously in its micro-sectoral accomplishments, it must also be taken seriously in its macro-sectoral claims. The Movement urges that a new social order—for nations as for the world—be founded on these four principles of personal reawakening. Only if nations and the world rally to this model of development, can human beings inhabit a planet where violence does not rule, where selfish competition does not destroy solidarity, and where no pretext based on doctrine or considerations of utility can justify hierarchic inequalities among people. The Movement radically challenges, not only prevailing canons of development, but also conventional wisdom as to the nature of politics. For this reason the future performance of this unique Sri Lankan people's movement vitally interests students of development worldwide.

One question is especially vital for students of alternative development strategies. Can Sarvodaya harness the latent dynamisms present in Sri Lankan tradition so as to resist the adverse impact of outside values? During the 1950s and 1960s Burma's leaders chose to promote a form of development—albeit not a very dynamic one—in harmony with the land's historical past and indigenous values. But they did so by creating a closed society, barred from contact with outsiders. Sarvodaya is undertaking a similar aim within an open society presently subject to massive foreign influences. If Sarvodaya succeeds, perhaps other movements in other countries can also hope to succeed.

Theravada Buddhism, the philosophical matrix out of which Sarvodaya derives its model of development, condemns that "dynamism of desire" which is the motorforce of Western development aspirations, capitalistic and socialistic alike. The dynamism of desire starts from the premise that development can come about only if hitherto passive people are taught to want more; their desires must be awakened, either by the revolutionary denunciation of exploitative oppressors, or by holding out to them prospects of abundant goods. While it does not romanticize austerity or condone poverty, Sarvodaya nonetheless offers people a philosophical and psychological basis for choosing to "have enough" in order to "be more" instead of perpetually craving "to have more" with the end result that they become less human than before. This pathway to development lays a foundation for a sustained commitment to social justice and environmental wisdom far deeper than approaches based on the fear of ecological catastrophe. Many social critics in developed countries advocate simple living out of fear of environmental collapse, not out of a profound understanding of the illusions perpetuated by the dynamism of desire. Thanks to its reasonable interpretation of Theravada Buddhism, on the other hand, Sarvodaya possesses a holistic rationale for adopting an active development stance which is neither complacent about existing social structures nor indulgent toward technocratic means of achieving abundance.[6] If Sarvodaya successfully crosses its new phase, it will offer qualitatively important lessons to many outside Sri Lanka who search for new models of human fulfillment, social organization, and environmental wisdom.

Sarvodaya is, in one sense, a 'modest' development actor, leaving center stage to people themselves. For this very reason it appeals to champions of alternative development strategies. Moreover, such modesty might well be emulated by experts who pride themselves on knowing what needs to be done. Sarvodaya's example is a salutary remainder to experts, and to those who observe them, that they probably do not know what truly needs to be done. Yet, paradoxically and from an opposite vantage point, Sarvodaya is also supremely ambitious in its development aspirations. In 1980 the following statement was made.

> The movement is preparing a total development plan for Sri Lanka from a people's point of view. . . . It is the Movement's intention to publish this in the form of a book which can easily be understood by the common man in the village. This is an attempt to make the people think about their own development. In this way, they might pose some critical questions for the politicians who will contest the elections in 1983. This is done with the intention of raising the consciousness of all people pertaining to the development of their country.[7]

For its audacity no less than for its modesty, Sarvodaya bears special watching by students of development. The immediate goals of this remarkable Sri Lankan people's movement is to raise the consciousness "of all people pertaining to the development of their country." Its ultimate goal, however, is to arouse "all people pertaining to the development of the entire world."

Notes

1. Address to the Society for International Development, Sri Lanka Chapter, entitled "Integrating National Development with the Rural Sector," 8 November

1979, at Bandaranaike Memorial International Conference Hall, Colombo, p. 2.

2. Sarvodaya Development Education Institute, *Ten Basic Human Needs and Their Satisfaction.* Sarvodaya Community Education Series #26, Moratuwa, S.L.: Sarvodaya Press.

3. Sarvodaya report entitled *Ethos and Work Plan* (Utrecht, Netherlands: n.d.), p. 6.

4. The concepts of ego-focused and group-focused images of change are drawn from Albert O. Hirschman, *The Strategy of Economic Development* (New Haven: Yale University Press, 1958), pp. 11–23.

5. Interview with author 29 July 1980.

6. David Riesman, (ed.). *Abundance for What?* (New York: Doubleday, Anchor Books, 1964). Cf. Denis Goulet, "Development for What?" *Comparative Political Studies,* Vol. 1, No. 2 (July 1968), pp. 295–312; Anthony Arblaster and Steven Lukes (eds.), *The Good Society* (New York: Harper Torchbooks, 1972); Marilyn B. Chandler, et al., *Working Papers on the Good Society* (University of California, Los Angeles, School of Architecture and Urban Planning); and *An Anthology of Selected Readings for the Quality of Life Concept,* 29–31 August 1972 at Airlie House, Warrenston, Virginia, sponsored by the Environmental Protection Agency, Office of Research and Monitoring, Environmental Studies Division.

7. Remarks by A.T. Ariyaratne in *Minutes of the Fifth Meeting of the NOVIB-Sarvodaya Commission of Dialogue,* Colombo, 27–28 June 1980, p. 5.

References

Adelman, Irma 1977 "Redistribution Before Growth—A Strategy for Developing Countries." Working paper 78–14. Department of Economics and Bureau of Business and Economic Research: University of Maryland.

Ariyaratne, A.T. 1978 *A Struggle to Awaken.* Colombo, S.L.: Sarvodaya Press.

1983 "Sarvodaya Approach Towards a Lasting Solution to the Present National Crisis," *DANA* (International Journal of the Sarvodaya Shramadana Movement) Vol. IX, No. 9, September.

n.d. *Collected Works.* Vol. I. Dehiwala, S.L.: Sarvodaya Research Centre.

n.d. *Sarvodaya and Development.* Moratuwa, S.L.: Sarvodaya Press.

Central Bank of Ceylon 1979 *Annual Report for the Year 1979.* Colombo: Central Bank of Ceylon.

Corea, Gamani 1975 *The Instability of an Export Economy.* Colombo: Marga Institute.

Economic Review 1978 "The Mahaveli Project." Special Issue. Vol. 4, Nos. 8/9. Colombo: The People's Bank.

1979 "Tourism." Special Issue. Vol. 5, Nos. 3/4. Colombo: The People's Bank.

1980 "The Economy in 1979." Special Issue, Vol. 6, No. 3. Colombo: The People's Bank.

Goulet, Denis 1981 *Survival with Integrity: Sarvodaya at the Crossroads.* Colombo: Marga Institute.

Hirschman, Albert O. 1958 *The Strategy of Economic Development*. New Haven: Yale University Press.

Kantowsky, Detlef 1980 *Sarvodaya, The Other Development*. New Delhi: Vikas Publishing House.

Lipton, Michael 1977 *Why Poor People Stay Poor: Urban Bias in World Development*. Cambridge, Mass.: Harvard University Press.

Marga Institute 1979 *Welfare and Growth in Sri Lanka*. 2nd ed. Colombo: Marga Institute.

Ministry of Finance and Planning 1980 *Public Investment 1980-84*. Colombo: National Planning Division.

Ratnapala, Nandasena 1979 *Sarvodaya and the Rodiyas, Birth of Sarvodaya*. Dehiwala, S.L.: Sarvodaya Research Institute.

World Bank 1980 "Self-help in Sri Lanka." *World Development Report*. Washington, D.C.: The World Bank.

4

MEMORIES OF DEVELOPMENT: THE RISE AND FALL OF A PARTICIPATORY PROJECT AMONG THE DINKA, 1977-1981

Richard Huntington

The Abyei Rural Development Project among the Dinka of Sudan was cancelled by USAID in 1981 amid bureaucratic controversy and ethnic violence. It had been a controversial project from the start, both in Sudan and in the American AID organization. Within Sudan the very idea (in 1976) of a development activity in Abyei stirred up emotions and resentment because the area was a disputed borderland between the recently warring 'Arab' north and 'African' south. The issue of project participation of local people (which local people?) and their representatives (who properly represents them?) reopened as yet unhealed political and ethnic wounds. Meanwhile, within the Washington AID bureaucracy the early plans for the Abyei project also stirred up emotions and conflicts. The Harvard Institute for International Development stressed the then current issues of "popular participation," "appropriate technology," and "integrated development." This touched a raw nerve in Washington AID which felt itself being forced in this direction by a Congressional mandate. At the heart of these new directions of American policy was the vague and idealistic question of "participation of the poorest of the poor" in development projects to their benefit. Harvard led many people to view the tiny Abyei project as some sort of test case in the continuing debate over the direction of development policy for rural Africa. Throughout the life of the project it was embroiled in disputes quite out of proportion to its modest budget and rather standard development activities.

It is important to indicate my own anthropological vantage point. It is impossible to study development programs with quite the same sympathetic detachment one adopts when studying lineage systems or religions. Development programs, even those less controversial than the Abyei project, are part of an adversarial political process in which activities are frequently and prematurely labelled as successes or failures by the interested parties. In such a context the usual anthropological guise of participant observation wears thin. Even if one avoids choosing sides, sides usually choose the anthropologist, and participant observation is transformed into observant participation.

In my first such experience, villagers of the Bara people of Madagascar chose me, in a sense, as their development consultant. I had lived and worked among them for some time (1969–1971), studying their religion and social organization, and when I returned several times over the following years they requested my advice on how they should respond to the development initiatives coming from the new post-revolution government (Huntington 1973). It was not a role in which I felt comfortable. I saw myself as a researcher and a scholar and suddenly I found that I had a client to whom I owed (by dint of all they had done for me) the best advice I could give, regardless of my own political persuasions or negative attitudes towards 'development' programs in general. I was also ambivalent about how my advice seemed to alter behavior and events in the village in a way that my previous research had never done to their religion or social structure. Furthermore, the political dimensions of the matter made me uneasy. This feeling was reaffirmed when shortly after my return to the United States, I heard that the body of a friend, a German anthropologist connected with this development program at the national level, was found floating in a river under suspicious circumstances ("Madagascar: Herz des Volkes" in *Der Spiegel* nr. 11/1975).

My situation regarding the Dinka of Sudan was different. In this case I was part of "the project" and as such unavoidably partisan. The normal adversarial relations between different levels and sections of the various bureaucracies often placed me in an ambiguous position. Policies tentatively begun would need to be prematurely rationalized and defended, and, more importantly, it was sometimes necessary to forestall the imposition of alternate policies that had not been thought out at all but which satisfied some distant mandate. One maneuvered and negotiated to save half-baked programs from being replaced by those that were either raw or guaranteed to offend the local people. I shall return to such issues, but the reader is alerted that what follows is of necessity a somewhat partisan report. To pretend otherwise would be unscientific and not very revealing of the development process.[1]

A development project is an international bureaucratic phenomenon of considerable complexity. For the Abyei project there were four major actors: the Sudanese government, American AID, the Ngok Dinka people and Harvard University. Each of these parties inevitably had a somewhat different view of and interest in the project, and each of them was itself internally divided on how to achieve their goals. Not only were there different parties with their divergent stakes, but there were also important factional divisions as well as factions which pre-dated the project and had little to do with project goals or structure, but which were part of the political landscape and greatly affected the project activities. These factions include the structural jealousies between AID-Sudan and the Khartoum American Embassy, the Ngok Dinka and the Humr Arabs, the central ministry and the provincial government, Harvard economists and anthropologists, etc. Furthermore, development projects are tightly circumscribed by time. This more than any other factor puts all the interested parties and pre-existing factions into a pressure cooker situation which forces and constrains decisionmaking at all levels. The sequence of events and crises often has more impact on immediate decisions than does informed analysis, and many decisions were made in response to a previous event or crisis. Finally, to this pressure cooker is added the unreality of the basically irreconcilable contradictions upon which some international development policies rest: local participation mandated from abroad and popular participation without politicization, to name two.

Additionally, the Abyei project belonged to the genre called "integrated rural development" which meant that it was charged not with a simple, single objective such as expanding agriculture or setting up a health care system or running a training program, but was to cover all these areas in a quixotic search for that perfect synergy of local activities which produces that most desirable end: an egalitarian improvement in the basic quality of rural life as well as demonstrable economic advance. Toward this end the Abyei project conducted activities in the areas of agriculture and livestock, training, construction, water supply, health, transportation and communication, and field studies.[2]

Harvard's philosophy was that in extremely remote and difficult rural areas such as Abyei the appropriate development activities must be discovered through a pragmatic program of action-research and the trial and error adaptation of technologies and institutions to the realities of the local environment. This philosophy was embodied in the official documents setting up the project and in the approved patterns of funding and personnel allotment. Although this philosophy was shared by the Ministry of Agriculture responsible for the project, it was never fully accepted either by AID-Sudan or, more importantly, by the Ngok Dinka leadership.

I will explain in this chapter some of the roles played by Ngok Dinka, and some of the issues and events in which the contradictions and complexities of a 'participation' policy reveal themselves. Specifically I will consider the role of the Dinka political patron, the problem of setting up a permanent local development organization, a clash between the development program and traditional religious values, and the operation of village cooperative organizations.

Political Origins of the Abyei Project

The Abyei project had an important local participatory agenda from its very inception. The rationale for the project derived from local political and economic problems; local leaders pushed for the project to be approved and funded. Situated in South Kordofan Province, Abyei is in the northern part of Sudan at the border of the southern region; its people represent both of these regions. The great majority of its permanent residents are Dinka people whose cultural and linguistic ties are with the Nilotic peoples of the south. At the same time, Arabic speaking northerners (actually western Sudanese), nomadic Humr, have long relied on this area for seasonal cattle grazing during the dry months. Thus both populations have an attachment to the area. The Dinka practice a mixed economy of sorghum production and transhumant cattle herding. During the wet season they keep their cattle near their compounds and work in the fields. During the dry season, Dinka youths take the herds south, while the Humr Arabs bring their herds down from the north to graze in the Abyei area. Clashes over grazing land and competition for scarce resources threaten always to rekindle the hostilities between these peoples.

After the Sudanese civil war (1955–1972) between north and south, the Ngok Dinka in particular felt vulnerable as a southern people under the jurisdiction of a northern province. The leading spokesman for the Ngok Dinka, Francis Deng, worked to establish a development project for this area—a project which he claimed would help both peoples of the area and be a symbol of Sudan's tenuously established unity between north and south (Deng 1973).

At the highest level of participation stood Francis Deng. A son of the late paramount chief of the Ngok Dinka, Deng is a Sudanese diplomat and an internationally known scholar of Dinka and African culture. He served Sudan as its ambassador to the United States and was instrumental in reestablishing ties between the two nations. Next he served as State Minister for Foreign Affairs, and as such was the most prominent non-Arab in the central Sudanese government. At the national level Deng embodied an important link between north and south. Internationally, he provided an important tie between Sudan and the United States.

It is not surprising that with the resumption of the USAID program in Sudan, its first project was in Deng's home area of Abyei. Nor was it unexpected that this project would be justified as a symbol of north/south unity. The project began shortly after Deng became a cabinet minister and was terminated by AID shortly after he resigned his post to become ambassador to Canada. Because of his pivotal position and deep concern for the welfare of the Ngok Dinka, Francis Deng's participation made the Abyei project possible. To his frustration and regret, Deng was not in a position to make the project actually succeed, politically or economically.

One can appreciate the cultural implications and personal linkages of the Abyei project by comparing it to the other integrated rural development project USAID funded during the same period. The Blue Nile project provides an example of a development scheme whose location was largely accidental. In the spring of 1977 AID-Washington sent out a team charged with planning the whole American program for "AID to Traditional Agriculture." Due to transportation problems, the most experienced and senior member of that team was marooned in Khartoum while his colleagues were out west. The Aid Affairs Office of the American Embassy (there was as yet no AID Mission) thus sent him on an unplanned trip to a more accessible area in the Blue Nile Province. He returned to Khartoum and submitted a project proposal for one of the villages he had just visited. When the team was finally reunited, his proposal was added to the others because the team leader was expected to produce at least twelve "project identification documents" (PIDs) during this six week first visit to a vast and complex country. To the gratification of the villagers of Abu Gemai in the Blue Nile Province, the proposal was subsequently approved and Uncle Sam landed a twelve million dollar project in their area.

Abyei Peoples' Development Organization

In the project paper, Harvard proposed that an Abyei Peoples' Development Organization be negotiated and set up during the first phase of the project. The exact details of such a structure were not in Harvard's power to arrange, for this involved a Sudanese constitutional and political issue of some sensitivity. Philosophically Harvard had two criteria in mind. One was that any such organization should be linked to some regular government apparatus. Remote rural areas frequently suffer from a certain detachment from the central government, and development projects which set up a totally separate channel of support only increase this sense of isolation. The other criterion was that the APDO should in some sense be representative of and responsive to the local Abyei populations. Harvard knew rather little about the political realities of Abyei at that time, but they were under pressures from Washington to press the issue of local participation in order to secure support and get the project signed. The proposal suggested a somewhat complicated arrangement with a largely local technical and managerial senior staff, some kind of a local advisory council, and a policy-making board of directors.

After but a few weeks in Abyei, the Harvard team realized that establishing an APDO as originally proposed was impractical, unwise, and perhaps even dangerous. The local factionalism in Abyei was so intense that the project needed all of its political energies just to maintain neutrality and flexibility. Forcing the establishment of an APDO would have precipitated a crisis, thereby allowing one or the other of the shifting local factions control of the project. And such a narrow identification would have invalidated the project in the eyes of most local residents. The project (three young American technical advisors, six Ngok Dinka civil servants, two northern Sudanese agriculturalists) spent its first six months desperately trying to avoid local politicization, while simultaneously attempting to establish some basis for public participation.

The project stayed in a state of suspended animation during the first rainy season, avoiding politicization, but at the same time untouched by all shades of Abyei power, authority and influence. However, using subtle diplomacy and persistence, the Sudanese senior staff gradually managed to attract local officials and widen their base of support. It was a stunning political accomplishment performed in the space of one year. All segments of the Abyei population began to complain that the project was not doing enough for them vis-à-vis what it was doing for some other village, clan, ethnic group or government unit. Whereas at first all the local interests had studiously ignored the project, a year later everyone was trying to climb aboard.

The political accomplishment brought its own problems of mediating access to project activities, problems which might have been handled by some sort of local development council as foreseen in the project paper. However, it was still impossible to set up such an organization because an official locally-based organization would have been unconstitutional and contrary to the letter and spirit of the Sudanese Local Government Act of 1971 and the Decentralization Act of 1976.

When the British withdrew from Sudan they left behind two separate power elites. To one, the educated civil service class of the city, they ceded the government bureaucracy. To the other, the chiefly families of the rural areas, they bequeathed the system of native administration and chiefs' council, i.e., effective control of the countryside. The purpose of the Local Government Act was to extend the power of the urban based government bureaucracy to the rural areas and to dissolve any locally based power structures which were viewed as archaic, feudal, and colonial (Gaafar Mohamed Ali Bakheit 1974). The 1971 law dissolved the system of local chiefs (*nazirs*) and their councils and placed all authority with the provincial commissioner, who is a direct appointee of the president (Howell 1974). But the locally based chiefs still managed to maintain their considerable influence in the vast rural areas of Sudan. The Decentralization Act of 1976 attempted to remedy this by bringing the power of the provincial commissioner closer to the local arenas by doubling the number of provinces.

The commissioner of the new province of South Kordofan resented any incursion into his supposed realm of control. He worked against two kinds of incursion. One was from the central government, especially from large agricultural schemes that reported directly to the Ministry of Agriculture or to its semi-autonomous corporations in Khartoum. The other interference he resented was any continuation of the influence of the old local chiefly families, or, for that matter, any locally based organization. The Abyei project combined both of these elements. The commissioner insisted, quite correctly, that only he had the authority to appoint local development committees in South Kordofan. He had in mind an appointed local committee which would report to a provincial committee of which he would be the chair—a pyramidal structure mirroring that of the Sudan Socialist Union and 'peoples' councils.'

In addition to this constitutional issue, there was, as in so much of Africa, an ethnic issue. South Kordofan is comprised of three ethnic groups: the Nuba, the 'Baggara Arabs' and the Dinka. It is said that the only way to stay in power there is to keep one foot among the Nuba and the other foot among the Arabs, one hand in the pockets of the merchants, and the other hand beating down the Dinka. Because of this ethnic split, it was not practical for a project to be both a local Dinka project and part of the provincial government structure. An "Abyei Peoples' Development Organization" had a nice ring to it; unfortunately, it was not a viable way to link Dinka participation to a permanent governmental framework.

What emerged from the realities of negotiation and institution building was a somewhat different organization to fulfill the twin goals of providing local participation and sensitivity with a stable institutional tie to the national government. It was a regular project of the Ministry of Agriculture with an experienced and respected ministry man as director. At the same time, the senior field staff consisted largely of educated Dinka from Abyei on secondment from their regular departments and ministries, with a senior Abyei man as deputy director. The staff consisted of people trained in practical areas such as agriculture, forestry, livestock, community organization, health care and accountancy. It is important to realize that the arrangement functioned rather well after the shakedown period of the first rainy season and the ox plow crisis (to be discussed next). It was not a perfect solution, but it was far better than the naive proposal for an Abyei Peoples' Development Organization.

AID-Sudan continually faulted Harvard for failing to create the APDO promised in the project paper. The final project evaluation report by a company called Development Alternatives, Inc. gave this failure as a main reason for terminating Harvard's involvement with the project, and ending American technical assistance to the Ngok Dinka area. The Ngok Dinka did not want authority placed in a board of directors, either as Harvard had originally proposed or as the hated provincial commissioner was likely to set up. The provincial commissioner, for his own reasons, purposely never moved to create any such organization. The Ministry of Agriculture certainly did not want it, and, under the circumstances, neither did Harvard. AID alone insisted upon it.

Ox Plow Program: Sacred Cow or White Elephant?

A participation issue of a different kind emerged in an early crisis over choice of technology. The project was supposed to experiment with various agricultural technologies to adapt each more effectively to the local situation or to determine which were essentially unfeasible. This program resulted from the local Dinka people's original insistence that increasing grain production and local food security was their highest priority. The project decided to work with three farming techniques: tractors, ox plows and hand tools. This choice was not the result of any agricultural theories from Harvard, but simply reflected the fact that these were the technologies being extended to Dinka areas by the ministries and development organizations in northern and southern Sudan. Harvard, fully aware of the intensely emotional, religious, and esthetic aspects of Dinka attitudes towards cattle, was cautious about the ox plow work and stated in the project paper that this would take place only "if the cultural barriers did not appear to be too great."

One of the first American technical advisors was chosen because he had previously had experience in successfully introducing animal traction systems among the Afars of Ethiopia, who also have strong feelings about using cattle as beasts of labor. During the first rainy season in Abyei, he busied himself purchasing a few oxen, training them, experimenting with fodder systems and discussing ox plow technology. During those early days this was almost the only visible project activity. The issue loomed larger than it really was, and it seemed to many Dinka that this development project was there mainly to impose an unwanted ox plow program upon them. The somewhat messianic attitude of the young American ox plow advisor raised Dinka objections to an even higher pitch.

When the rainy season cleared, people from Abyei converged upon the house of Francis Deng in Khartoum and camped in his yard, demanding that he put a stop to the ox program. Deng complained to the director of the American AID program who in turn contacted me, Harvard's newly arrived representative in Khartoum. Why, he complained echoing Francis Deng, was Harvard threatening traditional values? The AID director said that if pressure from the Dinka forced the dropping of the ox plow program, then he felt that the entire character of the project was altered so that its original premises were not longer valid. I reminded him that it was a Ministry of Agriculture project with a largely Dinka Senior staff who were quite aware of the cultural issues. It seemed to me that these men had decided to continue with the activity, and I suggested that he speak with them. (Although this was supposedly a participatory project, the American AID officials in Khartoum never seemed to accept the idea that Harvard was not 'in charge.' A number of times I was requested not to bring the Sudanese project director to meetings "so we can talk more freely," even when the topic to be discussed was the allocation of local currency funds over which the Sudanese director had sole authority).

The next day three Dinka staff members spoke to the AID director like "born again" ox plow advocates. Yes, they said, they shared the Dinka feelings about cattle, but they were willing to have the project examine all possible ways of progress and development. They respected their own traditional values, but they also had confidence in the Dinka's ability to adapt and adopt new ways if offered a better future. Dinka are accomplished orators, and these staff members were extremely convincing. Apparently, after this meeting the AID director turned the ultimatum on Francis Deng saying that if he wanted the project to continue at all, it must include the ox plow program.

A face saving compromise was reached in which the Dinka leaders agreed that the ox trials could continue (they had no choice) but with the proviso that Dinka cattle be spared the indignity. The trials were to be done only with "Arab" cattle! (It was specifically stipulated that Nuer cattle also could not be used since they are related to Dinka cattle.)

One theory, and the one which AID seemed to accept, was that it was the Dinka elite (minus those working with the project) who were most adamant against the ox plow program. Those who were farthest from traditional religious values and lifeways seemed the most disturbed

that such values should be weakened by development activity. Economic
motives were seen to underlie this outcry. These Dinka leaders wanted
a real development program with tractors and modern agricultural
machinery, not low key 'appropriate' technology left over from the
European middle ages. Additionally, some of the protesters may have
had personal economic reasons for wanting tractors, since in recent years
entrepreneurs in rural Sudan had profited hugely from subsidized tractor
programs. On the other hand, the farmers themselves seemed neither
greatly interested nor greatly offended by the little bit of experimental
ox plowing taking place in Abyei.

There was some truth to this theory of the ox plow crisis (and this
theory was discussed by AID officials in Washington as well as in
Khartoum), but it was an unfair oversimplification. There was a range
of reasons cited by Dinka leaders for their opposition to the program.
They wanted this program to succeed and feared that a project predicated
upon ox plowing would fail ultimately to involve and benefit the people.
They cited the example of the failed Sudan Council of Churches' ox
plow project in another Dinka area. Another aspect was that educated
Dinka, removed from their traditional culture, maintain an emotional
stake in those values which is perhaps made even stronger by the
ambiguities of their life styles.

Village Cooperatives

At the village level other types of community organizations existed
which were not unique to the Abyei Development Program—consumer
cooperatives and group (block) farms. Neither organization was created
by the project, but, in the case of the group farms, was inherited by
the project from previous government development activity in the area.
The consumer cooperatives were never part of the AID project; they
were, however, run by the government in some of the same villages that
had direct project contact.

Both of these types of village level development cooperatives are
common programs throughout Sudan and elsewhere in Africa. And both
quite regularly fail to achieve the seemingly modest functional goals set
for them, especially in the more remote, poorer and less populous areas.
Such programs fail so regularly that one wonders why they are recreated
over and over. The answer is that they fulfill an important political
function. In the remote pastoral areas of extremely poor countries
government resources are unable to provide real services, but the political
stability of such nations is too fragile for them to ignore these large
open areas completely. And so committees are ordained, promising
'development' in various isolated villages. Thus, symbolic gestures fre-

quently serve as a useful style of administrative activity and a minimal hegemony is maintained over vast areas.

Having suggested why such 'cooperative' organizations are repeatedly set up, let me turn my attention to why they repeatedly fail. It is because they are simultaneously antithetical to traditional cultural systems, marginal to the market economic system, and incidental to the functioning government bureaucracy. No motives—moral, political or economic—systematically operate to make for success or even institutional survival.

Not all the cooperatives and village development councils in Africa are failures. There are classic cases of 'successes' which for good or ill at least functioned vibrantly for quite a time. For instance, the African local government in Busoga, Uganda (Fallers 1965) had its problems, but it was a central part of the bureaucratic enterprise of late colonial Uganda. Or, for an economic example, the system of peanut cooperatives of Senegal (Cruise O'Brien 1975) was a vast exploitive institution, but it was profitable, viable and successful at least for some people for a considerable time. And there are accounts of traditional "councils in action" (Richards and Kuper eds. 1971) adapting deep cultural values and institutions to the changing times. Most such examples come from the more densely populated or more complexly organized societies of Africa, rather than from pastoral areas. However many of the poorest areas of the continent resemble Dinka territory—a remote, sparsely populated region that has now witnessed over two decades of difficult national independence, much of it marred by devastating civil war. One can hardly blame the people there for not believing in the promise of 'development.' And yet, we shall see, the village group organizations exhibited more local élan and expertise than anyone could reasonably expect. If they seem to have 'failed,' it is not due to lack of effort or skill on the part of the local participants. The village organizations were set up in the midst of an economic, bureaucratic, and cultural vacuum.

Following a pattern used elsewhere in Sudan, government officials had attempted to organize some Dinka farmers into group farms in Sudan. It may be recalled that such block farming set ups had been a staple of mechanization schemes in much of British Africa in the late 1940s and 1950s. For each of these farms, it was envisioned that fifty men would work to clear one thousand acres, a size which had been deemed necessary for the efficient use of one tractor. It was assumed that each man and his family would weed and harvest his own twenty acre section of the field.

In the Ngok area now, two group farms were organized by the Dinka district commissioner, Justin Deng, in 1976. Two more were organized by the Abyei Development Project in 1979, and the project assumed the task of supporting these four groups with the necessary technical services. All four farms failed to operate in the way the government officials had hoped. The largest cleared field was fifty acres rather than a thousand. However, of these four groups, two failed less completely than the others. Among the Ngok Dinka, coherence, allegiance and identity are strong within each of the nine subtribal territorial groupings. Each of the two more successful group farms was situated well within a traditional subtribal area, and its members were entirely from that group. One of these was of the most prestigious subtribe, the one associated with the chiefly family. The other was of the least prestigious subtribe. Within each of these two groups, there was a sense of the legitimacy of the group leadership and a consensus about group activities. The least prestigious group revolved around a single charismatic and innovative leader, whereas the farm in the chiefly subtribe had a more diffuse leadership. The men of this prestigious family were not in the habit of relinquishing their prerogatives. This group, while not as innovative as the other, exhibited a strong sense of consensus and a steady involvement with the farm. Between these two groups there was a certain spirit of rivalry.

The other two group farms barely functioned in four years. One never cleared so much as five acres of new land, but insisted that the tractor plant a large infertile area of abandoned farmsites. The other group managed to clear twenty acres in four years at which point its members found themselves unable to agree upon what day of the week they would do the weeding, etc., and they distrusted their elected leadership. Both of these groups were riven by bitter factions. These two groups were located in the areas that straddle the boundaries between subtribes, and their group membership also cut across traditional social divisions. This was not accidental: the Ngok Dinka district commissioner, Justin Deng, had intended that these activities help diffuse inter-subtribal animosities and create a more modern type of social identity for development.

All of these group farms demanded styles of cooperation and organization unknown in the traditional culture. Deng has noted that the Dinka are individualistic, secretive, and competitive concerning economic matters. Furthermore, the Dinka have very little tradition of fixed cooperative groups or identity at the village level. All of the farms were marginal to traditional Dinka culture; two farms were simply less marginal than the others.

Regarding politics and bureaucracy, the two more successful farms were also more strongly linked to the local elite family which includes Francis Deng, who was seen as ultimately responsible for these development activities, the (former) district commissioner who initiated some of these activities, and the staff of the development project who held governmental responsibility for these group farms. These two group farms were within the modern political orbit of influence of the local elite members of the civil service. The situation in the other group farms was more complicated. Both of these areas were divided by conflicting subtribal loyalties, as I mentioned. But more importantly, they were divided by forces in support of and in strong opposition to the policies of Francis Deng and his father's family regarding the Ngok's position vis-à-vis the split between northern and southern Sudan. The situation was a bit complex because the position of the Deng family and that of the opposition have reversed in recent years. It is possible that Justin Deng, in setting up the two groups which did less well, hoped to diffuse a very modern political opposition in those areas as well as transcend traditional rivalries.

Finally, it is in economic terms that these group farms were most marginal. The greatest problem faced in their initial years was the fact that the government tractors were repeatedly delayed and did not arrive in time for planting. These small plots were understandably low on the priority list of the ministry officials and when spares, fuel, and tractors themselves were in short supply, it made no economic sense to send them down to Dinka land. When the Harvard-advised development project was fully funded in 1979, tractors, fuels, seeds, lubricants were all available. Nonetheless, it was found to be extremely difficult technically (due to rainfall patterns, soil type and topography) to cultivate effectively even these small fields. A large and talented support system managed to serve these fields so that at best their yields were half that of traditional fields and the cost per acre very high. None of this is or was surprising to anyone familiar with the extensive literature on rain-fed mechanization programs in Africa. However, the political value of visible tractors outweighs the economic drawbacks. And, as yet, there is no economically viable alternative.

Regardless of the cultural, bureaucratic, and economic marginality of these group farms and in spite of the fact that they failed to fulfill the goals planned for them, much creative leadership and organization was apparent among two of the farms. They organized regular systems of contributory labor, record keeping systems, fines for non-participation, and storing and marketing arrangements. Each of these farms independently evolved solutions to these issues in its own way. One group worked as a unit two mornings a week. The other opted to allow members to work semi-independently at their convenience (a sort of flex-time arrangement). Both groups faced a critical shortage of weeding labor at certain times and resorted to hiring visiting Twic Dinka from the south to supplement the work. One group paid these outsiders a daily rate to join them on their work days; the other carefully contracted out piece work. Both groups found ways to pay these laborers out of common stocks of grain or cash. The degree of successful organizational innovation at this level was impressive. These group farms were not viable for the many reasons I have stressed, yet their failure was clearly not the result of any inability of traditional Dinka farmers to meet challenging new situations more than halfway. The failure derived from their doomed position in the overall bureaucratic, cultural, and economic systems.

My information on the Dinka consumer cooperatives is less complete than on the group farms for they were not a program of the Abyei Project. I was studying traditional farming and living in a small village when a young man arrived to begin a new cooperative program among the Ngok. For his own kinship reasons, he chose 'my' village as the site of his first effort. There was initial skepticism, but he came out from town repeatedly to encourage people to sign up and to demonstrate his seriousness. He came out on foot in all sorts of weather and visited each homestead personally. He knew the local cleavages which he skillfully worked around and balanced. This man had been with the ministry of cooperatives for some time and had experience organizing similar groups among the Nuba. He carefully mended his political fences in town with the Sudan Socialist Union, the only legal political party. This village was one of the do-nothing group farm sites, but within a month a rather large sum of money was collected, a steering committee was elected, and the cooperative was on its way. He went on to organize similar groups in two other villages. Barely two months later, however, the program was finished, embroiled in politics, and all activity was suspended.

Such consumer cooperatives may have some success in areas of higher literacy and increased involvement in the cash economy. But as transplanted among the pastoral Dinka, they made little economic sense. They promised the people supplies of luxury items such as tea and sugar at government subsidized prices. Much of the initial receptivity on the part of villagers was due to the fact that the organizer was able to offer government sugar at a good price. However, even at half the market price, most of the people of the village could only afford tiny amounts of this coveted and scarce item. As much as they might desire these luxury comestibles, the Dinka villagers could hardly afford them. Moreover, there was no way the cooperative organizer could assure the purchase, transportation, and safe storage of such commodities; there was no budget, no procurement system, no access to vehicles. The only possible economic motivation relating to an organization such as this is the opportunity for fraud.

In the political factionalism of this region, accusation and counter accusation never cease. A previous cooperative had been closed down several years earlier due to the embezzlement of the funds. The new organizer was empowered by his ministry to go through the records and bring evidence against the guilty parties. Not by coincidence, he found evidence against the leader of the anti-Deng political opposition and had the man jailed. It was only a matter of time before the inevitable political backlash. Meanwhile the villagers withdrew their support because they distrusted the political motives of the over-zealous organizer.

Conclusions

What can one reasonably conclude from the experience of a development project such as this? There is a growing literature and even an AID-funded journal (*Rural Development Participation Review*, Committee on Rural Development, Cornell University) dedicated to the task of organizing local participation more effectively. This literature demonstrates the variety of local situations and explores the many impediments to local participation. The lesson I draw from these accounts and from the Abyei experience is that there must be more realistic and more flexible expectations for local participation in rural development projects, especially in the poorer and less accessible regions of Africa.

The first aspect of currently unrealistic expectation pertains to the nature of rural Africa. Do those who speak in such glowing terms of popular participation understand the dynamics of most rural social formations in remote and sparsely settled regions of the continent? From afar one may see in rural Africa an equality and uniformity born of poverty. But such a view is misleading, for the uniformity is often riven with deep factions and is bitterly competitive. Abyei may be an extreme case in this regard, but such inter-ethnic tensions, shifting intra-ethnic allegiances, and problematic central control are reported to be common situations throughout the length and breadth of sub-Saharan Africa. One cannot reasonably expect a participatory development project to erase these problems. Nor can local involvement be excluded because such schisms exist. However, local participation is not easily organized in resource-starved and factious areas of fragile nation states. One must be prepared (and donor agencies and national governments rarely are) for a lot of noisy jockeying for position and alternating involvement and disengagement of local interests, especially at the early stages of such a program.

Even under the best of conditions, such participatory local organizations have somewhat contradictory goals. They are supposed to provide a routinized and permanent institutional framework as well as serve as a creative local mobilizing force of popular action. General sociological theory (see for example, *Max Weber: On Charisma and Institution Building*, S.N. Eisenstadt, ed.) suggests that these goals are trade-offs, allowing but a partially satisfactory compromise which dynamically swings in a seemingly unstable way.

Next, the implicit contradictions between what African governments mean by 'participation' and what donor agencies have in mind must be taken into consideration. The governments of most African nations are socialist in flavor, and their notions of participation follow a generally Eastern model. This socialist model tends to view local participation as a means of mobilizing and channelling the energies of the masses to serve centrally defined developmental needs of the nation. The various vague Western notions held by donor agencies are rather different. The most idealistic version sees popular participation as a means whereby people at the local level will, in a great variety of locally determined ways, assume part of their own responsibility for economic development and avoid being a burden on the state. Another view of local participation sees it as a kind of consultation process which helps the donor agency avoid costly errors of inappropriate projects. And there is the view that regards local participation in terms of 'self help' contributions of free menial labor to reduce the costs of constructing public buildings.

In spite of the fundamental philosophical contradiction between the socialist and the Western views, these approaches frequently become confused in each others' rhetoric. At cocktail parties in African capitals one hears American AID economists unwittingly espousing the development theories of Mao Tse-Tung, and African socialist officials praising styles of management that are reminiscent of the corporate board room. It seems that many of the government decision-makers, expatriate and national, are unaware of any underlying policy contradictions, and not at all clear about what they expect from their 'policies' of local participation.

Finally let us return to the Abyei project. At the beginning AID, HIID, and Francis Deng had all created unrealistically high expectations. Even if the budget was modest and the fine print cautious, the expectations and the rhetoric were grand. Much of this was necessary to convince various parties to approve, allow, fund, or implement a patently difficult project. The project fell short of its own rhetoric as well as the vague idealism of the policies of participation of the "poorest of the poor."

When participatory projects fail to live up to these unrealistic expectations, they are often pronounced 'failures.' Several conclusions can then follow: one is that the local people are obviously not capable of handling matters and that what is needed are more competent outsiders, foreign or national. The other conclusion is that the project is not worthy of further support. For the Abyei project both of these pronouncements were made. AID could not publicly blame the inability of local people to manage their affairs, but they repeatedly stated that more outside experts were needed. The final AID evaluation report by Development Alternatives, Inc. criticized the lack of outside expertise in Abyei and the modest organization in Khartoum as well as the paucity of permanent staff members back at Harvard. Based on these managerial weaknesses and the failure of local development organizations to be properly formed, the recommendation was to terminate further funding.[3]

Putting aside the question of whether this particular project was worthy of support or too risky to maintain, let us consider the effects of this not uncommon on and then off pattern of development funding. Such a pattern encourages individuals and groups to take the shortest and narrowest view and get as much 'aid' as possible while the wind is blowing their way. This uncertainty and seeming capriciousness of development funding greatly intensifies the instability of the shifting power relations in rural areas where intense competition for resources and administrative instability are already the greatest barriers to any possible progress.

Notes

1. I was involved with the Abyei project in various capacities from the time of an early exploratory visit to Abyei in January 1977 until the project's termination in June 1981. As a faculty member in the Harvard anthropology department, I worked with the Harvard Institute for International Development (HIID) first as a consultant helping with project design (1977–78), then as HIID's representative and liaison officer in Khartoum where I had a visiting appointment at the University of Khartoum (1979–80), and as field research coordinator (1980–81). I was fortunate to be involved in both the operational and research aspects of the project for substantial periods in three of the crucial locations of activity: Abyei, Khartoum, and Harvard.

In several places in this chapter there appears to be criticism of actions taken by individuals and institutions, especially USAID. This does not mean that such actions by AID were ultimately incorrect or inexplicable. In a forthcoming work, I discuss the very difficult position of the AID Mission in Khartoum regarding this project in particular and their enormous task in general.

2. The Abyei Project, like most development projects, generated a great deal of written material: eight official and semi-official project documents, four evaluation reports, and seventeen research and technical reports. A complete list may be found in, HIID, "Abyei Integrated Rural Development Project, Final Report" December, 1981. The following reports reflect some of the work done in Abyei.

Moh. Salih Hassan, Akos Ostor, Lina Fruzzetti, "Abyei Project: Main Report of the Socio-Economic Survey," Khartoum, Development Studies and Research Center, University of Khartoum, August, 1978; and these Harvard Institute for International Development (HIID) publications: David C. Cole and David J. Vail, "Action Research in Abyei: An Approach to the Identification, Testing and

Selection of Appropriate Technologies in a Rural Development Context," March 1980; Richard Huntington (Wm. R.) "Popular Participation in the Abyei Project" May 1980; Dana Larson, "Abyei Rural Development Project, Report on the Health Program, June 1978—June 1979," October 1980; Jane J. Hayes, "Land Use Analysis/Population Survey: Abyei Study Area. South Korodofan, Sudan," October 1980; Miryam Niamir, "Animal Husbandry Among Ngok Dinka of the Sudan: Report of a Field Study," December 1981; Richard Fuller, "Report on the Agriculture Program in Abyei," December 1981; William J. Donovann, "Report on the Training Program in Abyei," December 1981; Joseph Sharp, "Report on the Construction Program in Abyei," December 1981; Bruce Eaton and David Cole, "Report on the Water Program in Abyei," September 1981; Jay Ackroyd, "The Traditional Village Economy of Abyei," December 1981; Ann Byerly, "Report on the Health Program in Abyei," December 1981.

3. The Ministry of Agriculture continued the project, using local currency funds received from AID. According to USAID reports, the staff and the project infrastructure remained largely intact one year after termination of the Harvard contract.

References

Cruise O'Brien, Donal B. 1975 *Saints and Politicians: Essays in the Organization of a Senegalese Peasant Society.* Cambridge, London, New York: Cambridge University Press.

Deng, Francis M. 1973 *Dynamics of Identification: A Basis for National Integration in the Sudan.* Khartoum: Khartoum University Press.

Eisenstadt, S.N. (ed.) 1968 *Max Weber: On Charisma and Institution Building.* Chicago: University of Chicago Press.

Fallers, Lloyd 1965 *Bantu Bureaucracy.* Chicago: University of Chicago Press.

Gaafar Mohamed Ali Bakheit 1974 "The Politics of Native Administration, 1954–60," in J. Howell (ed.), *Local Government and Politics in the Sudan.* Khartoum: Khartoum University Press.

Hopkins, Nicholas S. 1969 "Leadership and Consensus in Two Malian Cooperatives," in D. Brokensha and M. Pearsall (eds.), *The Anthropology of Development in Sub-Saharan Africa.* Society for Applied Anthropology, Monograph 10.

Howell, John 1974 "The Reform of Local Government, 1971," in J. Howell (ed.), *Local Government and Politics in the Sudan.* Khartoum: Khartoum University Press.

Huntington, Richard 1973 "Community Spirit in a Malagasy Village," in *Outlook: Focus on Development.* Cape Town: The Christian Institute.

Huntington, Richard, James Ackroyd and Luka Deng 1981 "The Challenge for Rainfed Agriculture in Western and Southern Sudan: Lessons from Abyei," *Africa Today* Vol. 28, No. 2.

James, Wendy 1972 "The Politics of Rain Control among the Uduk," in Cunnison and James (eds.), *Essays in Sudan Ethnography: Presented to Sir Edward Evans-Pritchard.* New York: Humanities Press.

Kramer, Ralph M. 1969 *Participation of the Poor: Comparative Community Case Studies in the War on Poverty.* Englewood Cliffs: Prentice-Hall.
Richards, Audrey and Adam Kuper (eds.) 1971 *Councils in Action.* Cambridge, London, New York: Cambridge University Press.
Der Spiegel 1975 "Herz des Volkes." Nr. 11.

5

ECONOMIC DEVELOPMENT AND SOCIAL CHANGE IN INDIAN AGRICULTURE: A HISTORICAL PERSPECTIVE

David E. Ludden

Indian cultivators work their fields in little social worlds suffused with the influence of national markets, administration, and politics. The agrarian system of India today is so integrated that it is reasonable to approach Indian agricultural development through a unified, national model of agricultural conditions. This approach, futhermore, is buttressed by cultural anthropologists and Indologists confirming the underlying unities of Indian civilization.[1] Scholars and politicians alike have thus spoken for many years about characteristically *Indian* agricultural problems, potentials and patterns of change. Scholarly discourse on development processes has generally moved directly from broad theoretical questions—concerning, for instance, the rationality of peasant enterprise, or the productivity and equity effects of specific technologies and customs—to empirical data drawn from India as a whole, or from its huge states, each holding many millions of farmers. Another approach has become more prominent in recent years, however; that is, to focus upon the diversity of Indian agriculture, and upon the little worlds of day-to-day agricultural activity. This move toward microcosmic studies—with efforts to systematize variations, and to unravel the many strands that tie little worlds to the agrarian system as a whole—may now have become pertinent to planners, too, because national development efforts must work locally to succeed.[2]

It was once commonplace to conceptualize the peasant's traditional world as an isolated village community, stagnant, homogeneous, and backward; and thus to see economic development and social change as the outcome of village inclusion within networks of political control and market exchange, which began, it was said, under British rule, c.1780 to 1947. In fact, however, few farmers even in the distant past lived detached from networks of social relations that tied villages to one another, and to urban centers. Networks of kinship, caste, religion, markets, migration and political authority extended from and encompassed villages at various levels of scale. Historians call the totality of networks involved in the flow and growth of agricultural wealth "the agrarian system," and they have shed considerable light in recent decades on the complexities of systemic structure and change in pre-British times. The peasant's little world was indeed shaped by the system in which he was embedded, and systems changed quite dramatically over the centuries.

At its widest extent, the Indian agrarian system today encompasses the entire nation and stretches outward into the world political economy. Within this national system, however, the individual states possess distinctive systemic characteristics for a variety of reasons: first of all, they were reorganized along linguistic grounds in 1956; they also are in charge of administering their respective development programs; and, lastly, of course, each retains its own legacy of disparate history with respect, for instance, to such matters as land law and water rights. Within states, there are regions that are similarly bounded by social networks, sometimes corresponding to administrative boundaries. These are regions defined by the distribution of dominant caste groups; by networks of marriage, pilgrimage and trade in dietary staples; by physical conditions bearing upon production, such as rainfall, soil type, slope, water table and drainage; and by traditional patterns of caste relations. These regions are comprised of agricultural communities with common traditions, technologies, social structures and patterns of change.

These lower reaches of the agrarian system are the subject of this chapter. Unlike wider realms, they characteristically have very long histories as arenas of agrarian organization, development and dominance. Policy interventions and market forces generated in distant metropolitan centers affect agricultural development, social stratification, income distribution and power in the countryside only by shaping relations within these small scale building blocks of India's political economy, within these historic arenas of agrarian civilization.

This local level of the agrarian system comprises a set of working relations among groups engaged in day-to-day agricultural operations. Such agrarian relations have in India been constructed over very long periods of time, in the context of quite specific physical conditions bearing upon social and technical solutions to survival problems. Agricultural communities are composed of groups conscious that they have struggled over generations to control natural and human forces so as to ensure group survival. And communities do not comprise a unity of interests among groups. Far from it. They seem always to contain differential access to the means of production and a varying set of converging and diverging interests. At the same time, however, within small scale agrarian regions there is a community of interest focussed upon very specific resources, relations and conflicts; and control of such resources in that specific context seems generally to be thought essential. Thus group pursuit of control within communities of interest provides the dynamic force in the little worlds of agriculture.

In the Indian context, agricultural communities are structured as a set of multiplex identities and relations, which are not dissected and analyzed separately in daily life, where social networks intertwine so tightly so as to lose much of their distinctiveness, and where caste, kinship, material exchange, political allegiance and sacred power combine over many generations in a specific agricultural milieu. In daily life, these various strands of human relations appear indistinguishable to the participants themselves, a fact that has generated unending debate about the relative significance of caste and class in Indian villages.

One agrarian system, then, can contain a variety of agricultural communities whose social relations are localized, intense, and tied to a specific set of productive operations. The networks that comprise the agrarian system fuse as they converge within a locality, so that, for example, political and economic trends with distinct origins in the system as a whole become one as they affect local relations. For political economy, the analytical distinction between communities and systems highlights the fact that power relations over wide spaces derive from the control of moveable resources, such as money, credit, ritual honors, loyalty and armies; whereas in a local context power depends on the control of immoveables, like land, and on resources extremely difficult to manipulate from a distance, i.e., water, animals, human labor and detailed knowledge of local production conditions and social customs. Power in an agrarian system must be translated into the language of local discourse, and exerted within the local scene, to effect local relations in agriculture.

Processes of development and change, therefore, look quite different when one focuses on communities rather than on systems. In South India, for example, the arena of my own research, the system evolved in definite stages from the ninth century onward. From the consolidation of early kingdoms throughout the peninsula around 800 A.D. until the middle of the eighteenth century, the system worked on emphatically Hindu lines. Hindu temples, for instance, and networks of authority based on patronage by notables of temples and Brahman landed elites, remained critical throughout this millenium of systemic evolution. After

1750, with the invasion of South India by British colonial capitalism, the system was thoroughly transformed. Religious institutions and ideologies lost their dominance in the integration of the system as a whole. The market economy and rationalized administrative institutions, both centred on colonial urban centers, took hold. Another phase of systemic development began with Indian Independence, in 1947, when native elites obtained new levers with which to protect national interests and develop agriculture. Today, vestiges of the past remain, but the institutions and organizing principles of the pre-colonial and colonial agrarian systems have faded into vague memories.

Continuities are much more pronounced, however, in the structure and workings of agricultural communities. Even after the transformative impact of colonialism and independence, local structures of agrarian relations are still visible which are quite as distinct from one another today as arenas of development and social change as they were in the ninth century. These local continuities have led me to formulate four general, comparative propositions about the social organization of Indian agriculture, viewed as a long-term, diverse human enterprise. Though these propositions are fitted most closely to data from South India, they can be applied more broadly to the localities of the subcontinent, as I will indicate with reference to recent work in agrarian history (Ludden 1984) and in development studies.

Technology

Broadly conceived to include all the materials and techniques employed in production, as these are fitted into a specific natural setting, agricultural technology becomes over time an integral part of local production relations. It follows from this that technologically uniform regions will assume system characteristics traceable to dominant agro-ecological elements and that technological change can be both cause and effect of changing agrarian relations.

This proposition is not deterministic, for it does not argue any one line of causation. It merely posits pervasive interpenetration between what is termed "social relations" and technological "software." The workings of agrarian relations as they pertain to agriculture and as they pertain to politics, kinship and so forth cannot be viewed separately. Consequently, just as one finds throughout the world a strong family resemblance among swidden agricultural regimes, a general correspondence between swidden agriculture and tribal organization, and an ancient social as well as technological chasm between swidden farmers, on the one hand, and settled peasant communities, on the other; within Indian peasant agriculture there are community structures associated with particular agro-technological regimes. Traditions of control over the material and symbolic elements of each regime have had a very strong tendency to persist over time, despite epochal changes in the agrarian system.

Taking a long-term perspective, we can categorize agro-technological regimes along a continuum from "wet" to "dry," based on the availability of a key scarce resource in Indian agriculture, water. Wet cultivation, over the centuries based on high rainfall and drainage irrigation, has characteristically centered on rice, which needs lots of water and heavy inputs of labor, and which can in turn support dense populations and relatively large numbers of non-cultivators, from artisans and priests to landlords and literati. Dry cultivation is simply the opposite extreme: extensive, often long-fallow, millet cultivation, combined of necessity with hunting and/or pastoralism, a regime that can support relatively thin populations, with little luxury or high civilization. As contexts for human survival and social development, local arenas of agrarian relations in India have social histories that diverge significantly when they are situated on opposite ends of this agro-technological spectrum from wet to dry.

Agricultural communities in wet localities—throughout Bengal, Bihar, Kerala, and scattered along the western and eastern peninsular coast—have tended to become dominated by non-cultivating, high-caste land-owners, often Brahmans, who have controlled over the centuries not only paddy lands and irrigation water in villages, but elite positions in the city, too. By contrast, dry communities—not only in arid Rajasthan and Sind, but in semi-arid tracts in the upper Indus and western Gangetic plains, and also in the interior uplands of the peninsula—have become the domain of rugged warrior and peasant castes, whose rustic lifestyle in the village sets them off both socially and culturally from the elites concentrated in major towns and cities.

To contrast wet and dry agro-technological features of such communities hardly suffices to depict their historical character, to be sure. But it brings out clearly the strong tendency for elements associated with wetness and dryness to cluster together and persist, even in technologically mixed regions, like the Punjab and western Uttar Pradesh, which have both been transformed by new agro-technology and, to a much lesser extent, by land legislation during the last century. Western U.P., Haryana, and the Indian Punjab today enjoy considerable supplies of water from dams, canals and tubewells, yet they also comprise, historically, a dry region; for despite recent trends, most irrigation in centuries past depended solely upon wells, most cultivation was carried on by a locally dominant warrior-peasant caste, the Jats, and the agrarian social world was characterized by sharp distinctions between city and village. The Gangetic Plain gets decidedly wetter toward Bihar and Bengal in the east. With the exception of the former kingdom of Oudh, north of the Ganges, western U.P. witnessed a steady decline in large landlord power after 1850; small-scale farms, owned by Jats, became the dominant unit of agricultural development. But not so in the east, where land legislation never succeeded in wresting control of the soil from non-cultivating elites.

Such contrasts have now become well-worn subjects of debate among historians and developmentalists (Stokes 1978). Paddy cultivation in India today seems to proceed in a social context of complex and rigid stratification. Landowners tend strongly to be non-cultivating elites who take little part in agricultural operations and often disdain to dirty their hands. There is a marked overlap of caste and class in agricultural communities, with a traditional, high-caste elite on top, and very low, often untouchable castes on the bottom. This situation arose from the ability of high-castes to capture the production process and the agricultural surplus through conquest, superstratification, elite solidarity and religious sanctions. For the lowly, survival became equated with subordination: to eat meant doing jobs deemed lowly, and hence to recreate one's lowliness each generation. In dry localities, by contrast, abundant land and family labor units working on a subsistence frontier created a landscape of hardy peasants and competing warrior elites; here agriculture is the work of almost all households, rich and poor alike, many descended from warriors of the past, and all unconstrained in their pursuit of opportunity by an elite stratum's unassailable control of the means of production. Peasants, in short, control the development process locally, in politics and in production.

Whole regions dominated by wet or dry conditions tend to assume distinctive systemic characteristics. Where population is very dense and paddy prevails, urban and rural life tend to blur at the edges for a variety of reasons: the rural elites are traditionally literate and mobile participants in high culture, and political integration has been achieved by continual absorption of prosperous families from various high castes into the elite strata. By contrast, cities and towns stand out much more in dry regions where the scale of central places depends more on linear, long-distance trade than on expanding output from the immediate hinterland. In these regions security was always at a premium in centuries past, so urban merchants clustered under the protection of local rulers in fortified centers. Though linked by various ties to the countryside, urban centers tended thus to stand out as nodes of a distinctly urban culture, much more so than cities in wet regions.

Technological change in Indian agriculture has for the most part been fitted locally into prevailing modes of production organization; partly because much of the new "hardware"—pumpsets, seeds, fertilizers, tractors, and so forth—has been selected for application by those in command of the production process; and partly because imposed projects such as massive irrigation works, railways and industry have been adapted in their managerial or "software" dimension to make them workable in various local milieus. This is not to say changes in production techniques have had no significant impact on production relations. Tubewells and tractors have changed land and labor relations in northern India, giving new power to those who command the new productive resources. Likewise, motorized pumpsets have enabled landowners once dependent on community irrigation facilities to manage their land and water resources with a new freedom in recent decades (Dasgupta 1977; Farmer 1977). Nonetheless, any generalization about the social impact of the Green Revolution loses merit to the extent that it ignores the variety of techniques included under that label and the great diversity of technical applications in practice. The so-called "Green Revolution" is a bundle of material inputs that have been applied variously according to the needs and aspirations of farmers in quite different milieus. These milieus must be seen historically to gauge the impact of the new technology on either production decisions or social relations.

Enterprise

Culturally, it seems, working the land in contrasting agro-technological regimes over centuries has produced a set of contrasting conceptions about agricultural enterprise itself, and quite different strategies that guide elite behavior in the process of economic development.

Notions of enterprise in the wet subculture of rice farming reflect the radical disjuncture in that regime between landowning and labor. Because working the land is the task of very low people, manual labor has heavy overtones of social degradation. Daily agricultural operations do not receive detailed attention, as a rule, from high-caste landowners, whose time and energy would tend to move toward higher pursuits, and who view the land basically as a source of wealth, food and status. The production process thus does not figure prominently in the musing of landlords, whose efforts to intensify land-use and to increase profits tend to focus on problems of social control: how to extract more, where possible, from labor, and, where this meets resistance, to displace workers. A smoothly running paddy regime in India presupposes, as a rule, successful management of poor, undernourished, economically disenfranchised workers by a traditional landed elite who are more concerned with matters of order and status than actual land productivity.

In contrast, the warrior-peasants and present day commercial peasants who farm the drier parts of the subcontinent have built their enterprise

on a core of family labor, even if their operations do not exactly correspond
to Chayanov's model of the peasant family farm (Thorner et al. 1966).
Even where agricultural laborers have emerged as critical in cash crop
farming, the ethos of the peasant cultivator continues to suffuse daily
work among Jats, Marathas, Reddis, Kammas, Kongu Vellalas, and other,
similar castes. They take to farming as they would to war. They look
for ways to retain and improve their land, to increase their families'
stature on the land, and to increase their income from the soil. For
them, power has always meant landed wealth, and in turn effort to
increase output, most often through their own work.

This contrast does not mean that only peasant castes are enterprising,
only that enterprise assumes different directions among landowners who
traditionally have worked the soil. In drier parts of India, villages were
for centuries relatively isolated, fortified bastions of warrior-peasant
control. They fitted much more closely than those in paddy-growing
tracts the image of the "self-sufficient village republic" made famous by
Sir Charles Metcalfe in the nineteenth century. Even as railways, trucks,
buses, telegraphs and telephones tied villagers more and more closely
into marketing networks and thus to towns, peasant enterprise tended
to focus on the farm and to exploit market opportunities for making
profits in the village. Social discontinuities and disruption emerged as
mercantile enterprise gained supremacy and displaced warrior enterprise
under British rule; this was reflected in a variety of violent outbreaks:
grain riots, credit riots, Hindu-Muslim conflicts and caste conflicts.
Political conflict suffused with specifically urban-versus-rural overtones
continues in some dry regions even today, now elevated to the status
of state or even national significance.

By contrast, the traditional literacy, urbanity and social mobility of
high-caste landowners in rice-growing regions made it logical and painless
for them to pursue opportunities in town and city, in professions,
politics, commerce and industry. The land became a financial base, but
aspirations for wealth focussed rather on city lights. It became common
for agrarian elites to maintain moorings in urban and rural milieus, and
for their sons to become prominent in politics. They assumed a role
out of all proportion to their numbers in the nationalist movement and
are the mainstay of what we call the Indian "middle class." The highway
of opportunity for elites was paralleled by paths of labor migration, so
urban and rural proletariats came to closely resemble one another as
well. As a result, class conflict and political alliances across the urban-
rural divide became characteristic of such regions, best exemplified in
West Bengal and in Kerala.

Mobility

Participation in the development process moves along avenues of mobility established within each production regime, so that trends in the agrarian system tend to trigger changes locally that recapitulate the distinctive character of regimes over time.

Karl Marx once argued that British commerce, railways and private property would revolutionize social relations in village India (Avineri 1969). The reality was much less exciting. Private property relations merely cemented the position of peasant cultivators in dry farming regions; in some, like the Punjab, Jat political power had put peasant control in the forefront even before British rule (Banga 1974; Dasgupta 1977). In Bengal, many families alleged to be landlords (*zamindars*) were in fact unable to exercise dominant economic and political power in their estates; and new markets for agricultural products and labor were contained within existing networks of local control.[3] In South India, breaking up the collective control of landlords in irrigated villages primarily meant that they henceforth exercised local control individually, retaining, as a status elite, control over land, water and labor in their villages (Ludden 1978; Washbrook 1976). Even "the rise of the rich peasant" has been questioned of late by historians who argue that dominant peasant families merely converted control of the grainheap to control of local markets for land, labor, and credit during the course of commercialization (Charlesworth 1980). Historical revisions of classical sociological generalizations, in short, should caution scholars who would find radical social change in the Indian countryside today. Change will probably look less drastic with a longer term and comparative perspective.[4]

The structure of paddy-cultivating communities has certainly become, in André Béteille's phrase, more "open" in the last decades. Village workers can look for employment in town; landowning has shifted away from some elites, especially Brahmans, and toward others, especially the higher castes of non-Brahmans; and political power has gravitated leftward in Kerala and West Bengal. Nonetheless, such change has not altered the essence of the local production regimen characteristic of these regions: hence, they continue to resemble one another much more than they do dry farming regions in many important respects. Landless laborers, for example, continue to represent a large percentage of the population, forced to make in each generation the trade off between subsistence and social status that keeps them both lowly and dirt poor. Population pressure, rising paddy prices and intensified land use give new incentives for landowners to maintain or tighten control over workers. Thus, a vicious cycle of mass poverty, low technological change, class conflict and slow, even negligible development characteristically afflicts the classically wet regions of India, once the breadbaskets of the civilization, once the magnets for enterprise and social mobility. Today it seems that mobility remains a strong likelihood primarily for the old status elite, except where political change has made real reform in land relations as may be happening in Kerala. But very slow growth means little real mobility for everyone.

The dry regions are of course poor, too. But here above all it is the land that is poor, and thirsty; the social structure, though hardly egalitarian, tends more to spread poverty around than to rigidify distinctions between well-fed and hungry families. More importantly, family enterprise has often involved technical change and social mobility for well-placed peasant families. Not all warrior-peasants fared well in the course of commercialization, to be sure. Some, like the Maravas of South India, prized martial more than peasant virtues, and have struggled in the political arena to regain what they have lost in the economic one over the last century. The pacification of the subcontinent meant that warriors, in order to retain and expand routes for family mobility, had to use the market as they once did the battlefield. It meant, thus, that they faced a new style of competition. The peasant castes that took first to commercial agriculture were often not the warriors, in fact, but relatively low-status garden cultivators who had long experience in working the land and the marketplace simultaneously (Attwood 1984). Maravas resisted this new role model, but other warrior-peasants made the market their new frontier.

The successful competitors became those we know today as "rich peasants," or, as Lloyd and Susanne Rudolph (1984) like to call them, "bullock capitalists." Many of them no doubt came from the ranks of former village magnates, traditionally martial leaders who had set up little fiefs for themselves in the village. But new opportunities for investing in land, trade and moneylending, as well as, eventually, in industry, provided new routes to riches for families that could make it. Caste and kin networks among peasant farmers in dry South Asia allowed families to start a slow, fitful, precarious, but definitely upward movement in their agrarian stature.

Rising rich peasants established for themselves a firm presence not only in the agrarian economy, but in politics. After Independence, they became the center of attention for planners, economists, and politicians alike. Today, there are no doubt communities dominated by single families or by rich peasant oligarchies that throttle the aspirations of poorer farmers. At the same time, however, dry communities have become famous for feuds between old guard families and rising competitors for power. Enterprising commercial peasants generate a subtle pattern of circulation in dry communities, which, though hard to measure, (Attwood 1979), and though constrained by overall poverty, reflects the kind of mobility, with all its ups and downs, that would be expected in a competitive market economy. Not surprisingly, dry communities have been the most successful arenas for technological innovation during the Green Revolution.

Development

In prescriptions for the future, as in descriptions of the past, contrasting agrarian milieus in India fit contrasting theoretical models of economic development.

Patterns of development and change in wet and dry regimes have wreaked havoc with attempts to characterize *the* mode of production in Indian agriculture. On the one hand, landowning elites in wet communities often appear highly modernized and rational in western terms. They often speak English, and participate excitedly and knowledgeably in commerce and politics. Yet in their landowning role they often look more like feudal barons, dependent upon the labor of half-starved workers, constrained in enterprise by considerations of caste and custom. Many a refined, broad-minded—even revolutionary—member of the urban intelligentsia lives off a family estate worked by virtually bonded labor, or by tenants who regard him as lord. Such relations of production have generated the image of Indian semi-feudalism (Rudra et al. 1978). An alternate, and probably more useful, characterization of these relations pinpoints the critical linkage among markets for land, labor, credit and food, and thus turns attention toward structural changes necessary to generate the dynamism theoretically inherent in the market system.

In dry regions, on the other hand, agrarian elite values based on martial virtues and frontier justice imbue many peasants with what might be seen as an economically irrational passion for self-reliance and dominance, but also drive farmers headlong into the market economy. Moreover, caste and kin networks provide the highly valued and hence consistently maintained social base for individual enterprise. Jat cultivators in the Punjab, no matter how much they look like individualistic peasant capitalists, rely on their families, and invest, above all else, in family ties (Kessinger 1974). Martial virtues and traditional values thus mingle freely with capitalist ones, and capitalist agriculture never quite assumes the social character one expects on the basis of models derived from European experience. At the same time, economic differentiation never generates stratified relations characteristic of wet communities.

It would seem that a survey of historical experience and inquiries into contemporary events in agrarian India support the proposition that no single model of agricultural development can fit the diversity of milieus in which development in agriculture actually takes place. For historians, the lesson is clear: a comparative framework needs to be elaborated for studying change in the Indian countryside. The distinction between "wet" and "dry" localities is only the beginning, and a crude one at that. There are a great variety of "mixed" regimes in the subcontinent. Industrialization complicates the matter still further. The comparative model presented here is in fact best applicable to pre-industrial conditions, though, as indicated, it may shed light on an industrializing economy still dominated by agriculture. The discussion here has also omitted the local influence of particular caste, merchant and political networks, though I have tried to indicate where they would enter into comparative analysis.

For social scientists and planners my argument is simply that abstraction and model-building should not proceed without attention to the critical distinction between an agrarian system and its agricultural communities. India is highly integrated as a national economy, yet it contains little worlds of agricultural life for which the forty-year nationhood is but the most recent hour in many centuries of development. These little worlds, though still very poorly understood, and barely perceived in circles of academic discourse, are in fact the social context of future development in agriculture. Theories, models and plans must somehow take them into account, for they will not disappear.

Notes

1. See, for instance, Louis Dumont, *Homo Hierarchicus*, Chicago, 1970; McKim Marriott, "Hindu Transactions: Diversity Without Dualism," in Bruce Kapferer (ed.), *Transaction and Meaning: Directions in the Anthropology of Exchange and Symbolic Behavior*, Philadelphia, 1976, pp. 109–42; and W. Norman Brown, "The Content of Cultural Continuity in India," in Thomas R. Metcalf (ed.), *Modern India: An Interpretive Anthology*, London, 1971, pp. 12–21.

2. Recent discussions of this issue include Theodore W. Schultz (ed.), *Distortions of Agricultural Incentives*, Bloomington, 1978; and E. Walter Coward (ed.), *Irrigation and Agricultural Development in Asia: Perspectives from the Social Sciences*, Ithaca, 1980, reviewed with interesting comments by Benjamin Ward in *Journal of Asian Studies* Vol. 40 No. 2, February 1981. pp 335–37.

3. Rajat and Ratna Ray, "The Dynamics of Continuity in Rural Bengal under British Imperium: A Study of Quasi-Stable Equilibrium in Underdeveloped Societies in a Changing World," *Indian Economic and Social History Review* Vol. 10 No. 2, June 1973. pp. 103–29. For the variability of developments in Bengal, see Ratnalekha Ray, *Change in Bengal Agrarian Society, 1760–1850*, Delhi, 1979.

4. For such a perspective on recent ethnographic accounts, see David E. Ludden, "Dimensions of Agrarian Political Economy: Focus on Tamil Nadu," *Peasant Studies.* Vol. 8 No. 4, Fall 1979. pp. 19–30.

References

Arnold, David 1979 "Looting, Grain Riots, and Government Policy in South India, 1918," *Past and Present* Vol. 84, August. pp. 111–145.

Attwood, Donald W. 1979 "Why Some of the Poor Get Richer: Economic Change and Mobility in Rural Western India," *Current Anthropology* Vol. 20. pp. 495–516, 657–58.

1984 "Capital and the Transformation of Agrarian Class Systems: Sugar Production in India," in M. Desai, S.H. Rudolph and A. Rudra (eds.), *Agrarian Power and Agricultural Productivity in South Asia.* Delhi: Oxford University Press.

Avineri, Shlomo (ed.) 1969 *Karl Marx on Colonialism and Modernization.* Garden City, New York: Doubleday.

Banga, Indu 1974 *Agrarian System of the Sikhs: Late Eighteenth and Early Nineteenth Century.* Delhi: Manohar Publishers.

Barrier, N. Gerald 1974 "The Punjab Disturbances of 1907: The Response of the British Government in India to Agrarian Unrest," *Punjab Past and Present* Vol. 8 No. 2. pp. 444–477.

Brown, W. Norman 1971 "The Content of Cultural Continuity in India," in Thomas R. Metcalf (ed.), *Modern India: An Interpretive Anthology.* New York: Macmillan.

Charlesworth, Neil 1972 "The Myth of the Deccan Riots," *Modern Asian Studies* Vol. 6 No. 4. pp. 401–421.

1980 "Rich Peasants and Poor Peasants in Late Nineteenth Century Maharashtra," in C. Dewey and A.G. Hopkins (eds.), *The Imperial Impact: Studies in the Economic History of Africa and India.* London: Althone.

Coward, E. Walter (ed.) 1980 *Irrigation and Agricultural Development in Asia: Perspectives from the Social Sciences.* Ithaca: Cornell University Press.

Dasgupta, Biplab 1977 *Agrarian Change and the New Technology in India.* Geneva: United Nations Research Institute for Social Development.

Dewey, Clive 1972 "Images of the Village Community: A Study in Anglo-Indian Thought," *Modern Asian Studies* Vol. 6 No. 3. pp. 291–328.

Dumont, Louis 1970 *Homo Hierarchicus.* Chicago: University of Chicago Press.

Farmer, B.H. (ed.) 1977 *Green Revolution? Technology and Change in Rice-growing Areas of Tamil Nadu and Sri Lanka.* London: Macmillan.

Kessinger, Thomas G. 1974 *Vilyatpur, 1848–1968: Social and Economic Change in a North Indian Village.* Berkeley: University of California Press.

Ludden, David E. 1978 "Agrarian Organization in Tinnevelly District, 800 to 1900 A.D." Unpublished Ph.D. dissertation. University of Pennsylvania.

1979 "Dimensions of Agrarian Political Economy: Focus on Tamil Nadu," *Peasant Studies.* Vol. 8 No. 4, Fall. pp. 19–30.

1984 "Productive Power in Agriculture: A Survey of Work on the Local History of British India," in M. Desai, S.H. Rudolph, and A. Rudra (eds.), *Agrarian Power and Agricultural Productivity in South Asia*. Delhi: Oxford University Press.

Marriott, McKim 1976 "Hindu Transactions: Diversity Without Dualism," in Bruce Kapferer (ed.), *Transaction and Meaning: Directions in the Anthropology of Exchange and Symbolic Behaviour*. Philadelphia: Institute for the Study of Human Issues.

Ray, Rajat and Ratna Ray 1973 "The Dynamics of Continuity in Rural Bengal under British Imperium: A Study of Quasi-Stable Equilibrium in Underdeveloped Societies in a Changing World," *Indian Economic and Social History Review* Vol. 10 No. 2. pp. 103–129.

Ray, Ratnalekha 1979 *Change in Bengal Agrarian Society, 1760–1850*. Delhi: Manohar Press.

Rudolph, Susanne H. and Lloyd I. Rudolph 1984 "Determinants and Varieties of Agrarian Mobilization," in M. Desai, S.H. Rudolph and A. Rudra (eds.), *Agrarian Power and Agricultural Productivity in South Asia*. Delhi: Oxford University Press.

Rudra, Ashok, A. Majid et al. 1978 *Studies in the Development of Capitalism in India*. Lahore.

Rudra, Ashok 1984 "Local Power and Farm Level Decision Making," in M. Desai, S.H. Rudolph and A. Rudra (eds.), *Agrarian Power and Agricultural Productivity in South Asia*. Delhi: Oxford University Press.

Schultz, Theodore W. (ed.) 1978 *Distortions of Agricultural Incentives*. Bloomington, Indiana: University of Indiana Press.

Stokes, Eric 1978 "Dynamism and Enervation in North Indian Agriculture," in *The Peasant and The Raj*. Cambridge: Cambridge University Press.

Thorner, Daniel, Basil Kerblay and R.E.F. Smith (eds.) 1966. *The Theory of Peasant Economy*. Homewood, Illinois: R.D. Irwin.

Washbrook, David A. 1976 *The Emergence of Provincial Politics: The Madras Presidency, 1870 to 1920*. Cambridge: Cambridge University Press.

6

INVESTING IN INEQUALITY: CLASS FORMATION IN UPPER VOLTA

S. P. Reyna

This chapter examines the influence of international donor investments on class formation in the savanna nation of Upper Volta.[1] The analysis will show that dependence on donor investment facilitates state and private class formation through the articulation of state, private and domestic production relations. This casts doubt on the argument that the process of underdevelopment acts to maintain pre-capitalist modes of production.

Preliminary Observations

The economic prospects for Upper Volta are bleak . . . The economy generates little capital for . . . expansion (McFarland 1976).

The West African savanna nation of Upper Volta consists of two distinct ecological zones: riverine lands near the Volta Rivers and their tributaries, and the dry interior. In general, the former lands are more fertile than the latter. Since the early 1970s, donor investments have been skewed in favor of the riverine lands. The *Autorité des Aménagements des Vallées des Volta* (AVV), for example, is a parastatal Voltaic resettlement scheme centered on a rainfed, cash-crop production program near the Volta Rivers and supported by French, German, Dutch and EEC donors. AVV's budget for 1980 was reportedly about $15 million, nearly 8% of the proposed national budget for that same year. Of about $76 million invested annually in Upper Volta's rural development (USAID 1980:25), fully one-fifth went to AVV; yet during 1978, AVV had only 3,750 hectares in production (Sorgho and Richet 1979:4). By 1979, then, some 20 percent of Upper Volta's rural investment was being spent on 40 out of the country's 274,000 square kilometers. Further donor investments in Upper Volta have also been in other parastatal river valley agro-enterprises (Ouedragogo 1979:555).

Class Analysis in West Africa

Three sets of institutions promote class formation in West Africa: state bureaucracies, parastatals and private landowners.[2] These generate a dual process of class formation resulting from the influence of donor investments.

Some conceptual clarification is needed in order to proceed. The analysis of class formation is concerned with how classes evolve, that is, how differential control over property and surplus appropriation emerge, and also with how classes come to exhibit common action through class consciousness—a subject which is beyond the scope of this chapter. Private class relations are those in which a surplus is appropriated by private individuals. State class relations occur when a surplus is appropriated through a hierarchy of state offices. Bureaucracies, parastatals and private landowners are seen here as components of a dual process of state and private class formation.

Dual class formation is explained through the articulation of modes of production, as suggested by Rey (1971, 1973) and discussed in Wolpe (1980). Articulation is used in Wolpe's sense as: "the relationship between the reproduction of the capitalist economy on the one hand and the reproduction of production units organized to pre-capitalist relations and forces of production on the other" (1980:41). Articulation theorists view articulation, rather than dependency, as the "fundamental cause of underdevelopment" (Meillassoux 1981:95). On this view, underdevelopment is a phase of the articulation of pre-capitalist with capitalist economies in which the latter maintain the former in order to derive certain resources necessary for their reproduction (Rey 1973). This chapter explores articulation in the post-colonial period, a period not well represented in the literature. The following section shows how donor investment in agro-parastatals facilitates the emergence of state class relations.

State Class Relations: Establishment of AVV

The French bilateral development agency, *Fonds d'Aide et de Coopération* (FAC), recommended the creation of a parastatal agency with development responsibility in valleys along the Volta Rivers (Maton et al. 1971), and

Upper Volta accepted FAC's recommendations. In September 1974, a presidential decree created the AVV and transferred ownership of Volta River valley lands to the state. By 1979, these lands included roughly 30,000 square kilometers, or about 12 percent of the country. A 1976 decree authorized two levels of control: the first, consisting of AVV and other government officials, was given control of land utilization; the second, consisting of tenants, was obliged to work the land under conditions set by AVV.

AVV's establishment hinged upon a convergence of EEC and Voltaic interests that had been developing since colonial times. Early in the twentieth century, French colonial administrators judged Upper Volta to be econmically "non-viable" (Songre et al. 1974). This meant that investments were diverted to more attractive areas, generally located on the coast, and that Upper Volta was used as early as the 1920s to supply laborers for those areas (Londres 1929). At roughly the same time, Voltaics were obliged to grow cotton to pay taxes and to supply the French textile industry with inexpensive fiber. Cotton was cultivated using the existing technology and organization of production (Ossendowski 1928:276), and prices were set at low levels dictated by cotton purchasing monopsonies. The few investments made in Upper Volta at that time were predominantly in road and rail links needed to transport labor and cotton. French merchant capital offered consumer goods under near monopoly conditions.

Such policies moved Upper Volta into the French portion of the world capitalist economy and obliged existing farming systems to produce additional outputs demanded by metropolitan capital, while simultaneously diverting labor to more lucrative, coastal investments. Hence, commoditization was intensified under colonial terms-of-trade in which Voltaics sold labor and commodities cheap, while buying French goods and services dear.

For the first decade following independence in 1970, Volta's development strategy followed the colonial pattern. Rural investments were limited and were mainly implemented by French enterprises, such as the *Compagnie Française pour le Développement des Fibres Textiles* (CFDT), and others like it. Emphasis continued on the cultivation of cash crops using the existing production organization, with limited technological improvements (Marchal 1977:85). Although CFDT was able to increase cotton production, other successes were minimal. Productivity of food crops generally stagnated or declined (Savonnet 1976:507–12), and most alarmingly, soil deterioration increased on the Mossi Plateau, the most densely populated region of the nation.

Since agriculture was the main source of government revenue, these conditions resulted in fiscal problems. As ecological pressures on the

Mossi Plateau increased, demands on the bureaucracy to resolve these problems intensified (personal communication, E. Skinner). The 1972–73 drought greatly exacerbated both the fiscal and ecological concerns; thus by 1973 it was in the government's interest to develop the agricultural sector in Upper Volta.

In 1973, the World Health Organization began a program to control the blackfly which breeds along the banks of the Volta Rivers and is the vector for river blindness (onchoceriasis). This program altered the economic attractiveness of riverine areas because, "With control of the vector, the valleys . . . [could] be resettled, thereby generating new output on 'new lands' . . . " (Berg 1978). France and other EEC nations were not indifferent as to how these "new lands" should be developed. During the first decade of independence, CFDT had demonstrated that it could grow cotton. Not only would EEC textile concerns benefit from the cotton, but multinational industry could potentially sell products and allied services to Upper Volta's cotton sector. Estimates based on projections of AVV investment and operational costs indicate that EEC firms could conservatively do $125 million worth of business by installing the AVV and could thereafter conservatively realize $3.5 million annually by selling farm equipment and supplies to the AVV (Reyna 1983).

The creation of AVV met EEC interests through providing new markets and an increased supply of cotton. The FAC mission reported to the Voltaic government that "Government revenues from a parastatal would be approximately 3.7 billion Central African francs (F CFA) over twenty-five years" and that 150,000 individuals could be resettled from the Mossi Plateau into the parastatal's domain, reducing the Plateau's overpopulation (Maton et al. 1971:22). Thus the AVV would at the same time address the nation's pressing need for agricultural revenue and its ecological needs. This conjuncture of EEC and Voltaic interests influenced the creation of AVV.

AVV was in full operation by 1978 with the average tenant farm family cultivating six hectares, 40 percent of which was cotton (Murphy and Sprey 1980). With respect to land control, I have argued elsewhere (Reyna 1983) that AVV tenants were obliged to contribute financially to uncertain agricultural decisions in which they did not participate, and which offered no protection should these decisions go awry. AVV managers, on the other hand, were shown to enjoy greater *de jure* control over land use than private landowners. It was estimated for 1978 that 63 percent of the income received for the sale of AVV cotton was appropriated by the Voltaic state. Under these conditions, a majority of the tenants were in debt and exhibited an *"insécurité fondamentale"* (Kattenberg 1979:40).

Wallerstein suggests that, following capitalist core expansion, coerced cash-crop systems emerge in the periphery, where the peasants are required by legal processes enforced by the state to labor at least part of the time on large domains producing products for sale on the world market (1974). A defining feature of such class systems is that actions by the state directly set the rate of surplus labor appropriation. The AVV tenant class is legally coerced into cultivating cotton. Because of the direct participation of the state in production relations, it is appropriate to speak of coercive state class relations on AVV lands.

Stagnation and Migration in the Interior

As a result of riverine donor investments, little capital is available for development in the interior. Fertilizers and other inputs are allocated first to agro-parastatals. As interior incomes are exceptionally low, farmers cannot afford those few inputs that are available. Agricultural technicians are disproportionately assigned to agro-parastatals, reducing the quality of agricultural services available in the interior. If new inputs and services are necessary for increases in productivity, stagnation in the interior is a consequence of favoring the parastatals. Stagnation, in the presence of population growth, harms both the environment and farming systems, driving people from their land.

Upper Volta's last national census indicates a high population growth rate of 2.6 percent per annum. These rates apparently extend back into the colonial era (Marchal 1977:75; Kohler 1972), and may result from colonial policies which appear to have encouraged high levels of fertility. French administrators forced Voltaic farmers to cultivate cash as well as food crops, while providing no labor-saving tools; and they imposed *corvée* labor on the population, while reducing the work force by organizing migration. Suret-Canale concludes that colonial policy, by creating more work and fewer workers to do it, intensified agrarian labor requirements (1976). Some scholars have argued that the demand for child labor in agriculture, and hence fertility, is likely to increase under conditions of decreasing agricultural productivity due to over-exploitation of the land and male out-migration (Cleveland 1979; Faulkingham 1977; Handwerker 1977; Reyna 1977; Deere 1978; and Javillonar 1979:Ch. 2). Population and emigration increased during the colonial period in Upper Volta, while mortality and immigration remained roughly constant, suggesting that population increases were due to changes in fertility. It appears, then, that increased labor demand during colonial times contributed to Upper Volta's population problem.

Population growth resulted in increased density on the Mossi Plateau (Marchal 1977:75), a situation which led to restricted access to farmland

(Boutillier 1964; Kohler 1971; Swanson 1979). Kohler describes a
sequence of tenure changes he observed among Mossi at Dakola. As
population density increased, control over land passed from lineage to
household heads (1971:151). Household elders should not deny access
to household members, but can and do exclude other lineage members.
Access is thus narrowed, and individuals are deprived of guaranteed
access to former lineage lands.

Land scarcity, in the absence of new technology, leads to soil deterioration and productivity declines. This is the case on the Mossi Plateau,
where productivity has decreased considerably (Marchal 1977). Under
demographic conditions prevalent on the Plateau, households are thus
faced with less arable land and fewer ways to increase their holdings to
alleviate this problem. This process separates people from their land and
results in a supply of migrant labor searching for subsistence.

Emigration from the Mossi Plateau can be interpreted as an indicator
of the magnitude of this problem. There is a relatively large literature
concerning Upper Volta's migration, reviewed in Gregory (1974), and
Piche, Gregory and Coulibaly (1980), which establishes three points.
First, the volume of intra- and international migration is great, including
perhaps 12 percent of the total male Voltaic population (Courel and
Pool 1973:10-13; Upper Volta 1979). Second, migration is highest among
productive age-groups in the most densely populated regions (Piche,
Gregory and Coulibaly 1980). Third, emigrants are motivated to leave
Upper Volta either to augment incomes or to avoid the consequences
of population pressure. These points suggest that "migration is the
principal process by which Africa is being proletarianized" (Gregory
1979:82).

Private Class Formation

Labor pushed off the land becomes available to individuals or agencies
who control land. A part of this work force supplies labor to the
agricultural parastatals, including the AVV; the majority, however, are
employed by private individuals. Studies in different interior areas suggest
how donor investment preference affects the rate of private class formation.

The Eastern Regional Development Organization (ORD) is an area
with low demand for agricultural commodities, according to data collected
by the Michigan State University farm-level survey (personal communication: G. Lassiter). Nevertheless, Swanson observes that "traders and
functionaries in large communities . . . use their influence and wealth
to secure for themselves valuable property" such as land (1979:6). This
land is then worked by wage laborers, usually paid in kind, mainly to
produce foodstuffs for local markets. Individuals acquiring land in this

manner are government officials, traders, 'traditional' rulers or veterans who have greater access to financial capital. Land is often acquired simply by requesting it from individuals in authority, who are usually pleased to oblige in expectation of future services from the recipient.

However, only a very small percentage of the farms employ wage labor. Preliminary results from the survey by Michigan State University suggest that 10 percent of the labor supplied to farms is some form of wage labor (personal communication: G. Lassiter). Sharecropping is not reported. In Fada N'Gourma, for example, which is the largest town in the Eastern ORD, an informant estimated there were twenty to thirty farms of from twenty to thirty hectares employing wage labor. If a liberal assumption is made that there are twenty farms of the same size near each of the other large towns in the Eastern ORD, then five hundred such farms occupy a total of 125 square kilometers, which means that less than 1 percent of the Eastern ORD's 50,000 square kilometers is given over to wage-labor farming.

The Mossi Plateau is also a region of relatively low demand for agricultural commodities, but one of far greater population density than the eastern region. Evidence suggests that private class relations are forming here, but this involves a different mechanism of land acquisition. During the late 1960s and early 1970s, Claude Remy studied farming in the densely populated region of Nobere. He showed that farms with more high-quality land belonged to families from founding lineages and/or lineages with lower growth rates, while those with lesser amounts of fertile land were owned by more recently arrived lineages (1972:87–95).

A study by James Smith suggests that, "the decision to grow or not to grow a cash crop clearly distinguishes two types of household. The first has more than enough resources to assure its survival and growth, while the second is closer to the subsistence level." The first type "hires more labor and owns more equipment than the average household" and sells a larger proportion of its crops. The second type allocates "its resources to subsistence activities" and probably sells labor to other households (Smith 1977:88).

Smith and Remy thus suggest that families with greater amounts of land are descended from earlier arriving lineages which occupied the most and best land and then multiplied at slower rates. Families with smaller holdings are later arrivals with higher growth rates. Laborers from these disadvantaged families are hired by the larger landholders to grow cash crops. Class relations are thus at least partially formed as a result of differentials in lineage land occupation and growth rates.

Officials and traders also use their resources to acquire land and establish private class relations on the Plateau. This occurs near large communities where the demand for foodstuffs is greater. For example, there is a small dam at Mogtedo, eighty paved kilometers from the capital, Ouagadougou, where according to Dumont "more than half the dam's irrigated fields were the property of urban dwellers" (1978:308) and were worked by wage labor. At Boulbi, immediately south of Ouagadougou, a dam was constructed and irrigated rice cultivation begun. Fields were originally allocated to local farmers, but, according to Dumont, "their plots were given to someone else who was in reality the figurehead for a bureaucrat" (1978:308).

Dumont also reports on the situation from around Banfora and Bobo Dioulasso in southwest Upper Volta. This area has lower population densities than the Plateau, but, due to proximity to Ivory Coast markets, has a stronger demand for agricultural commodities. He states: "One sees appearing more and more orchards, often of mangoes . . . planted above all by those with money: urbanites, bureaucrats, soldiers. These new non-peasant farms are thus the work of a new category of absentee landlords . . . who have land 'attributed' to them by customary authorities. These developing enterprises create a new category of workers, proletarians, detached from their means of production: agricultural wage laborers, often paid 100 F CFA plus a meal" (1978:309). Likewise, Finnegan observed the existence in southeastern Upper Volta at Tenkodogo of several mango orchards of perhaps eighty trees per orchard. However, he reports that the owners experienced difficulties in finding a market (1980:317), unlike the mango plantation owners in Dumont's area. Such contrasts suggest that a brisk demand for cash crops may catalyze class formation.

There is another area where class formation has been affected by Voltaic labor migration. This is in the coastal forests of Ghana and the Ivory Coast. Perhaps one-sixth of Upper Volta's inhabitants have migrated to these coastal countries. A 1960 survey found that most were agricultural workers (Courel and Pool 1973:1003). Campbell documented the growth of an Ivorian "planter class" that expanded from an estimated three hundred families in 1950 to twenty thousand wealthy families who "controlled about one-fourth of cultivated land, [and] employed two-thirds of salaried labor" in 1965 (1978:72–73). This labor was supplied by foreign migrants drawn almost exclusively from Upper Volta (Foltz 1967:47). Changing demand for agricultural commodities in the form of rising coffee and cocoa prices hastened the emergence of this class formation after 1946 (Campbell 1978:72).

In summary, private land ownership differentials are established in two ways: either officials or traders acquire large holdings, or farmers retain unequal control over fertile land due to the history of their lineage's land occupation. Once land differentials emerge, the demand for cash crops influences the rate of private class formation. In areas of higher agricultural commodity demand (the southwest and the coastal forest), farms based on wage labor developed rapidly, while in those of lower demand (the Mossi Plateau, the Eastern ORD, and Tenkodogo), such farms grew more slowly. These processes are conditioned by Upper Volta's position in the world capitalist economy.

Finally, what happens to the interior labor which does not migrate and is supplied to the domestic economy? Here there is evidence of a "profound disorganization of productive structures" (Ancy 1977:6). The individualization of land tenure around Dakola (Kohler 1971) in conjunction with Ancy's observation that 40 percent of the fields around Koudougou are *beolse* (individual), worked largely by women whose husbands are away on migration, suggests, contrary to Meillassoux (1981), that underdevelopment in Upper Volta does not preserve the communal production relations which characterized its domestic economies.

The System of Articulation

The dual class formation process has its roots in Upper Volta's high level of dependency on donor financing of development in conjunction with the EEC's and Upper Volta's shared economic interest in parastatals. This has resulted in a preference for investment in riverine lands, which has two consequences: interior lands suffer from a lack of capital, and the development of agro-parastatals in the riverine zone has given rise to the emergence of state class relations. In the underdeveloped interior, the absence of investment continues to inhibit capital accumulation and constrains productivity. Increased labor demands generated by colonial policies are hypothesized to have supported population growth, a situation which, in the presence of agrarian stagnation, resulted in overcrowding and migration. This process is characterized by increased environmental degradation, restricted land tenure and the removal of farmers from the land, as manifested by the high rate of emigration.

This 'freed' labor accrues to both private and state class relations, under four conditions:

a. Laborers migrate into areas with higher demand for agricultural commodities, facilitating private class formation (e.g., in the coastal forest).
b. In areas with weaker demand for agricultural commodities and scarcity of finance capital, wage labor moves more slowly into private class relations (e.g., in the Eastern ORD and the Mossi Plateau).

c. Some labor is supplied to agro-parastatals, thus facilitating the emergence of state class relations.

d. Finally, some labor remains in existing domestic production relations which function under increasingly marginal conditions.

Colonial policies in Upper Volta and the contemporary plan of preferring investments in parastatals were and are designed to incorporate Upper Volta into a capitalist world economy. The colonial policies described above provided inexpensive labor in order to hold down primary commodity costs to French industry while simultaneously ensuring a monopoly over the sale of French goods to Voltaics. This favored French capital accumulation by helping French capital to buy cheap and sell dear. Under neo-colonial conditions, production can be externally controlled even after direct political authority is lost. In parastatals such as AVV, the scale of operations is so great that nations like Upper Volta lack the capability to manage them, necessitating affiliation with a dominant industrialized economy. Further, as reported in Reyna (1983), the rate of remuneration to labor in a parastatal like AVV is not above Third World poverty levels. Parastatals tend to produce commodities required by industrialized countries; because of low labor costs, these can be offered at lower prices. At the same time, the scale of parastatal operations permits the purchase of higher technology commodities from core industries. Hence, colonial and neo-colonial policies which lead to dual class formation continue to assist capital accumulation in the core.

These tactics have 'squeezed' domestic production relations and articulated new ones in Upper Volta. Bernstein (1977) introduced the notion of a simple reproduction 'squeeze' to help explain what frequently happens to domestic economies experiencing commoditization. Simple reproduction is a situation in which a succession of production cycles results in no net investment and capital accumulation (Marx 1970:567). The economy simply reproduces itself. A 'squeeze' occurs when the system has difficulty doing even that (Bernstein 1977:64–65).

The interactions described above between population, land tenure and labor supply can be regarded as such a squeeze. The domestic economy cannot reproduce itself because the population expands at rates which exceed those of agricultural production. Between 1951 and 1975, population grew at 2.3 percent and agricultural production at only about 1 percent per annum (Dumont 1978:269). During the post-colonial period, finance capital has been diverted to agro-parastatals thereby denying productivity-raising inputs to domestic economies. Thus a simple reproduction squeeze arose in Voltaic domestic economies because co-

lonial policy, designed to stimulate French industry, concurrently pro-
voked soil deterioration and population growth. The squeeze continues
due to post-colonial investment preferences.

Investment tactics by the core result in new articulations between
savanna and forest, and between domestic, state and private production
relations. Both state and private classes emerge from core investment
patterns. Upper Volta created the juridical codes and institutional structures which encourage donor investment in parastatals, resulting in
coerced state class relations. Likewise, the demand for cash crops and
the availability of finance capital catalyze private class relations in areas
which produce commodities demanded by core economies.

There is, moreover, evidence that the two class systems are articulated:

> A small but influential group of *fonctionnaires* in Ouagadougou has become
> 'gentlemen farmers' or 'civil servant farmers' . . . As members of the group
> in Ouagadougou, these men have had little difficulty obtaining land—
> even valuable rice land—from peri-urban and rural chiefs. They either
> bring rural relatives to settle on these farms as cultivators or hire youths
> in Ouagadougou to go work there (Skinner 1974:51).

Donor investments make possible agricultural parastatals in which the
state appropriates surplus product from its tenants. Bureaucrats invest
some of this surplus, which they obtain as salary, into land. State and
private relations of production are thus articulated.

Domestic production relations are part of this system of articulation
because they supply labor to state and private class formations. The
domestic economy is motivated to provide labor by forces different from
those operative during the transition to capitalism in Europe. In the
latter case, the flow of labor to the nascent capitalist system resulted
from the expulsion of peasants from aristocratic domains (Rey 1973).
In Upper Volta, there is no landed aristocracy forcing farmers from the
land, so the simple reproduction squeeze does the job.

Thus, four sets of class relations are articulated in Upper Volta and
certain areas of the coastal forest. Core capitalism, through its donor
investments, provides crucial capital to the Voltaic state class. The Voltaic
state class, in turn, provides capital to purchase private landholdings.
Private and state classes both sell primary commodities to, and purchase
inputs from, core capital. And finally, impoverished domestic economies
supply labor for both state and private classes. The dynamics of this
system of articulation are dominated by core capital, which squeezes
domestic economies to expand state and private class relations.

Upper Volta—A Museum of Antique Modes?

Donor investment preferences have helped create new state and private production relations in Upper Volta, thereby causing simple reproduction squeezes which remove land and labor from domestic modes of production. Relations of production dominated by a gentry consisting of bureaucratic managers and private owners are emerging in Upper Volta.

Finally, these findings bear on arguments that underdevelopment is a phase in the transition to capitalism during which pre-capitalist modes are 'maintained.' The underdeveloped world, in this view, is a museum teeming with antique modes of production. Voltaic evidence does not support such a position. Rather, whatever transition is occurring there involves pre-capitalist modes whose productive forces and relations appear to be experiencing rapid change as a consequence of their articulation with emerging state and private production relations.

Notes

1. Data are derived, first, from published and unpublished documentary material. For a discussion of the quality of this data, especially as it pertains to the AVV, see Reyna (1980). The second data source is from participant observation and interviews conducted in the course of three missions to Upper Volta as Regional Anthropologist for the Regional Economic Development Services Office, West Africa of USAID.

2. Discussion of the literature which explores class formation in terms of West African bureaucracies, parastatals, and private land owners can be found in Reyna (1983).

References

Althusser, L. and E. Balibar 1970 *Reading Capital.* London: New Elft Books.

Ancy, G. 1977 "Variation Mossi sur le thème: reproduction de milieux ruraux mis en contact avec le système capitaliste extérieur," *Travaux et Documents* No. 64. Paris: ORSTOM.

Berg, E. 1978 "Onchocerciasis Control Program: Economic Review Mission." Ann Arbor: Department of Economics, University of Michigan. Unpublished manuscript.

Bernstein, H. 1977 "Notes on Capital and Peasantry," *Review of African Political Economy,* Vol. 10.

Boutillier, J.L. 1964 "Les Structures Foncières en Haute Volta," *Etudes Voltaiques.* Mémoire No. 5. Ougadougou: CVRS.

Bradby, B. 1980 "The Destruction of Natural Economy," in H. Wolpe (ed.), *The Articulation of Modes of Production.* London: Routledge and Kegan Paul.

Campbell, B. 1974 "Social Change and Class Formation in a French West African State," *Canadian Journal of African Studies*. Vol. 8.
1978 "The Ivory Coast," in J. Dunn (ed.), *West African States*. Cambridge: Cambridge University Press.
Cleveland, D. 1979 "Fertility and the Value of Children in Subsistence Agriculture: Savanna West Africa." Paper delivered to the Annual Meeting of the American Anthropological Association, 1979.
Courel, A. and I. Pool 1973 "Haute-Volta," in J.C. Caldwell et al. (eds.), *Croissance Démographique et Evolution Socio-Economique en Afrique de l'Ouest*. New York: Population Council.
Deere, C. 1978 "Intra-Familial Labor Deployment and the Formation of Peasant Household Income: A Case Study of the Peruvian Sierra." Amherst: Department of Anthropology, University of Massachusetts. Unpublished manuscript.
Delgado, C. 1978 *The Southern Fulani Farming System in Upper Volta: A New Old Model for the Integration of Crop and Livestock Production in the West African Savannah*. Ann Arbor: Center for Research on Economic Development, University of Michigan.
Dumont, R. 1978 *Paysans Ecrasés, Terres Massacrées*. Paris: Laffont.
Faulkingham, R. 1977 "Fertility in Tudu: An Analysis of Constraints on Fertility in a Village in Niger," in J.C. Caldwell (ed.), *The Persistence of High Fertility*. Canberra: ANU Press.
Finnegan, G. 1976 "Population Movement, Labor Migration, and Social Structure in a Mossi Village." Ph.D. dissertation. Ann Arbor: University Microfilms International.
1980 "Employment Opportunity and Migration among the Mossi of Upper Volta," *Research in Economic Anthropology*. Volume 3.
Foltz, W.J. 1967 *From French West Africa to the Mali Federation*. New Haven: Yale University Press.
Foster-Carter, A. 1978 *The Modes of Production Controversy*. New Left Review 107.
Gregory, J.W. 1974 "Development and In-Migration in Upper Volta," in S. Amin (ed.), *Modern Migrations in Western Africa*. London: Oxford University Press.
1979 "Underdevelopment, Dependence and Migration in Upper Volta." in T. Shaw and K. Heard (eds.). London: Longman *The Politics of African Dependence and Development*.
Gregory, J. and V. Piche 1978 "African Migration and Peripheral Capitalism," *African Perspectives*. Vol. 1.
Handwerker, W.P. 1977 "Family, Fertility and Economics," *Current Anthropology*. Vol. 18, No. 2.
Javillonar, G. 1979 *Rural Development, Women's Roles and Fertility in Developing Countries: Review of the Literature*. Chapel Hill: Research Triangle Institute.
Kattenberg, D. 1979 *Quelques Aspects de la Culture Mossi*. Ouagadougou: AVV, Ministère du développement rural.
Kohler, J.M. 1971 *Activities Agricoles et Changements Sociaux dans l'Ouest Mossi*. Paris: ORSTOM.

1972 *Les Migrations des Mossi de l'Ouest*. Paris: ORSTOM.

Lavroff, D.M. 1979 *Les Entreprises Publiques en Afrique Noire*. Vol 1. Série Afrique Noire no. 9. Paris: Editions A. Pedone.

Londres, A. 1929 *Terre d'Ebène*. Paris: Presses Universitaire de France.

Ly, A. 1958 *L'état et la Production Paysanne*. Paris: Présence Africaine.

Marchal, J.Y. 1977 "The Evolution of Agrarian Systems in Yatenga," *African Environment*. Vol. II, III and IV. pp. 73–87.

Marx, K. 1970 *Capital*. Vol. 1. Moscow: Foreign Languages Publishing House.

Maton, Claude et al. (FAC) 1971 *Etudes de Pré-Factibilité: Projet d'Aménagement et de Mise en Valeur des Vallées des Volta*. Ouagadougou: Ministère du Plan, de l'Industrie et des Mines.

McClelland, S. 1979 "Political Economy and Dependence in Africa: An Annotated Bibliography," in R. Cruise O'Brien (ed.), *The Political Economy of Under-development*. Beverly Hills: Sage Publications.

McFarland, D. 1976 *Historical Dictionary of Upper Volta*. Meuchen, N.J.: Scarecrow Press.

Meillassoux, C. 1970 "A Class Analysis of the Bureaucratic Process in Mali," *Journal of Development Studies*. Vol. 6, pp. 97–110.

1972 "From Reproduction to Production: A Marxist Approach to Economic Anthropology," *Economy and Society*. Vol. 9, No. 1.

1981 *Maidens, Meal and Money*. New York: Cambridge University Press.

Murphy, J. 1980 "Volta Valley Development Project: Preliminary Project Paper." Ouagadougou: USAID. Unpublished working paper.

Murphy, J. and L. Sprey 1979 *Results of the 1978 Agricultural Season in Villages Created by the Volta Valley Authority, Upper Volta*. West Lafayette: Department of Agricultural Economics, Purdue University.

1980 *The Volta Valley Authority: Socio-Economic Evaluation of a Resettlement Project in Upper Volta*. West Lafayette: Department of Agricultural Economics, Purdue University.

ORSTOM 1979 "Stratégies d'Aménagement et de Mise en Valeur des Zones Libérées de l'Onchocercose en Haute Volta," *ORSTOM Mémoire No. 89*. pp. 275–80. Paris: ORSTOM.

Ossendowski, F. 1928 *Slaves of the Sun*. New York: Dutton.

Ouedragogo, D. 1979 "Genèse et Structure d'un Espace Enclavé: La Haute Volta," *ORSTOM Mémoire No. 89*, pp. 553–59. Paris: ORSTOM.

Piche, V., J. Gregory, and S. Coulibaly 1980 "Vers une explication des courants migratoire voltaiques," *Labour, Capital and Society*. Vol. XIII, No. 1.

Remy, C. 1972 *Donsin, Les Structures Agraires d'un Village Mossi de la Région de Nobere*. Ouagadougou: ORSTOM.

Rey, P.P. 1971 *Colonialisme, Neo-colonialisme et Transition au capitalisme: example de la Camilog au Congo-Brazzaville*. Paris: Maspero.

1973 *Les Alliances de Classe*. Paris: Maspero.

Reyna, S.P. 1977 "Economics and Fertility: Waiting for the Demographic Transition in the Dry Zone of Francophone West Africa," in J.C. Caldwell (ed.), *The Persistence of High Fertility*. Canberra: ANU Press.

1980 "Impact of Autorité des Aménagements des Vallées des Volta." Abidjan: REDSO/WA. USAID.

1983 "Dual Class Formation and Agrarian Underdevelopment: An Analysis of the Articulation of Production Relations in Upper Volta," *Canadian Journal of African Studies.* Vol. 17 No. 2.

Sarraut, A. 1923 *La Mise en Valeur des Colonies Françaises.* Paris: Payot.

Savonnet, G. 1976 (No title available). Vol. 13, No. 1. Ouagadougou: ORSTOM.

Skinner, E.P. 1967 *The Mossi of Upper Volta.* Stanford: Stanford University Press.

1974 *African Urban Life: The Transformation of Ouagadougou.* Princeton: Princeton University Press.

1980 "A Brief History of the Sahel," in S.P. Reyna (ed.), *Sahelian Social Development.* Abidjan: REDSO/WA.

Smith, James 1977 "Economy and Demography in a Mossi Village." Ph.D. dissertation. Ann Arbor: University Microfilms International.

Songre, A., et al. 1974 "Réalités et Effet de l'Emigration Massive des Voltaiques dans le Contexte de l'Afrique Occidentale," in S. Amir (ed.), *Modern Migration in Western Africa.* London: Oxford University Press.

Sorgho, J. and O. Richet 1979 *Les Coûts Récurrents d'une Installation en Culture Sèche, de 15,000 Familles sur des Terres Neuves Aménagées par l'Autorité des Aménagements des Vallées des Volta.* Ouagadougou: CILSS.

Suret-Canale, J. 1976 *French Colonialism in Tropical Africa 1900-1945.* London: Heinemann.

Swanson, R. 1979 "Gourmantche Agriculture. Part I. Land Tenure and Field Cultivation." Fada N'Gourma: EORD. Mission document.

Terray, E. 1972 *Marxism and "Primitive" Societies.* New York: Monthly Review Press.

Upper Volta 1979 *Recencement National 1975. Résultats Provisoires.* Ouagadougou: Bureau Statistique.

USAID 1980 *Country Development Strategy Statement: Upper Volta.* Ouagadougou: USAID.

Wallerstein, I. 1974 *The Modern World-System.* New York: Academic Press.

Wolpe, H. 1980 "Introduction," in H. Wolpe (ed.), *The Articulation of Modes of Production.* London: Routledge Kegan Paul.

7

A CASE STUDY OF THE CLOSING FRONTIER IN BRAZIL

Marianne Schmink

In Brazil the 'moving frontier' has long been the motor of agricultural growth. Since the surge of industrialization and urbanization in Brazil beginning about 1930, a specifically 'pioneer frontier' cycle has emerged, due to the internal migratory movements of surplus populations in the country. At least three distinct frontier cycles have occurred since that date: Parana, 1945–1970; Mato Grosso, 1955–1975; Amazonia, 1965–present. Despite the differences in location and historical period, each frontier moved through a similar set of stages which make up the recurring frontier cycle in Brazil (Foweraker 1981).

The first stage is the penetration of extractive industries for such items as lumber, minerals and rubber. The second features the immigration of small farmer migrants, the beginnings of a subsistence-and-surplus agriculture and the first indications of the development of a market in land and labor. This is followed in the third stage by the consolidation of a capitalistic market in land and labor, the concentration of landholdings in the hands of large companies and the demise of the small farmer. Roads permit access to the national economy, population grows rapidly and a reserve of landless workers is created. In general it is recognized that by the end of the frontier process the historical tendency has been to evolve into a 'big man's frontier.' Landholdings and investments are progressively concentrated, and the *latifundio/minifundio* pattern which persists in Brazil's other regions is reproduced on the frontier.

Studies of the Brazilian frontier have demonstrated the contradictions and social conflicts which have accompanied this process. In the scramble for a foothold on the new frontier, the interests of bureaucrats, professionals, businessmen, small farmers, workers and Indians are often in conflict. The outcome of these interactions is determined by the relative power and resources available to particular classes or groups involved in the frontier expansion process at each particular stage. During the second stage of the pioneer cycle, the primary conflict is between indigenous groups and those involved in extractive and speculatory interests, on the one hand, and peasants and capitalists interested in securing access to land, on the other. The move to consolidate a capitalistic market in land and labor during the cycle's third stage brings peasants and capitalists into direct opposition (Foweraker 1981; Schmink 1982).

State agencies and policies mediate the different interests represented in frontier struggles and movements (Bunker 1979; Schmink 1982; Foweraker 1981). The outcome of a given situation depends on the extent to which different social classes or class factions are able to influence policy content and/or utilize its provisions to their specific interests (Pompermayer 1984). This ability, in turn, is broadly determined by the prevailing form of the state, or the system of power and domination by which diverse social classes are articulated. In Brazil since 1930, and particularly since 1964, the economically dominant classes have included military and civilian government bureaucrats, executives, policy-makers in state-owned enterprises, large-scale national and foreign entrepreneurs and the professionals and technicians linked to these sectors. During most of this period, the interests of these groups were politically represented by the bureaucratic-authoritarian state, which helped to guarantee social domination by these classes, to ensure favorable conditions for the accumulation of capital, and to impede the formation of a power base for those classes excluded from power (Cardoso 1975; Foweraker 1981; Pompermayer 1984).

On the other hand, peasants have remained a subordinate group with no effective representation within the state. One of the motivating factors in the 1964 military takeover was the increasing organization and militancy of peasant groups in the Northeast region. Afterwards the government took steps to prevent the re-emergence of a threatening level of peasant mobilization. Rural unions have little power and under the military regime were directly controlled and manipulated by federal regulation and intervention. Although the Brazilian Land Statute of 1964 provides a firm basis for the defense of small farmer agriculture, many of its provisions have not been implemented. Hence it is not surprising that the outcome of state mediation in the conflicts generated during frontier expansion has favored the interests of large-scale capitalist enterprises rather than those of the small farmer migrant.

The Amazon Frontier

In the Amazon region the government has played a strong, direct role in stimulating and orienting frontier occupation. This has accelerated the frontier cycle in the Amazon, so that stages have succeeded one another very rapidly or partially overlapped, intensifying and complicating patterns of conflict between different social groups. The Amazon region assumes a special role as Brazil's last major frontier. The historically moving frontier has reached its end in the Amazon, where the accumulated problems and tensions from other regions of rural Brazil have come to be played out in dramatic fashion. Thus the consolidation of the Amazon frontier represents the 'closing' of Brazil's historical pioneer frontier cycle (Silva 1979).

Two years after the military takeover in Brazil, a consistent national policy for the Amazon region was defined in the "Operation Amazonia." A "gradual and irreversible" occupation of the region by private enterprise was to be induced through three measures which would implement this initiative: the creation of SUDAM (the regional development agency), BASA (the Amazon bank) and the generous fiscal incentives programs designed to attract investments by national and multinational firms (Andreazza 1979:4). Alongside measures to encourage private investment, the government also took an aggressive role in providing the necessary infrastructure in roads, beginning with the Belem-Brasilia highway. This basic strategy has continued until the present, with periodic shifts in emphasis.

Business interests have actively participated in the formulation of Amazon policy, primarily through their alliance within the relevant government agencies. The community of interest between large-scale capitalists and the state bureaucracy has produced a kind of 'bureaucratic entrepreneurship' in which agencies act in the interests of their capitalist allies with respect to specific policies (Cardoso 1975; Foweraker 1981; Pompermayer 1984). Aside from individual contacts, two hundred of the country's largest economic groups (nearly all national) have also operated through the Association of Amazon Entrepreneurs (AEA), a formalized Sao Paulo-based lobby group. The AEA promoted cattle raising as the 'vocation' of the Amazon as a means of obtaining access to substantial expanses of land with as much as 75 percent of investment costs provided through SUDAM's fiscal incentives program (Horak 1984; Pompermayer 1980; 1984).

Before 1970 government policy favored the construction of roads to permit 'spontaneous' occupation of new areas and fostered a program of inducing new economic investments through fiscal incentives administered by SUDAM. Small farmer migrants expanded into the center-west region during this period, quickly followed by large enterprises which gradually came to dominate in the areas occupied during the 1950s and 1960s (Foweraker 1981; Hebette and Acevedo 1979; Lisansky 1980). These patterns soon extended into the southern Para region of the Amazon.

The announcement of the widely-publicized National Integration Policy in 1970 gave the appearance of a significant shift in the direction of policy initiatives for the Amazon region. The core of the program was the construction of major highways in the Amazon region and the commitment to finance and directly administer the colonization of lands made accessible by the new roads. The colonization effort was designed to relieve pressures in the highly concentrated agrarian sector of the Northeast by transferring 'men without land' there to the 'land without men' of Amazonia. Directed colonization was favored as a means of reducing the potentially explosive social tensions in the Northeast region, where poverty and exploitation had generated threatening peasant and worker organizations in the 1960s, and reorienting northeast emigration away from the crowded metropolitan centers of the center-south. In this sense the colonization plan was to function as a 'counter-land-reform' by avoiding reforms in the Northeast while giving the impression that the government was responding to the needs of the poor peasant (Ianni 1979) through the National Institute for Colonization and Agrarian Reform (INCRA).

While colonization was emphasized in INCRA policy pronouncements after 1970, the parallel fiscal incentives program under SUDAM continued to stimulate the establishment of large capitalist enterprises as an alternative to the solution of absorbing Brazil's excess rural population. By 1973, just a few years after they had begun, the colonization projects along the Transamazon highway were being strongly criticized. Numerous problems confronted the official colonization effort, including the lack of realistic planning and bottlenecks in implementing the complex system of bureaucratic and administrative supports foreseen in the original proposal. In the tradition of "blaming the victim," the colonists themselves were often faulted for the project's lack of success, citing their lack of management abilities, technological sophistication or persistence (Wood and Schmink 1978). Alternatively, the blame was laid on the state agencies, especially INCRA, which were responsible for the programs (Bunker 1979).

By 1974, the new policy priorities for the region spelled out in the "Polamazonia" five-year plan (1975–1979) indicated an abandonment of the offical colonization initiative in favor of a renewed emphasis on the role of the large enterprise. Since this policy reversal came far too soon to allow for the correction of the project's many difficulties in planning and implementation, the viability of colonization and the program's capacity for adjustment and adaptation remained untested. By the mid-1970s, new official colonization projects were confined to Rondonia, where growing migratory pressure had stimulated an effort to try to absorb the thousands of families seeking land in western Amazonia.

The rapidity of this shift called into question the political will behind the original colonization plan, which was certainly controversial from its inception. At the same time, the widely-publicized colonization effort itself had stimulated changes in the region which contributed to the subsequent shift in policy emphasis. Of the large numbers of migrants to the region, only a small proportion were ever absorbed in the INCRA projects; the remainder sought to stake out independent claims. Simultaneously, the massive road-building effort led to a rapid increase in land values which further attracted the attention of large-scale investors. As the pace of occupation escalated, so did tension and conflicts over land. Together these trends contributed to the mid-1970s shift in policy emphasis (Schmink 1982).

As the official colonization projects came under criticism, business interests proposed an alternative model of small farmer settlement which would be carried out not by the government but by private enterprise. State agencies would play a supportive role in providing long-term financing for land, infrastructural investments, access to credit, and assistance in the selection and training of colonists. But the task of subdividing land and administering the project, and the profits generated by the sale of lots, would fall to private business. Proponents of this model made use of studies which have concluded that state involvement has negative consequences for the success of colonists, and that earlier 'spontaneous' or privately-run colonization models are preferable. Both are believed to promise more efficient and rational colonization projects through a better colonist selection process, among other things (Nelson 1973:51). Since as early as 1973 these arguments in favor of a 'selective' colonization to be carried out by private firms have been advanced by Sao Paulo investors and their bureaucratic allies (Pompermayer 1984). Although it was never approved, the AEA presented an extremely ambitious proposal for the private colonization of thirty-four million hectares of land by a consortium of large enterprises, along the margins of the Cuiaba-Santarem highway. In 1976, private colonization was given a more clearly delineated role in Amazon occupation, to be carried out with the guidance of the National Institute for Colonization and Agrarian Reform (INCRA). The agency was authorized to approve sales of up to five hundred thousand hectares in certain priority areas for private colonization, and by the end of the decade twenty-five projects had been authorized in northern Mato Grosso and southern Para (Arruda 1979, cited in Skillings and Tchegan 1979:84).

The private colonization model purported to respond to a complex set of goals, as outlined in both business and official documents. The first was the occupation of the Amazon region in such a way that a favorable rate of economic return is assured. Second, private colonization was touted as a means of simultaneously colonizing the Amazon and resolving the pressures for land reform in other regions of Brazil. This time the target was not so much the impoverished Northeast as the more developed central and southern states (Rio Grande do Sul, Santa Catarina, Parana, Minas Gerais and Espirito Santo) where a variety of changes had caused increasing emigration. The three goals of private colonization in the Amazon, as spelled out by INCRA in 1976, included: a) the transference of *minifundista* cultivators, with their skills and resources, from the agricultural cooperatives of the south to an Amazonia with improved infrastructure; b) to thereby allow the 'regrouping' of rural properties in their place of origin; and c) hence to raise national agricultural production (quoted in Ianni 1979:86).

The state, in favoring private colonization, cannot only save heavy direct costs and avoid further criticism for its own failures, but also directly support those groups on whom the dominant class alliance rests, even if the projects fail. Investors can reap the profits of these land development projects, and a middle-class group of merchants, bureaucrats and technicians can be expected to emerge either directly or indirectly associated with the projects (Miller 1980). These same groups will benefit from the growing emphasis on mining and lumbering projects, now the centerpiece of Amazon planning agendas.

As for the small farmer migrant, a 'select' few will be able to buy lots in the private colonization projects, while settlement of official colonists is increasingly restricted. Thousands of resource poor migrants already in the Amazon region seeking land have little recourse but temporary employment in gold prospecting or in the large projects currently being favored. Yet cattle ranching, mining and lumbering are activities which absorb relatively little labor, and the history of large capitalist projects in the region has failed to demonstrate their ability to attract a stable and satisfied labor force. The vast majority of migrants moved to the region with the single objective of obtaining rights to their own land for farming; for the most part, wage labor is viewed merely as a temporary means of subsisting while waiting to attain that goal.

It is specifically with respect to the small farmer migrant that the Amazon frontier may be said to be undergoing a new and final stage which 'closes' the pioneer frontier cycle. On earlier frontiers, it was the *posseiro,* with only usufruct rights, who first occupied new lands which were later usurped by expanding capitalist enterprises during the third phase of consolidation of the market in land and labor. The frontier cycle has historically been perpetuated in spite of this patterned outcome because of the subsequent movement of *posseiros* into the next expanding area where the cycle begins anew (Martins 1980). By acting as the

advance guard for larger-scale operators, the pioneer peasant has historically contributed through his own labor to the primitive accumulation
of capital on the frontier (Foweraker 1981; Ianni 1979).

In the Amazon region, state provision of subsidies and infrastructure
make investment opportunities so attractive that the expropriation of
peasant lands represents only a minimal advantage (Pompermayer 1984).
At the same time, the rapidity of the frontier expansion process in the
region has increased the level of conflict between different groups of
frontier actors. Peasant and capitalist 'fronts' have not so much succeeded
one another as they have come into direct opposition. The response of
the state to this threatening situation has been to seek to consolidate
the central role to be played by large-scale enterprises. It is in this sense
that policy trends have signified an institutional 'closing' of the Amazon
frontier to the traditional Brazilian pioneer, the *posseiro*. The concrete
impact of the closing of the frontier is illustrated by the case study
material which follows.

The New Frontier in Sao Felix do Xingu

Sao Felix do Xingu provides a focal point from which to trace the
impact of the major structural changes currently underway in Amazonia.
It is an area rich in exploitable resources which have been the focus of
shifting government policy priorities. A sleepy riverside community dating
from the rubber boom, it has been recently swept into the frontier
process due to its continuity with the southern Para frontier area. Located
near the confluence of the Xingu and Fresco rivers in south-central Para,
Sao Felix is now connected to the Belem-Brasilia highway by a new state
road.

The earliest inhabitants of the Sao Felix do Xingu area were Indians
from a variety of groups which splintered off from the Cayapo tribes,
moving into the Xingu region from the direction of the Araguaia River
probably around the turn of the nineteenth century (Vidal 1977). Near
the end of that century, Brazilian rubber gatherers first entered the
middle Xingu, finding both *seringa* and *caucho* rubber trees. During the
first decade of the twentieth century, a rubber trading post was set up
by a former National Guard Colonel, Tancredo Martins Jorge, on the
island of Ilhota near present-day Sao Felix. After a flood in 1914 wiped
out the post, the settlement was moved to Sao Felix which provided
better access to the mule trail along which rubber was transported to
Conceicao do Araguaia. The settlement took its name from the image
of Saint Felix brought by Coronel Tancredo to his new *barracao*. Until
after World War I when world rubber prices plummeted, Sao Felix was
the scene of brisk traffic in rubber and goods, regulated by a complex

credit and labor system *(aviamento)* under the monopoloy control of Colonel Tancredo.

With the decline of rubber, productive activities were diversified, as in other parts of Para (Weinstein 1983). Brazil nut extraction began to be important in about 1928, and nuts are still collected by Sao Felix residents although production has fallen off recently. During the Second World War, when Asian sources of natural latex were cut off, there was a renewed demand for rubber, and many of the old *seringais* were again exploited. Hunting of wild animal skins also began in the post-war period, and flourished in the 1960s when the demand for rare pelts made it a very profitable business. After the skin trade was outlawed in 1970, it ceased to play an important economic role in the area. Finally, residents typically combined these varied activities with hunting, fishing and small plots of food crops, nearly always less than one hectare in size. Despite the area's endowment with relatively good soils, agricultural production was minimal and restricted to subsistence crops of rice, beans, manioc and corn, and some fruits (bananas and citrus).

Sao Felix do Xingu began to attract the attention of regional planners during the most volatile period of policy shifts, as is evident in the evolution of planning for the area. A preliminary Integrated Development Report on Sao Felix in 1970 recommended research on the area's resource potential and infrastructural investments which would link the municipality to Maraba and Conceicao do Araguaia. As it became evident that the area offered rich potential for the exploitation of mineral, lumber, and soil resources, interest in investment there grew quickly. Research carried out after 1970 revealed deposits of gold, silver, lead, zinc, diamonds, copper, manganese, nickel and cassiterite (from which tin is made). Part of the mineral complex associated with the rich Serra do Carajas is located in the municipality of Sao Felix. As early as 1975 hundreds of requests for mineral research permits had been filed with the National Mineral Research Department for Sao Felix. Several national and multinational firms had set up temporary operations in the town and hired local residents to help them carry out their research.

Similarly, the area's soils appeared fertile by Amazon standards from 1974 RADAM photographs, and began to interest planners and investors. Approximately 10 percent of the municipality's soils are fertile *terra roxa,* although these soils are discontinuous and partly undulating. Fully half of the one and a half million hectares are suitable for cultivation of perennial or annual crops, and an additional two hundred thousand hectares could be used for pastures or reforestation (SUDAM 1976). By 1973 more than two thousand land requests had been filed with state agencies, and would-be owners were beginning to stake their claims by marking off and occupying land in the area. Thus, even before government planning for Sao Felix was formulated, " . . . although still imprecisely, a new pioneer front of Amazonia was beginning to take shape" (Pinto 1980:194–95).

With the Polamazonia program, published mid-decade, the first concrete plans for Sao Felix emerged. The municipality was not initally included in any of the ten designated development poles, but later the limits of the Polo Carajas were extended to include it. The object was to break the *municipio's* isolation and backwardness by linking it to projected road networks, and to take advantage of the area's resource potential. Nearly one hundred and fifty million cruzeiros were allocated to projects in Sao Felix, including a new airport, land demarcation, an urban development plan, a colonization feasibility study, and the construction of the PA-279 to link Sao Felix to the frontier road network of Maraba and Conceicao do Araguaia.

The road was the key stimulus to a "rush" to occupy Sao Felix by competing groups. Construction actually began in 1976 and continued in fits and starts over the next seven years (Vidal 1981). During this period, the promise of improved transportation attracted potential investors and created a market for land. Whereas in 1972 one hectare of land cost slightly more than one dollar, five years later the official asking price was nearly $25 (Pinto 1980:197). Signs erected in nearby frontier towns by land surveyors invited investors to "Visit Sao Felix do Xingu, the best land in the Amazon." A number of large enterprises began to stake their claim to Sao Felix lands.

A more visible and immediate impact of the road was the attraction of thousands of migrants in search of land to till. At the junction of the new road with the PA-150 (linking Maraba and Conceicao do Araguaia), a new community of approximately eight thousand people had sprung up by 1978 where none had existed two years earlier (Godfrey 1979). The community was first referred to simply as *"Entroncamento"* (or "Junction"); others like it became well-known in the previous frontiers such as Maranhao and Mato Grosso (Godfrey 1979; Lisansky 1980). Migrants were attracted to the town, which was later named Xinguara (from Xingu and Araguaia) by the promise of an official colonization project announced by the state which, however, never materialized. Since 1977, the Xinguara area has been the region of most intense migratory movements in the state of Para, as well as one of the areas of most tension and conflict. By 1983 there were an estimated twenty thousand migrants in Xinguara and the surrounding area, the vast majority waiting for some opportunity to claim their own farming land. A sizeable proportion of these migrants had come from Goias and Mato Grosso or from other areas of southern Para, where small farmers had virtually lost all possibility of gaining or retaining access to land. In these areas, the frontier cycle had run its course with the consolidation of large cattle ranches, and residents who remained were those who had given up hope of ever owning their own land (Lisansky 1980). Those who still pursued this dream had moved onto the new 'front' to try their luck, in this case in Xinguara and along the road which would lead to Sao Felix.

In the mid-1970's squatters began to penetrate into the municipality of Sao Felix on foot from the Araguaia area or by boat from Altamira. Others paid exorbitant prices to transport themselves and their possessions by private plane from the frontiers several hundred kilometers distant. These pioneers were hoping to clear and hold onto small agricultural plots by staking their claims before the completion of the road. In 1978, when the new road was still less than one-third complete, the town boasted a new neighborhood of approximately fifty households composed of such migrants. In 1980, with still nearly two hundred kilometers of road to be built, a second new neighborhood had been opened and over eighty new houses had been built there. By 1981, the new neighborhoods were filled in and the town boasted 366 residential households. In August of 1983, the road finally arrived in Sao Felix, if precariously. Thereafter migrants could take a bus or other vehicle from Tucuma, especially during the dry season. A year later the town contained 768 households and had expanded to two new areas several kilometers distant from the original town center. The proportion of residents who were born outside the state increased from 18% to 37% between 1970 and 1980; 58% of these non-natives had arrived since 1977 (Chase 1984:7).

The migrant families who entered Sao Felix after 1975 are distinct from the town's earlier residents, because of their specific relation to the frontier process in southern Para and northern Mato Grosso, where would-be small farmers had been pushed out. These pioneers had complex migratory histories, especially in the recent past. They primarily came from the adjacent frontier area, soon to be directly joined by the road, including the towns of Conceicao do Araguaia, Redencao, Rio Maria, and Xinguara.

Many Sao Felix pioneers are from earlier frontier areas where there is no land for small farmers, and are a self-selected group who have chosen not to give up hope of securing a plot of land of their own. Nearly one-third of the recent migrants in Sao Felix specifically gave the desire for land as their reason for leaving their last place of residence, and for choosing Sao Felix as a destination (Table 7.1). They lost no time in staking out claims in the municipal government's agricultural 'colony' which was formed in the mid-1970s, but which still has ambiguous legal status. Located along a narrow strip of land between the Rio Fresco and the Xingu, in 1980 this 'colony' consisted of between

Table 7.1. Motivation for Migration

(Expressed in percent)

	Reason for Leaving Last Place of Residence			Reason for Choosing Sao Felix		
	Earlier Residents	Recent Migrants*	Total	Earlier Residents	Recent Migrants	Total
Work						
Desire for Land	13.3	30.8	25.9	11.8	30.2	25.0
Loss of Land	6.7	7.7	7.4	-	-	-
Lack Job Opportunities	-	12.9	9.3	-	-	-
Self-Employment Aspiration	6.7	7.7	7.4	5.9	4.7	5.0
Prospecting Opportunities	-	5.1	3.7	5.9	4.7	5.0
Drought	-	2.6	1.9	-	-	-
Prospects for Improvement ("Melhorar")	6.7	17.9	14.8	11.8	16.3	15.0
Better Health, Education, Infrastructure	6.7	7.7	7.4	11.8	7.0	8.3
Contacts in Sao Felix						
Family	20.0	7.7	11.1	23.5	20.9	21.7
Mayor	6.7	-	1.9	11.8	2.3	5.0
Acquaintances	-	-	-	5.9	7.0	6.7
Other	33.3	-	9.3	11.8	7.0	8.3
TOTAL	100.1	100.1	100.1	100.2	100.1	100.0
(N)	(15)	(39)	(54)	(17)	(43)	(60)

*Arrived in Sao Felix since 1975.

Source: Original Survey Data, 1978

one hundred and two hundred colonists located within a thirty kilometer zone along the municipality's one road. The most accessible lots were owned and leased by local elites (merchants and municipal employees).

In 1978, subsistence plots were cultivated by approximately half of Sao Felix's households—either newly-arrived migrants in the "colony" or earlier residents who had plots in riverside locations near the town. Most planted the staple crops of manioc, corn, rice, beans and fruits. Plots planted by more recent migrant families differed from this traditional picture in that nearly one-quarter had planted pasture, and two-thirds had planted crops other than the staples and fruit crops (Table 7.2). Compared to the earlier residents, a much higher proportion of newcomers had plots beyond a ten kilometer radius of the town, and the plots themselves tended to be somewhat larger, although still well below the established minimum of one hundred hectares for the Amazon region. Furthermore, recent migrants were more likely to have 'purchased' their lots, a term referring to some monetary transaction in the absence of definitive legal title. The recent migrants thus showed a greater commitment to small-scale surplus agriculture and to securing rights to land. The immigration of small farmer migrants, the beginnings of a subsistence-and-surplus agriculture, and the first indications of the development of a market in land and labor all demonstrate that by 1978 Sao Felix had moved from the first to the second stage of frontier expansion.

The recent group of migrants who were the principal agents of this change had systematically lower levels of resources when compared even with the small, nearly homogeneously poor population of earlier Sao Felix residents. The town's already precarious urban infrastructure has failed to keep pace with expanding occupation, so that new neighborhoods had virtually no access to electricity and piped water, and almost all houses were constructed of mud walls, beaten earth floors and thatch roofs. Thus, while housing quality had improved slightly for the town as a whole, conditions were worse than ever in the new neighborhoods. Moreover, while most of Sao Felix residents owned their own homes and residential lots, the proportion of homeowners was lower for recent migrants, and their homes had a lower declared market value; they were less likely to own other assets or to have supplementary monetary income aside from the earnings of household members (Schmink 1980). The more recent migrants were also probably less linked into the community's exchange networks through which goods and services are transferred.

Thus in 1978 Sao Felix was already receiving migrants who had been pushed out of earlier frontier areas in the eastern Amazon region. Desperately hoping to find a foothold in this latest front, they had been drawn to the area by the promise of official colonization projects which

Table 7.2. Characteristics of Subsistence Plots Owned by
Recent Migrants and Earlier Residents, Sao Felix, 1978

(Expressed in percent)	Earlier Residents	Recent Migrants	Total
1. Distance from Residence:			
0-10 km.	85.6	45.4	61.0
Over 10 km.	14.3	54.5	39.0
Total	99.9	99.9	100.0
(N)	(14)	(22)	(36)
2. Size of Plot:			
Less than 1 hectare	50.0	30.0	39.5
1-20 hectares	33.5	35.0	34.0
Over 20 hectares	16.8	35.0	26.2
Total	100.3	100.0	99.7
(N)	(18)	(20)	(38)
3. How Plot Acquired:			
Occupied	47.8	34.8	41.3
Purchased	21.5	43.5	32.6
Ceded (By Others)	21.7	4.3	13.0
Ceded by Prefecture	8.6	8.7	8.7
Others	–	8.6	4.4
Total	99.6	99.9	100.0
(N)	(23)	(23)	(46)
4. Subsistence Crops Planted (Percentage of Households with Subsistence Plots Planting Each):			
Manioc	64.7	73.3	72.5
Corn	62.5	66.7	71.8
Rice	50.0	53.3	51.3
Beans	56.3	40.0	48.7
Fruits	64.7	73.3	24.8
Pasture	6.3	23.1	11.1
Other Crops	23.5	66.7	14.0

would offer them land. But as described above, they brought with them
such minimal resources that even the traditionally poor Sao Felix population seemed relatively well-off by comparison. These findings contradict
the findings from other sites that suggest that spontaneous colonization
selects for those with a history of stable residence and previous ownership
of land or durable goods (Dozier 1969 and Nelson 1973, cited in Moran
1979). The term 'spontaneous' is probably misleading when applied to

Amazon frontier migrants who may have few other options besides repeated migrations (Foweraker 1981; Sawyer 1980).

Given the rapid influx of settlers into Sao Felix and the Xinguara area, by 1977 it was clear that " . . . with the road, Sao Felix is going to explode" (Pinto 1980:193). Small farmer migrants, Sao Felix residents and officials, and would-be large investors were concerned about the impending deluge. At first, this concern was shared by planners who believed that the area's expanses of fertile soils made it an appropriate site for a colonization project for small farmers. Part of the original Polamazonia funds were allocated to a feasibility study, and the program went as far as the pre-proposal stage, but the complete proposal was never elaborated. The Sao Felix area represented an excellent chance to benefit from earlier experiences and outline a more rational colonization plan which might be able to succeed.

> For the patterns of history of Amazonia, the government has a rare opportunity: to plan the occupation of an exceptionally well-endowed area, avoiding there the repetition of phenomena lamented and condemned in other regions. Although the frontier is rushing over Sao Felix do Xingu already, it is controllable and there is still time to define which economic activities can be developed, which modules are to be used and—a precious thing in our predatory days—establish a precise zoning of the soils, according to their aptitudes and in accordance with the best colonization project (Pinto 1980:202; translation mine).

As had happened at a national level, however, the enthusiasm for official small farmer colonization in Sao Felix was short-lived. A variety of factors impeded the colonization plan. First, the more detailed assessment of *terra roxa* provided a less optimistic picture of the potential for the project than had originally been estimated. Second, although the project was to be established, at least in part, on lands owned by the state of Para, the state land agency ITERPA was more interested in selling this land to private investors. Finally, at a time when small farmer colonization was receding from Amazon development priorities, funds could not be guaranteed to establish the project. In the end the official plan was abandoned, although much of the municipality's land has since passed into the federal domain.

Other kinds of urgently needed programs also failed to materialize for Sao Felix. A preliminary urban plan commissioned in 1976 was carried out but never made public. The plan emphasized the need for stimulating local food production and marketing, and improving the urban, health and educational infrastructure. Yet in 1980 the existing hospital was still closed for lack of a public doctor, water and electric systems were more precarious than ever, and the legal patrimony of the urban center and the agricultural 'colony' were still in doubt. Until after the road arrived in 1983, there were virtually no federal agencies present in the town, and whatever improvements were made had to be taken out of the municipal budget, which was only about ten million cruzeiros (or about $200,000) in 1980.

Of the goals set in the mid-1970s for the Polamazonia program, by 1980 the new airport had been built, some land had been demarcated, and the road was moving ahead rapidly. All of these activities were crucial in serving the interests of big investors in the area. Over five hundred thousand hectares of land across the Xingu river from Sao Felix had been sold by the state in lots of up to three thousand hectares to bidders evaluated mainly on the basis of the price offered and their ability to pay. Several groups had purchased multiple lots, and most buyers planned to install cattle ranches in the area. The federal colonization agency, INCRA, had supported the sale of four hundred throusand hectares to the Brazilian firm Construtora Andrade Gutierrez for the establishment of a private colonization project to settle three thousand families on the municipality's largest continuous expanse of *terra roxa*. Winning final approval of their proposal cost the Construtora many months of intensive lobbying, as the purchase had to be approved by the national Senate. One of the nation's ten largest firms and a member of the Association of Amazon Entrepreneurs, Andrade Gutierrez also won the contract to build the road to Sao Felix, which would go through their lands. Despite the company's heavy investments in planning and infrastructure, however, the colonization project would never succeed.

In the 'new frontier' area surrounding Sao Felix and the road, there was little place for the typical small farmer migrant. About two-thirds of the *municipio's* lands were reserved for the big investors. The *municipio* also contains two large indigenous reserves (Gorotire and Xikrin). Small farmers in Sao Felix were concentrated in a small area between the two rivers, which officially belonged to a national forest reserve, hemmed in by a small mountain chain. This reserve would become Sao Felix's colony, to accommodate about two hundred families. The remaining lands surrounding Sao Felix were in hot dispute by dozens of active *grileiros,* or land-grabbers, who first buzzed around the lands later granted to the Projeto Tucuma. This lack of alternatives for small farmer migrants was the on-the-ground expression of the closing out of the small farmer migrant from the planning process.

At least temporarily, many would-be farmers have found work in the 'boom' of placer mining of cassiterite and gold in the rich mountain chains of the area. These operations will eventually be mechanized, thus displacing the prospector (*garimpeiro*). Cattle ranches similarly provide employment only during the initial land clearing phase. Long-term employment possibilities will be in construction, commerce and services, and the wood processing industries which have already begun to expand in some towns. Yet these activities will hardly absorb the thousands of migrants already in the area. With the closing of the frontier to the small farmer, the Amazon frontier can expect to witness a growing problem of hyperurbanization and underemployment (Mougeot 1985).

The Closing Frontier

Sao Felix represents a case of the closing of the frontier to penetration by the small farmer migrant, and its analysis permits a better understanding of the structural changes which are implied by this concept. It has been argued that frontier expansion is a historical process which has played an important function as a 'safety valve' for excess population movement in Brazil. The process typically moves through a series of stages culminating in the appropriation of small farmer plots by capitalist enterprises, providing them with already-cleared land and at the same time freeing an unemcumbered and mobile labor force to be absorbed partially by these enterprises at different moments. But the frontier cycle has also continually recreated a pioneering peasantry which moves to the next historically expanding frontier (Foweraker 1981).

On the Amazon frontier, however, an expanded government role in building infrastructure and providing credit and other incentives has been successful in attracting investments on a scale large enough to make the appropriation of land cleared by peasants only marginal to profits (Pompermayer 1984). To the large enterprise, which has now consolidated a central role in Amazon development, the certainty of access to land is paramount. Particularly where conflicts are likely, it is therefore more rational to avoid conflict by excluding peasants from entering an area. Sao Felix is a good illustration of the attempt to create a 'safe zone' for large-scale projects—thereby avoiding the tensions existent in the adjacent frontier areas. Initial plans to settle resource-poor farmers in the area were scrapped in favor of a strategy permitting the prior appropriation of most available land for capitalist firms before the completion of the road.

The closing of the frontier alters the class relationships on the frontier, seeking to avoid the central conflict between *posseiros* and capitalists by eliminating the pioneering farmer from his historic role on the frontier. The closing of the frontier signifies its transformation to an essentially capitalistic one, with conflicts occurring between capitalist interests and extractive, speculative, or indigenous interests in land. As the Sao Felix case illustrates, the option for pioneers to move to the next frontier area becomes increasingly less feasible.

The tensions associated with these conditions should not be underestimated; the Araguaia-Xingu area has been the site of escalating violence related to land conflicts for years. In 1980 the area suffered two massacres of white persons on Indian lands, murders of ranch employees, and the assassination of the opposition candidate to the presidency of the Rural Worker's Union, to cite only the most dramatic examples of what is standard fare. In February of that year, a new agency was created primarily to defuse tension by resolving the most persistent and threatening cases of land conflict in a four hundred and fifty thousand square kilometer area. The Executive Group on Land in the Araguaia-Tocantins (GETAT) is a special commission connected directly to the Presidency and to the National Security Council of Brazil's military government. Its function is to carry out a sort of 'crisis colonization' program which entails the expeditious settlement of migrants on legalized plots of land in areas currently under litigation. In its first four years of operations, GETAT handed out over 40,000 titles to land.

With the support of the Catholic Church, Amazon migrant groups have successfully organized to demand attention to their plight, and the 'crisis colonization' approach can be accurately viewed as a direct response to these demands. The degree to which such limited reforms can effectively defuse the most serious threats to frontier order is still to be tested. Certainly among a growing opposition movement, a broader class consciousness has begun to emerge which will not stop with the satisfaction of localized problems. These long-standing tensions crystallized in the struggle over a new Agrarian Reform policy announced by the civilian government which took power in 1985. The outcome will depend on the political fortunes of the new government, and on the relative strength of an armed group of landowners determined to protect their property, versus an increasingly organized migrant population with a shared history of violent expulsion and the knowledge that their options for survival are few.

References

Andreazza, Mario David 1979 "Projeto Jari." Speech of the Ministry of the Interior in the National Security Commission of the House of Representatives, Brasilia, October 23.

Arruda, Helio Palma de 1977 *Projetos de Colonizacao. Exposicao a Comissao de Agricultura de Senado Federal.* Brasilia: INCRA.

Bunker, Stephen G. 1979 "Power Structures and Exchange between Government Agencies in the Expansion of the Agricultural Sector," *Studies in Comparative International Development.* Vol XIV, No. 1. pp. 56–76.

Cardoso, Fernando Henrique 1975 *Autoritarismo e Democratizacao*. Rio de Janeiro: Paz e Terra.

Chase, Jacquelyn 1984 "Evolucao demografica no municipio de Sao Felix do Xingu, 1970–1980," Unpublished research report.

Dozier, Craig 1969 *Land Development and Colonization in Latin America*. New York: Praeger.

Foweraker, Joe 1981 *The Struggle for Land: A Political Economy of the Pioneer Frontier in Brazil, 1930 to the Present*. London: Cambridge University Press.

Godfrey, Brian John 1979 "Road to the Xingu: Frontier Settlement in Southern Para, Brasil." M.S. Thesis. University of Calfornia, Berkeley.

Hebette, Jean and Rosa Acevedo 1979 "Colonizacao Para Quem?" *Amazonia/ NAEA*, Research Series Vol. 1, No. 1. Belem.

Horak, Christine A. 1984 *The Formation of Public Policy on the Amazon Frontier: The Rise of the Association of Amazonian Entrepreneurs:* MA Thesis, University of Florida.

Ianni, Octavio 1979 *Colonizacao e Contra-Reforma Agraria na Amazonia*. Petropolis: Vozes.

Lisansky, Judith M. 1980 "Santa Terezinha: Life in a Brazilian Frontier Town." Ph.D. Dissertation, University of Florida.

Martine, George 1980 "Recent Colonization Experiences in Brazil: Expectations versus Reality," in Françoise Barbira-Scazzocchio (ed.), *Land, People and Planning in Contemporary Amazonia*. Cambridge: Cambridge University Press.

Martins, Jose de Souza 1980 *Expropriacao e Violencia; A Questao Politica no Campo*. Sao Paulo: Hucitec.

Miller, Darrell 1980 "The Middle-Class Niche on the Transamazon: Adaptation to Rapid Growth." Presented at the Latin American Studies Association Meeting, Bloomington, Indiana.

Moran, Emilio F. 1979 "Criteria for Choosing Successful Homesteaders in Brazil," *Research in Economic Anthropology*. Vol. 2, pp. 339–359.

Mougeot, Luc J.A. 1985 "Alternative Migration Targets and Brazilian Amazonia's Closing Frontier," in John Hemming (ed.), *The Frontier After a Decade of Colonisation*. Manchester: Manchester University Press.

Nelson, Michael 1973 *The Development of Tropical Lands*. Baltimore: The Johns Hopkins University Press.

Pinto, Lucio Flavio 1980 *Amazonia: No Rastro do Saque*. Sao Paulo: Hucitec.

Pompermayer, Malori Jose 1980 "Agrarian Structure and State Policies in Brazil." Presented at the Latin American Studies Association meeting, Bloomington, Indiana.

1984 "Strategies of Private Capital in the Brazilian Amazon," in Marianne Schmink and Charles H. Wood (eds.). *Frontier Expansion in Amazonia*. Gainsville: University of Florida Press.

Sawyer, Donald R. 1980 "Mobilidade espacial da populacao e estrutura produtiva na Amazonia Brasileira: Nota de pesquisa." Presented at the VII meeting of the Working Group on Migration of the CLACSO Population and Development Council, Buenos Aires, August.

Schmink, Marianne 1980 "Sao Felix do Xingu: A sociodemographic and economic profile." Presented at the I NAEA/CEDEPLAR Seminar on Population Dynamics in the Amazon Region, Belem, Brazil, July.

1982 "Land conflicts in Amazonia." *American Ethnologist.* Vol. 9, No. 2, (May), pp. 341–57.

Silva, Jose Graziano da 1979 "A porteira ja esta fechando" *Revista Ensaios de Opiniao.* March.

Skillings, Robert F. and Nils O. Tcheyan 1979 "Economic development prospects of the Amazon region of Brazil," *Occasional Papers Series No. 9.* Center of Brazilian Studies, School of Advanced International Studies, The Johns Hopkins University.

SUDAM (Superintendencia do Desenvolimento da Amazonia) 1976 *Area de Sao Felix do Xinga-PA. Reconhecimento Pedologico.* Belem: SUDAM.

Vidal, Lux 1977 *Morte e Vida de uma Sociedade Indigena Brasileira.* Sao Paulo: Hucitec.

1981 "Pequeno Guia Practico de Como Invadir uma Area Indigena," in D. de A. Dalari, M.C. da Cunha and L. Vidal (eds.). *A Questao de Terra Indigena,* Cadernos da Comissao Pro-Indio, No. 2. San Paulo: Global.

Weinstein, Barbara 1983 *The Amazon Rubber Boom, 1850–1920.* Stanford: Stanford University Press.

Wood, Charles H. and Marianne Schmink 1978 "Blaming the Victim: Small Farmer Production in an Amazon Colonization Project," in Changing Agricultural Systems in Latin America (special issue). *Studies in Third World Societies.* No. 7, pp. 77–93.

8

LIVESTOCK POLICY AND DEVELOPMENT IDEOLOGY IN BOTSWANA

Eric Worby

Rural development policies are sometimes reformulated in popular ideological terms in order to convince rural dwellers that the government is acting in their interests, and therefore deserves their cooperation. More than mere rhetoric, the way in which development problems and solutions are dressed up for public consumption reveals just how unpalatable a government fears its policies might turn out to be, and gives an indication of where fundamental contradictions between state and peoples, and between social classes, ultimately lie.

In 1970, Botswana's Ministry of Finance and Development Planning issued a 'popular' version of its newly fashioned five-year development plan. The document includes a prominent section concerned with the future of livestock production in the country. The concern is hardly surprising; at the time, earnings from the sale of livestock and livestock products constituted 75 percent of Botswana's foreign exchange earnings. The paper therefore exhorts the people of Botswana to "continue to change our way of thinking about cattle. Many of us tend to keep cattle without using them to earn money. . . . We must use our cattle to have a regular income so we can improve our way of life." (Government of Botswana 1970).

The commoditization of cattle is, of course, only partly predicated on a change in popular attitudes. The Ministry document suggests, for example, that changes must also be made in the use of tribal land for grazing,[1] in the distribution of crop growing and cattle grazing areas, and in the technology and techniques of production itself. These and other proposals were formally articulated in the Tribal Grazing Land Policy (TGLP) enacted in 1975. The import of the policy ostensibly

155

lies in its legitimation of leasehold property rights to tracts of tribal land for individual cattle owners. By providing the legal means for the consolidation of capitalist relations of production for the first time, the TGLP has had, and will continue to have, far-reaching implications for Botswana's rural population.

Yet it would be misleading to find the source and the nature of these implications in the substantive proposals of the policy itself. By asking whether rural development policy is formulated on the basis of adequate data, sound economic analysis and stated social objectives and values, development analysts usually eclipse the possibility of examining how and why the problem of development is posed in the first place. The TGLP has received wide acclaim as an expression of government commitment to national land-use planning (Konzcacki 1978; Hartland-Thunberg 1977). Nevertheless, such planning hardly represents abstract, disinterested reflection on 'what's good for the nation' by local bureaucrats and expatriates. Development policy, as a form of government intervention legitimated by the structure of authority in the modern bourgeois state, often serves as a blueprint for political action; it is the internally directed counterpart of foreign policy. Development strategies are thus linked generically to the conditions of the emergence of the post-colonial state itself. Moreover, they reflect the class interests that predominate within the state structure and typically attempt to resolve inherent contradictions in the broader political economy, both national and international.

The land use policy put forward by the government of Botswana can hardly be expected to mirror that of, say, Kenya, in spite of some similarities in the ecological and technical constraints on agrarian production in each. The modern Kenyan state was formed against a background of ethnic diversity, extensive European settlement and anti-colonial struggle. Botswana, on the other hand, achieved independence peacefully in 1966 under conditions of relative ethnic homogeneity, colonial disinterest and deep dependence on external trade and finance. The complex relations between the presentation of a development policy, its implementation, and the response that it evokes from the people who are its object never originates in the office of development planning but derives from a specific history of class conflict and state formation.

This chapter attempts to link an analysis of contemporary rural development policy in Botswana to the history and evolving social organization of the nation's numerically and politically predominant Setswana-speaking people.[2] A modern division of academic labor tends to make such a linkage seem unnecessary or inappropriate. Development policy is usually allocated to economists and planners, leaving the study of the people to be developed to anthropologists and ethnohistorians.

The discipline of development economics, a child of the Keynesian revolution, is pursued as a positive science with pragmatic goals (Hirschman 1981:13). Social anthropology, in contrast, lends itself less to scientific determinations of cause and effect, and more to the interpretation of how historical contingencies are related to particular human social forms. The one discipline tends to rationalized interventions in the social order; the other, to reflections upon how that order is constituted, sustained and transformed. My purpose here is to show that *policy* interventions concretely express contemporary class relations and can be neither described, nor explained without reference to the historical constitution of the modern social formation.

The first part of this chapter attempts to excise the discussion of development policy in Botswana from its typically ahistorical and positivist context and to re-establish the analysis at the level of political economy and conflicting class interests. Why did the TGLP emerge *when* it did, and in the *form* that it did? What classes are liable to gain from it, and what are the historical contingencies that enable the post-colonial state to be used for their benefit? The evolution of a national development strategy, and especially of livestock management and land tenure policy in independent Botswana, illustrates when development economics merges with particular class interests, serving to justify political action through the agency of the state.

The second section brings the current debate over land tenure, water access and cattle ownership into historical perspective by viewing them at a higher level of abstraction. The story of the TGLP—its genesis and realization—recapitulates the more general rise of social and property relations dominated by capital throughout southern Africa. Indigenous African states based upon livestock and crop production and sustaining aristocracies through tribute were penetrated by European merchant capital, brought under European political hegemony, and subjected to the labor requirements of mining capital. These exogenous forces, together with the internal contradictions specific to these societies themselves, advance an ongoing process of commoditization—of the means of production, the products of labor and labor itself.[3]

The TGLP is only the most *recent* moment in this long historical process; it is part of an ongoing dialectic between a nascent capitalism and the ideological, jural and political forms that support its development. Particular property relations, modes of appropriation of surplus labor, and structures of political domination sustained and transformed Tswana chiefdoms in the past. These aspects of previous social formations provide the key to understanding the direction of change in Botswana today.

Origins of the TGLP: Dilemmas of
Drought and Independence, 1960–1966

Modern economic science always sets the stage for a discussion of development alternatives available to a government by assessing a country's economic profile in aggregate terms. Such a line of inquiry usually provides the statistical grist for the National Development Plans that third world governments produce every three to five years (Konzcacki 1978:137). By assuming the economist's view of Botswana, part of the rationale for government strategy can be understood, even as the social and political realities are set aside.

In the current struggle between north and south, the haves and have-nots, Botswana's development record shines like a bright light among a dim and flickering brethren of LDC's. A semi-arid, landlocked tableland, roughly the size of France, Botswana crowds 80 percent of its nearly one million inhabitants onto a fertile sliver of land east of the Kalahari sand veld. Materially, the country has two things in its favor: great herds of livestock that graze over its surface, and hordes of diamonds that lie beneath it. Until recently, the benefits yielded by mineral exploitation were limited by the absence of any domestic investment capital and the fluctuations in world demand. In the eyes of developers the herds of cattle have long represented a fund of indigenous productive capital with an immediate potential for large scale commercial production. The reproduction, distribution, and market or non-market disposition of cattle have long been at the heart of development policy in Botswana.[4]

At the time the Bechuanaland Protectorate achieved independence from the British in 1966, it bore all the marks of an economic welfare case. Already deeply dependent upon exports of labor and imports of foodstuffs and manufactures from South Africa, the new nation was born in the wake of an unprecedented trauma: between 1961 and 1966 the most severe drought since the nineteenth century had wiped out nearly one-third of the national herd at a time when the cattle industry supplied 85 percent of export earnings. Crops, too, were devastated. One in five persons, reduced to destitution, relied upon famine relief for survival. The prospects for rapid economic recovery and growth were deemed to be negligible, and long-term dependence upon infusions of British aid, inevitable (Colclough and McCarthy 1980:32, 54).

The British, eager to disburden themselves of a costly dependent, were interested in re-establishing Botswana's productive capacity as rapidly as possible. A British survey mission report in 1965 recommended the investment of aid for agricultural development primarily in shoring up the livestock sector. The report also cautioned that the exploitation of mineral resources such as nickel, copper and diamonds could yield significant returns only in the long run. The new government's early development planning nevertheless emphasized the mining sector and supporting infrastructure and the creation of internal sources of government revenue (Picard 1979:292). The possibilities for establishing a strong foundation for local government financing were limited indeed: the tax base was almost non-existent (per capital income at Independence was about US $80), as 91 percent of the labor force was still in agriculture; the nation was bound to an antiquated and inequitable Customs Union Agreement with South Africa, and the government was faced with the need to deliver services to a highly dispersed, mobile, and often inaccessible population. Botswana was little more than "an underdeveloped appendage of the South African economy" (Jones 1980:194).

Given this dismal background, the economic takeoff that followed in the next decade was remarkable by any standard. The annual rate of growth in real terms exceeded 15 percent on average between 1966 and 1973 and continued at a rate of 11 percent until 1976. The government balanced the recurrent budget in 1972-73 and has since had to justify a large and persistent surplus.[5] The government's fiscal strength during this period was attributable in large part to its successful renegotiation of the Customs Union Agreement in 1969 and to the income derived from the massive inflow of private investment and capital imports required for the mining sector. In addition, the United States, United Kingdom, Canada and the World Bank volunteered to bankroll the establishment of urban government and mining infrastructure. Formal sector employment grew rapidly, especially in government and in the construction industry. The estimated real value of domestic production doubled between 1965 and 1970 and had almost doubled again just four years later. (Colclough and McCarthy 1980: 55-62, 76-84).[6] In terming Botswana one of "the few success stories in black Africa, in terms of both economic development and political stability," one economist attributed its record of achievement to the pragmatism and foresight of government leadership, noting especially the government's receptivity to foreign expertise, aid and private investment (Hartland-Thunberg 1977: preface).

Botswana's torrid rate of growth, however, was generated in spite of—or even at the expense of—the rural economy. Livestock and crop production were not conspicuous concerns of the government's development effort in the first five years after independence, even though some 90 percent of the population were thought to depend to some degree on these sectors of the economy. Livestock production still accounted for about 40 percent of the GNP in the late 1960s, and although its relative share in total economic output has fallen, the absolute increase in production has been dramatic. The size of the national herd of cattle, for example, tripled to over three million head in the decade following the 1965 drought. The processing of livestock products continues to dominate manufacturing, and, until the mining industry became well established, accounted for virtually all of Botswana's exports.[7] Although some four hundred commercial freehold ranches, held mostly by non-tribesmen, contribute a disproportionately large share of beef production for export (about 40 percent in 1976–77), indigenous producers on tribal land hold over 80 percent of the national herd. Nearly all of the offtake from tribal herds (averaging about 8 percent annually) is eventually sold to the Botswana Meat Commission for export, an indication that the commercialization of livestock production is well advanced.

Given the apparent centrality of livestock to the welfare of the rural population, and the fact that cattle, in one sense, constitute the largest potential source of indigenous capital, the belated appearance of a policy to protect, and improve the efficiency of the livestock sector seems puzzling. The government's explicit rationale for putting investment in the rural economy on the back burner in the early years of development planning was based on a popular thesis of development economics at the time, namely, that revenues derived from rapid growth in the advanced sectors of the economy could subsequently be rechannelled into the less dynamic rural sectors. Essentially, this meant exploiting the nation's natural resource base as fully and rapidly as possible; funds derived from mineral exports could then be reinvested in education and training, labor-intensive manufacturing, agricultural development and the provision of rural services. The redistribution of resources to rural areas, in other words, would have to await rapid growth in mines and urban centres.

An alternative explanation of the government's policy of benign neglect toward agriculture generally, and livestock in particular, can be found in the dynamics of production and the property relations characteristic of the livestock sector itself. Not only did herds expand rapidly in the wake of the drought, but their ownership was becoming concentrated in fewer hands.[8] Moreover, it was the educated and salaried politicians and bureaucrats who were most able to invest in the accumulation of cattle. Although they envisioned the eventual conversion of the pastoral production system to the freehold model of private fenced ranching, for the time being they were content to rebuild policy that pointed toward the private appropriation of grazing lands in tribal territories. To have gone further would have alienated the rural constituency of the ruling Botswana Democratic Party (BDP). Chiefs and headmen, who retained a good deal of political legitimacy among rural tribesmen while having lost much of their effective authority, would also have been antagonized by such a policy, especially since they were still the nominal custodians of tribal land. Common political sense suggested that commercial livestock production should continue as an interest complementary to the government's revenue-building strategy, rather than as a direct means of achieving fiscal goals.

Ten years later the pendulum of development policy had swung from its initial urban-industrial focus to a preoccupation with range management, land-use planning and agricultural development. The conjuncture of events that led to this ideological shift, and culminated in a national grazing land policy, is best interpreted in the context of rapidly changing agrarian class relations.

For a variety of reasons, including a fortuitous succession of years with ample rainfall, the government's strategy of postponing major rural development enabled the emergent class of wealthy cattle owners to gain increasingly effective control over the essential means of cattle production—water, grazing land and the animals themselves. One source of the increasing disparity in cattle ownership inhered in the dynamics of herd reproduction; those with few cattle were forced to sell off their cattle for desperately needed cash during the drought. Large herd-owners, or those with alternative sources of income were able to maintain sufficient cattle for the future reproduction and expansion of the herd.

Having emerged from the drought relatively unscathed, these same cattle owners were in a position to reap the benefits of colonial livestock and water development policy. The Protectorate Administration sometimes spent more on veterinary services for tribal cattle than they did on medical care for the Tswana themselves. The widespread innoculation of cattle, coupled with strict quarantine practices, increased the potential for large-scale accumulation of cattle, and gave Botswana producers access to the lucrative European market for beef.

The accumulation of cattle was not effectively limited by the availability of pasture; the colonial interpretation of customary Tswana law[9] held that tribal producers were free to graze an unlimited number of cattle wherever they wished, and were enjoined from fencing grazing lands. For several years after Independence, cattle owners interested in building herds exclusively for commercial purposes seemed to support the ideology of free and equal access to pastures, under the aegis of local tribal authorities.[10] But this was not merely a gesture of good will in times of general prosperity, for they were able to secure control of large tracts of land through the more subtle control of watering points. Rangeland is rendered useless in the absence of an adequate water source, and these were scarce relative to the number of users in the traditional tribal grazing territories. While any tribesman was traditionally permitted unrestricted access to natural water sources, wells or boreholes were held to be the exclusive property of those who invested the labor and capital required for their construction and maintenance. Effective *use* of a particular stretch of rangeland could therefore be monopolized by the owner of a single water point, if that were the only one available for watering stock.

Here again, prior colonial policy played into the hands of the rural elite. The Protectorate Administration had, since the Second World War, financed the drilling of publicly owned boreholes in water deficient villages grazing areas of the eastern hardveld. In 1963, the Administration initiated a borehole drilling program for private cattle owners on a long term repayment basis. Over the next three years, when the drought was most severe, more than one thousand private boreholes were drilled. Many of these were sunk in the sparsely populated western sandveld regions with the intention of relieving grazing pressure from communal pastures near the large villages in the east. As the scarcity of water declined with the end of the drought in 1966, newly created District Councils began to sell off publicly managed boreholes to private syndicates or individuals as a source of revenue (Parson 1981:242). This policy set off a process of increasing *de facto* control of grazing lands by those with sufficient capital to purchase or drill, equip and operate boreholes. Meanwhile, those rural households impoverished by the drought were forced to purchase rights of access to water with cash, food, supplies or their own labor.

The conjunction of private water rights with an ideology of communal access to grazing land, however, embodied ecological, political, and social contradictions. The concentration of expanding herds around single water points severely degraded the range, especially in the vicinity of larger villages. While wealthy stockowners could move on to develop sandveld cattle posts, poorer tribesmen were left to graze their few stock on thorn bush and scrub. Politically, the stage was set for a confrontation between the chiefs, who had already been stripped of their legislative and executive powers by the new constitution, and the BDP government. As long as the state refrained from intervening directly in the economy's agricultural base, the residual authority of chiefs to distribute land remained unchallenged. But their ability to control land *use* was fast eroding, and with it their last remaining source of real political power. Finally, differential access to water and draft power implied the rapid polarization of classes in the rural areas, exacerbating the potential for effective dispossession and overt class conflict.

The Tribal Grazing Land Policy, and the process of its production, represents the response of the government to the heightening of these overlapping contradictions in the rural political economy. The intensification and expansion of pasture exploitation was in part the overt manifestation of an underlying conflict between rancher-bureaucrats and politicians with a new economic and political base on the one hand, and the tribal authorities on the other. The conflict was much more than mere competition between equivalent politial elites for power, for the systems of production from which each stood to gain differed fundamentally. Indeed, the entrenchment of ostensibly capitalist relations of production in the agrarian economy was at stake.

Birth of the TGLP: 1968–1975 State Intervention

Unlike the chiefdoms of the pre-colonial era and the subordinated tribal governments under the Protectorate, the very structure of the post-colonial state was predicated upon bourgeois legal and property relations (Odell and Odell 1980: 6). In spite of its continued reliance on British administrative staff, Botswana's new government was no empty shell, entirely dependent on the munificence of an ex-colonial power. An indigenous class of proto-capitalist ranchers, largely represented by highly paid civil servants and rural-based politicians, was prepared to use the agency of the state to grant itself exclusive title to grazing land. The story of how this came about, and of how it was nurtured, somewhat inadvertently, by expatriate development ideology, is the story of the TGLP.

The TGLP was presented as a highly rationalized form of land-use planning and management, the primary purpose of which was to solve an ecological crisis and to increase the efficiency of livestock production. This representation reflected the thinking of the expatriate administrative staff as well as the foreign aid agencies that established projects within the TGLP framework. It was the BDP government, however that saw the policy through the planning stages, was responsible for its final form and ultimately determined the manner of its implementation. By examining the micro history of the Policy's development, it can be seen just how the government utilized the discourse of its expatriate advisors as a rationale in making proposals for a transformation of rural property relations. The Policy's implicit class bias was in this way rationalized to foreign donors and justified to the rural population.

The government's early interventions in the rural economy proved to be of short term benefit to enterprising cattle owners, but they exacerbated ecological stress on the pastoral resource base. Throughout the colonial period, optimism regarding the expansion of the livestock industry was tempered by deep concern over the excessive concentration of cattle around water points and the deterioration of the range. It was the promise of expansion, rather than the ecological danger, however, that appears to have motivated government planners in the first years after

Independence. Stimulated by the increases in productivity achieved on fenced commercial ranches in the freehold farming blocks and on government test ranches, planners sought to develop fenced ranches for commercially-oriented herd owners. The problem was how to do this without violating the traditional junction against fencing grazing land, a rule likely to be jealously defended by chiefs and the majority of rural tribesmen. The exploitation of State Lands provided the solution, for the obvious reason that their allocation and management was beyond tribal control. An added incentive was the perception that these lands were sparsely populated, if inhabited at all, by nomadic hunter-gatherers who were incapable of political resistance.

The provision of ranches to tribesmen on State Land would, in theory, reduce the pressure to overstock in the east, and would also demonstrate the value of fencing, modern management and private ownership to less progressive stockholders in Tribal Areas. Armed with this rationale, the government drew up preliminary proposals for foreign assistance in 1968, and presented the World Bank with a formal request for funding in 1970.[11] This First Livestock Development Project was unequivocally directed at the prosperous and the progressive among Botswana livestock producers, although the hope was expressed that the benefits of a thriving commercial beef industry would touch the lives of the rural poor.

The government was not at first prepared to make similar investments in livestock production in the Tribal Areas; it was, however, anxious to secure the jurisdiction of the state over the disposition of tribal land, thus clearing the way for changes in the rules of tenure. The supposedly undemocratic and inefficient management of land by chiefs and their delegated headmen provided the justification for the Tribal Land Act of 1968 (effective in 1970). This critical piece of legislation wrested control over land and other natural resources of the tribe from the chiefs and placed it in the hands of Tribal Land Boards on which chiefs had limited representation.[12]

This last initiative made ever more apparent the contradiction between the BDP's policies and its conservative political base in the rural areas. The ruling party had come to power in 1965 with overwhelming rural support reflecting the backing of nearly all of the Tswana chiefs. Seretse Khama, the party's leader and first President of the Republic, commanded additional allegiance as the recognized heir to the chieftainship of the Ngwato, the nation's largest and historically most powerful tribe. Soon after taking office, however, the BDP stripped the chiefs of their residual legislative and executive powers, and all but a modicum of local judicial authority. The Tribal Land Act signalled the extinction of their control over the distribution and use of the means of agricultural production. In taking these measures, the BDP gambled on the rapid transferral of popular allegiance to elected District Councils and to local administrative organs of the state. The 1969 elections proved this to be a misjudgment, and the results motivated the Government to reassess its policies with respect to its rural constituents and their traditional leaders.

The announcement of the Tribal Land Act fueled the aspirations of wealthy cattle owners to gain control over tribal grazing land. Sensing the imminent granting of exclusive title, or at least permission to fence, these men embarked upon what many have called a massive land grab. In the late 1960s boreholes were drilled indiscriminately, often without the chief's permission. After 1970, Land Boards were bombarded with applications for more drilling rights, or for retroactive rights over boreholes drilled previously; the Land Boards, perhaps in the flush of their new mandate or under political pressure, were equally willing to grant such rights, usually without so much as a site inspection.[13] As a result, vast tracts of nominally communal lands fell under the *de facto* control of a rich minority, while poorer stockholders were required to pay watering fees or were excluded from grazing their stock in these areas altogether. Thus the pattern established after the drought was repeated and accelerated during the 1970s, only this time under the auspices of the state.

In sum, by the early 1970s, the government faced a political and economic dilemma on two fronts. On the one hand, it needed to contain any reactionary rural movements led by embittered tribal aristocrats. On the other, it was eager to promote private commerical ranching by extending the LDP I model into tribal areas. The key problem was how to accomplish this without lending credence to the fears of dispossession and the sense of neglect felt by the peasant majority. The first problem was solved by restructuring the district level bureaucracy to facilitate greater political control of rural areas still under the sway of traditional authorities. The question of how to advance commercialization without effecting wide scale dispossession, however, had to be answered with a carefully considered land and rural development policy. And the efficacy of such a policy would demand an equally compelling ideology asserting the impartiality of the state and the BDP.

Both an incentive and a leitmotif for such a policy were generated by an international Conference on Sustained Production from Semi-Arid Areas held in Botswana's capital late in 1971. The principal concerns of the participants—almost all of whom were expatriate civil servants and social or natural scientists—were ecological and economic: halting the deterioration in the environment and then expanding production to the maximum which the environment could carry. There apparently was little doubt in anyone's mind that, failing the adoption of stringent measures for range management and conservation, ecological disaster and profound social distress were imminent. All agreed that in the first analysis, both the source of and the solution to this crisis lay in the system of herd management and land tenure. The many government policy makers in attendance walked away armed with a new discourse— one that submerged the inherently political nature of a land policy within the neutral and unassailable rhetoric of ecological science and its pragmatic counterpart, social engineering.

While many of the discursive and theoretical elements of the 1975 Grazing Land Policy can be traced back to the 1971 Semi-Arid Lands Conference, one paper contained a precise, programmatic statement that foreshadows the actual strategy of the TGLP:

> For the big farmers who are keen to invest money in development, a survey of a vast grazing area should be made and liberal loans for the purchase of farms in this area should be advanced to farmers. Here land should be demarcated into well delineated farms which should be leased for long term and developed. The rest of the country should be left as rural tribal areas where traditional users of land should be encouraged to improve their agriculture and their animal husbandry (Khama 1971: 61).

The suggestion that emergent distinctions in social class be reinforced through government subsidies, and that the spheres of production of each class be mapped onto distinct geographical regions was to form the heart of the TGLP in its final form. Significantly, the author of this early formulation was at one time the Acting Tribal Authority for the Ngwato and a relative of the President; his views were probably representative of those held in the BDP cabinet.

The embryonic grazing land policy that appeared in the government's first national policy statement on rural development (White Paper No. 1: Rural Development in Botswana) published in March 1972 put forward essentially the same plan, but cast it in a complex ideological mold. The White Paper cannot be easily reduced to any particular class interests, either in substance or ideology. Its diagnosis and etiology of the crisis in the livestock sector links increasing rural inequality with a pattern of environmental abuse; the task it therefore sets for policy is to redress injuries to the rural poor and to the land. The paper contains, moreover, the first frank recognition of a causal relation between borehole drilling, the monopolization of range and water sources by wealthier farmers and the threat of permanent damage to pastures.[14]

The text of the White Paper indicates an implicit division of labor between expatriate bureaucrats and the Office of the President. The paper incorporates the apocalyptic, almost Darwinian discourse of the expatriates at the earlier Conference: "The situation facing us is one of an expanding population struggling to survive and improve their living standards in a harsh and deteriorating environment" (White Paper 1972:2). The substantive goals and strategies of the policy statement, moreover, bear the unmistakable stamp of expatriate thinking in key ministries. Conserving the land and raising agricultural productivity are given first priority. Improvements in marketing and credit facilities, the creation of new employment opportunities and the provision of social services in rural areas are the main subsidiary objectives. The instrumental language of these portions of the text are liberally seasoned with openly ideological passages from presidential speeches. These rhetorical interludes invoke the theme of 'social justice': the government would *not* pursue economic growth in the rural sector solely for the benefit of a privileged minority.

The wedding of techno-economic objectives with populist moral imperatives was to become the hallmark of the government's rural development ideology. Given sound planning and scientific management of the rural economy, the government claimed that growth *and* the more equitable distribution of its fruits could be achieved in tandem. Nowhere was this more apparent than in the discussion of the livestock sector. While recognising that the "uneven distribution of cattle makes it more difficult to achieve rural development in the interests of the majority," the paper adds that "we should, of course, do nothing which will make our cattle industry less productive, or which will reduce its income-earning capacity" (White Paper 1972:6).

The dual aims of social equity and increased productivity were never wholly reconciled in the initial White Paper. In fact, 'equity' became a code word for giving the poorer, 'traditional' stockholder a better chance at subsistence on tribal land, while 'productivity' was to be achieved by 'progressive' commercial livestock producers on land marked for their exclusive use (in 1972 still limited to State Land). Provision *was* made for mobility between these two arenas of production in the policy statement. Exclusive rights would gradually be granted to viable groups of small holders in both Tribal and State Land grazing areas. Legislation would also be enacted to enforce range conservation, limit stocking rates and grant corporate status to management associations composed of small holders, facilitating their acquisition of land and credit. But the essential vision was one of increasingly specialized livestock production and the economic stratification of rural dwellers into capitalist ranchers, small-scale crop producers and wage laborers.

In 1972, with support from the Ford Foundation, the government solicited a major consultancy from two planners with extensive East African experience to help them out of their quandary. The consultants' report (Chambers and Feldman 1973), though only partially heeded by the government, provided the groundwork for the TGLP. The consultants

pointed out that it was not possible to shape policy so as to maximize
the rate of economic growth without adversely affecting income distribution. Botswana, they suggested, was at a policy crossroads. Current
policy was concerned with creating an economic infrastructure to serve
the interests of foreign investors in mining, livestock products and
tourism. A desirable alternative, in their view, would be for the government
to actively intervene in the organization of rural production in order
to increase the quantity and equity of redistributive benefits. They
recommended that three steps be taken to achieve that goal: 1) Commercialization of livestock and crop production in the Tribal Areas; 2)
Diversification of rural income sources; and 3) Redistribution of resources,
opportunities and services in the rural sector of the economy. These
measures, according to the report, would increase Botswana's economic
autonomy from South Africa. At the same time they would alleviate the
deepening patterns of exploitation as Botswana becomes more stratified
between owners of capital and wage laborers; such exploitative relations
would be the inevitable result of an exclusive commitment to free
enterprise and capital accumulation, the authors warned.

The most sensitive, and in many ways the most critical arena for
government intervention, was in the property relations contingent upon
livestock production. Believing that "there is an inherent contradiction
between the present institutional structure of private herd ownership,
communal land control and the sustained development of the livestock
industry" (Chambers and Feldman 1973:57), the consultants recommended a strategy that would promote capitalist forms of land tenure
and investment policy, while simultaneously supporting the goal of social
equity in the livestock-dependent rural economy.

At the heart of the Policy lay a radical redefinition of land tenure in
Botswana's communally zoned or Tribal Land Areas where 85 percent
of the nation's population and an equal proportion of livestock reside.
The Tribal Lands were to be rezoned into three categories. Commercial
Farming Areas would be created, where large stock-holders and syndicates
of smaller owners would be encouraged to transfer their cattle onto
fenced lease-hold ranches; Communal Grazing Areas, which were to
remain accessible to the community at large for grazing purposes, would
preserve the rule interdicting individual enclosure of rangeland. Communities as a whole, however, would be encouraged to incorporate
modern ranching techniques. Lastly, Reserve Areas were to be set aside
for future grazing needs. The policy aspired to solve three of the nation's
most pressing problems in one fell swoop. First the privatization of
grazing land tenure in the commercially zoned regions was seen as a
sine qua non of rational herd management and especially of the prevention
of overstocking. Second, through careful land use planning, stock quotas

and the removal of large herds from severely pressed communal resources, the tendency toward rapid rangeland degradation would be reversed. And third, the dramatic disparities in rural incomes would be reduced by increasing general access to critical water and grazing resources, which had come under the *de facto* control of a few large herd owners, and by creating job opportunities in the newly commercialized livestock sector.

It is noteworthy that the similarities between the government's rural development proposals and the recommendations of the consultants were principally ones of form rather than of honest intention. The government seized on the opportunity to permit the private appropriation of grazing lands—hence the TGLP. Meanwhile, the larger contradiction between an export-based, free enterprise development strategy and the equitable distribution of income and opportunity was neither tackled nor even acknowledged. Picard suggests that the government ignored the main thrust of the consultancy recommendations, and substituted "a programme-oriented set of development schemes excised of any national commitment to social and economic change" (1979:296).

If the government was lacking in its commitment to change, it did its utmost to create just the opposite effect among its rural constituents. While beginning the extraordinary task of comprehensive land use planning for the TGLP, it launched a massive popular information campaign, lauded by one official as probably "the first large scale consultation programme in Africa as a whole" (Temane 1977:9). The Radio Learning Group Campaign alone involved some 50,000 citizens. The government clearly was greatly concerned that the uncomfortable *idea* of private rights to grazing land, and of 'scientific' herd management, be shown to be in the *national* interest and not merely in the interest of bureaucrats and ranchers.

It is not the primary purpose of this study to evaluate the success of the TGLP in terms of its stated objectives; nevertheless, it is instructive to look at the Policy's track record in order to get some idea of the government's sincerity, willpower and capability to actually implement change. Thus far, good intentions far outweigh concrete interventions. The technical and administrative means to survey land and allocate leasehold ranches proved to be insufficient. As of September 1979, only twenty-five ranches had actually been allocated and no leases had yet been signed (Sandford 1981:7). Of greater significance in the absence of limitations on ranch ownership by an individual was the inability or unwillingness of Land Boards to enforce stocking limitations either in communal areas or on commercial ranches.

There are several ways in which actual practice had directly contradicted the Policy's stated goals. First, the zoning of 'commercial' areas had largely been limited to land presently occupied by wealthy stockholders. The opportunity to liberate resources for small holder use in communal areas has consequently been lost; the evidence suggests that the commercial ranches being established have merely legalized *ownership* of cattle posts and boreholes already under private *control*. No effort has been made to force wealthier stockholders out of communal areas either. Second, the timorous approach of the Land Boards to the enforcement of lease obligations, not to mention the generous terms of the leases themselves, hardly augurs a revenue windfall for local development administrators to reinvest in communal livestock production. Third, no provision whatsoever was made for the fate of stockless persons—especially hunters and gatherers and dependent herders—who happen to reside on commercially zoned lands.

What then was the meaning of the TGLP? If its impact has been so muted, what motivated the government fanfare? Picard (1981:108) provides one interpretation:

> Public statements of political elites about the need for economic development in the rural areas have been supplanted by private policy decisions which have continued the high priority begun during the colonial period, of maintaining political control over the rural areas with a minimum of output in economic terms.

But the TGLP, as a blueprint for the recognition of private rights over land, represents a crucial stage in the formal penetration of capitalist relations of production where antithetical political structures, jural rights and ideologies had formally prevailed. The break was initiated and effected by the state, but only insofar as it aided the advance of the interests in capital accumulation by the cattle owning bourgeoisie.

The significance of the TGLP as an ideological and juridical transformation promoted by the state can become somewhat clearer if the process of class formation is traced from the period of increasing articulation of non-capitalist with capitalist modes of production during the colonial period of the nineteenth and twentieth centuries. Indeed, a look at Botswana history reveals that the issues of livestock and land tenure have been pivotal themes in the structuring of relations of production and in providing the ideological and juridical justifications for those relations.

Colonial Antecedents in the TGLP:
Property Forms and Socio-Political Relations

The British created the Colonial Protectorate in order to preserve the trade corridor to the north from Boer and German encroachment. Initially, they intended to cede control to Cecil Rhodes and the British South African Company. When missionaries and a group of Tswana chiefs lobbied the Crown to prevent such a move, the British had to satisfy themselves with trying to make the natives themselves bear the cost of administration. This was effected by imposing the characteristic *pax britannica,* creating Tribal Reserves and exacting revenue through a hut tax. Little attempt was made to interfere directly in either tribal administration or in production, though both were transformed because of British political hegemony.

The Ngwato under Khama endured both the rinderpest epidemic and the imposition of British rule considerably better than most of the other chiefdoms. Khama had forged out of his position in the trading nexus a kind of state-controlled mercantile capitalism. Most of the capital he managed to accumulate was reinvested in production: breeding cattle, plows, wagons and firearms were redistributed to producers to increase the self-sufficiency of the state. Larger cattle and grain producers profited enormously from the decimation of the herds of neighboring tribes, as the price of cattle sky-rocketed and grain for famine relief came to be in great demand. The Boer War reinforced the boom for the Ngwato, as producers engaged in military provisioning. After 1902, however, the weight of drought, market depression and escalating rates of colonial taxation bore down heavily on those who had formerly been able to dispose of a considerable surplus. Meanwhile, the railway link between the Cape and Rhodesia displaced the wagon trade entirely; although railway jobs permitted Khama to contain the labor market within the area of his jurisdiction, Ngwato men were starting to join other Tswana in the South African mines. The hut tax, which had to be paid in cash, was partly responsible for this development; insofar as the chief himself creamed off 10 percent of what he collected for the tax, he maintained an interest in the ability of households to pay. Indeed, not much coercion was necessary, as Massey (1980:11) points out:

> The relatively poor ecological base and the pre-existing situation of social and economic inequality lent themselves more readily to a process of proletarianization than . . . in other territories. Once cash needs had been created and the cooperation of the tribal authorities had been enlisted, it was relatively easy for the colonial administration in Botswana to induce people to seek employment. . . . Given the poverty of cash-earning opportunities in Botswana, taxation and labour migration were two sides of the same coin.

The process of proletarianization in the Protectorate was far from complete. As everywhere in southern Africa, wages paid to migrant

laborers were insufficient to both reproduce the family-group and to pay
the hut tax; with the exception of wealthy noble families, most households
depended upon the women to provide subsistence goods while men
were out on contract. Their task was made doubly difficult by the absence
of male labor for plowing and herding, and by the increasing distance
of arable and grazing lands. With the advent of wage labor, the chiefs,
having replaced traditional forms of tribute entirely by their access to
tax revenue, no longer were *obliged* to redistribute means of production.
The threat of tribal secession had disappeared with British administration,
and the need to appropriate surplus from the subsistence economy had
largely vanished. The chief no longer presided over a sovereign political
entity and was content to collect cash for purposes of private, as well
as public investment.

The only reliable source of cash other than wage labor for the majority
of the people during the colonial period was the sale of cattle. Although
the Customs Union Agreement of 1910 guaranteed free access to the
markets of Swaziland, Lesotho and South Africa, a series of measures
such as weight restrictions and quarantines effectively prevented the
Africans in the Protectorate from exporting very many cattle between
1924 and 1941. The sale of labor power became the only available
alternative; by 1943, after the cattle export restrictions were removed,
26 percent of all able bodied Ngwato men were working abroad—the
comparable figure for the southeastern tribes averaged 40 percent (Schapera 1953:31).

Up until the 1930s the British were content to have the tribes
administer their own affairs, so long as taxes flowed through the chiefs
to the Protectorate administration, stimulating in turn the flow of labor
to the Witwatersrand gold mines. But there were limits to this policy
of political laissez-faire. Chiefs, such as Khama, benefited mightily from
the commoditization of cattle and labor, and from the enforced peace;
the British finally were compelled to inhibit the tendency toward capital
accumulation and the consolidation of economic control in the hands
of the chiefs. In 1916, legislation was introduced restricting African
investment in trade, and during the 1930s the chief's judicial authority
and his tenure in office were officially subordinated to the colonial
administration.

Meanwhile, tax revenues were expended almost entirely on policy,
administration and the enclaves of European commercial agriculture.
Technical innovations and material inputs in the Tribal Reserves were
notably lacking in the Protectorate budget. Allocations for education
and health care favored the handful of Europeans over the mass of
Africans in gross disproportion.

Before the consolidation of British authority, chief Khama endeavored to increase the overall productivity of the Ngwato by adapting social, legal and political structures to enable tribal members to become petty commodity producers under the aegis of the Ngwato state. Continuous production of commodities would have required new means of exploiting increasingly scarce resources, and novel property relations defining access to land. Like nearly all Tswana chiefs, however, Khama was content to protect universal rights to arable and grazing lands based upon tribal membership. The chiefs were in no position to compete with European manufacturing and mining capital. Their power as a class still depended upon their political authority and would have been undermined by the legalization of individual property rights in land and the complete expropriation of poorer peasants. With their trading rights restricted and weight restrictions stifling the cattle trade, the independent hegemony of the chiefs began to wane. The state structure that had crystallized around their commercial and political dominance was formally subordinated to the wider South African political economy controlled by European industrial capital.

Nevertheless, the dissolution of the socio-political structures that had characterized Tswana states in the age of commodity trading left a developing class structure as a precipitate. Between the diminished authority of the chiefs and the disinterest of the British, the struggle for control over the means of production and labor was freed from some of its old political and ideological determinations. The process of rural differentiation based on the unequal distribution of cattle, the differential access to cash for taxes and consequent obligation to seek wage employment have already been mentioned. It was the intermediate estates of commoners and foreigners, *batlhanka* and *bafaldi,* whose security was most severely threatened by this trend.[15] Typically owning fewer than twenty cattle, the self-sufficiency of family groups in these strata were easily destroyed by the periodic droughts or crop failures; the availability of wage labor undermined the former obligation of the chief to provide for them from the tribal stores of surplus.

The dispersion of lands that followed upon the erosion of the tribal administrative structure by colonial authorities, as well as the erosion of the soils and range from prolonged immobility, made the task of production increasingly difficult for households lacking means of ploughing and transport. Building a herd for these purposes was frequently precluded by the absence of male laborers. And when labor or oxen was provided on loan, it was often only after their owners had attended to their own needs. The pre-colonial practice that suspended all stages of agricultural production until the chief has himself initiated them ceremonially was now insured by the facts of economic dependence alone.

The final nail in the coffin of subsistence agriculture based on equal rights of usufruct was provided by the introduction of British borehole technology. Financed by the protectorate authorities, the wells drilled by wealthier cattle owners became the wedge of capital investment and private property rights in grazing lands. Schapera (1955:210–11) provides an apt description of the transformation of property relations this entailed:

> All wells were formerly regarded as common property, where anybody grazing his cattle in that area could water them. But it has gradually become the law that only the people digging the well are entitled to water their cattle there. Anybody else wishing to use the well must obtain the owners permission failing which, if he trespasses, he can be ejected or punished.

Water in Botswana has always been the limiting factor in pastoral production. Though subject to the minimal spacing requirements established by the chief, individual borehole owners were able to gain *de facto* control of large stretches of grazing land, according to their capital means.

British investment in veterinary services early in the century and in the massive export abattoir at Lobatse in 1954 provided the other critical means to the realization of a fully commoditized livestock sector; though these were primarily intended to aid European free hold ranchers, the enhancement of marketing and processing facilities benefitted wealthier Tswana cattle holders as well, foreshadowing the commercialization of the pastoral economy in tribal areas after Independence.

British concern over capital accumulation by Africans abated as the long-standing possibility of incorporating the Protectorate into the Union of South Africa gave way to the certainty of independence in the late 1950s. Until that time "arable agriculture, education, health, and physical infrastructure remained almost completely neglected by the central administration" (Colclough and McCarthy 1980:31). But the task of constructing a stable and secure post-colonial state demanded greater colonial investment in these areas, and the benefits accrued mostly to wealthier farmers and livestock owners with the means to utilize capital inputs efficiently.

Supra-tribal political activity prior to elections under the new constitution in 1965 was dominated by the educated members of such wealthy families. The victorious Botswana Democratic Party (BDP), led by the British-educated heir to the Ngwato chieftanship, Seretse Khama, drew support both from the chiefs and from the emerging class of commercial livestock and crop producers. After the elections, a series of swiftly enacted legislative measures effectively dissolved the institutionalized authority of the chiefs and established the formal hegemony of the bourgeois democratic state. The consolidation of capitalist relations of production in agriculture and livestock production had only to await the extension of state power into the rural areas where the chiefs still commanded considerable political authority and formally controlled the distribution of land. Because the personnel in the state apparatus exercised considerable control over rural production already, their access to the legislative means for creating private property rights in land was all that was necessary to consolidate their class position.

Conclusion: The Dialectic of Class Formation and the Ideology of Development

The separation of producers from the means of production and the proletarianization of labor in rural Botswana is even today only partial. The roots of this process in the history of Tswana society are at least as deep as the appropriation of labor by nobles from the *malata* during the period of migration and expansion in the eighteenth century. The limits to capitalist development under the socio-political structure of Tswana chiefdoms was reached at the turn of the century by the Ngwato. But the interests of European trading and mining capital contradicted those of the Ngwato state, and the assymetry in power between the two secured the fate of the latter as a labour reserve for the former. Universal, though increasingly unequal, access to land ensured the durability of this arrangement. Moreover, the preservation in ideology and in law of rights of usufruct based on tribal citizenship continued to legitimate the political authority of the chief, while controlling the means of capital accumulation by those who were formally his political rivals in the nobility. The conflicting interests of those former aristocrats who sought education and civil service employment, giving them access to cash, boreholes and more cattle, and those of the tribal political structure preserved by the British, were resolved by the birth of the modern bureaucratic state.

Yet the bureaucratic capitalist class formed after independence had to attack the basis of peasant resistance to complete alienation from their means of subsistence. They did this juridically, through the agency of the state, by permitting the privatization of land in the TGLP. But the legitimacy of the democratic state depended upon the promotion of a new ideology of development that was largely contradicted in practice. Jack Parson (1981:238) has expressed the underlying logic of this process most acutely:

Concretely, in rural Botswana there is underway a land grab with many of the earmarks of an enclosure movement. More strongly, it has many of the characteristics of a capitalist 'primitive accumulation', a dispossession of direct producers. This process has centrally involved a capitalist class in the ownership of cattle and in positions of state, using the state to advance the process against the interests of the majority of rural dwellers. And it is the state, through its control of social resources (financial, regulatory, and coercive) which has been central to the whole movement despite its rhetoric to the contrary. In Botswana this process is known as the Tribal Grazing Lands Policy.

All too often, development policies and programs are examined *sui generis*, as if, like a new drug, they should be evaluated in terms of their stated objectives, their effectiveness in curing a perceived malady and the harmful side effects they may entail. Viewing the TGLP this way tells something about the relation of livestock production to resources and technical inputs; it indicates some of the admnistrative obstacles to restructuring a rural economy. But it fails to explain the rationale behind the policy's content and the motivations for its implementation.

It has been shown that the TGLP, far from being *in itself* a radical form of intervention in the Botswana rural economy, is largely an ideological and political tool for the consolidation of a centuries old dialectical relationship between socio-political structures and the relations of production. The initiation of long distance commodity trade, the imposition of the hut tax, and the introduction of borehole technology all represent earlier steps along the road to private property, commercial production and the dispossession of producers in rural Botswana. In a continuous evolution of political forms—from centralized chiefdom, to pre-capitalist state, to the colonial articulation of European with tribal administration, to the modern independent state—the disaggregation of labor from the means of its own reproduction was further enforced. Yet at each stage, the articulation of politics and production created contradictions, and these have increased with the polarization of social classes, as Cliffe and Moorsom (1979:42) have noted.

For the mass of peasantry, labour-service or wage labour is increasingly the only alternative. Although large numbers survive on the margins of rural production, the coincidence of the advanced penetration of commodity exchange and the monopolisation of the production resources with the small expansion of rural labour-demand has forced large numbers into oscillating labour migration or permanent emigration from the land.

The TGLP will hasten this process at the same time it tries to soften its impact on the dispossessed. As the antagonisisms between capitalist ranchers and the proleterianized peasantry increase, the TGLP cannot but bring about political transformations in the future just as they were called forth in the past.[16]

Notes

1. Seventy-one percent of Botswana's land area is designated Tribal Land and includes the eight Tribal Reserves demarcated during the early years of British rule for the principal Tswana tribes (Ngwato, Kwena, Ngwaketse, Tswana, Kgatla, Tshiidi-Rolong, Tlokwa, and Lete). The remaining area is either State (formerly Crown) Land (23 percent) or freehold farming blocks (6 percent).

2. I use the term 'Tswana' throughout to refer collectively to the Setswana-speaking peoples of contemporary Botswana and their ancestors, who are classified with the western branch of Sotho-speakers in Southern Africa. Other important linguistic groups represented in Botswana include the Kalanga, mixed farmers of the Northeast, Herero pastoralists in the Northwest and the San hunter-gatherers of the Kalahari desert. Most of these groups have historically been subordinated to the Tswana in the rural political economy.

3. J.K. Hart (1982), following some of Marx's key insights in the *Grundrisse,* has characterized the commoditization process as a universal tendency in human history, involving the increasing abstraction of labour from its original unity with the natural world and appearing under capitalism as the generalized production of goods for sale, or exchange value. (J.K. Hart, "On Commoditization", in E.N. Goody (ed.), *From Craft to Industry: The Ethnography of Proto Industrial Cloth Production.* Cambridge: Cambridge University Press, 1982, pp. 38–49.

4. Virtually every survey of the economic status of the Bechuanaland Protectorate by the Colonial Government suggested that cattle production was the only suitable basis for development (see E. Roe "Development of Livestock, Agriculture and Water Supplies in Eastern Botswana before Independence: A Short History and Policy Analysis" *Occasional Papers,* No. 10, Rural Development Committee, Cornell University, Ithaca, N.Y., 1980, esp. p. 8).

5. N.S. Makgatla notes that the recurrent surplus rose from P 14.7 million (one-third of the total recurrent revenue) to an estimated P 35.8 million (or 26 percent) in 1978–79 even though foreign loans and grants accounted for three-fifths of the development budget. Despite dramatic rises in budgeted development expenditure since 1976–77, "only about two-thirds of the total investment budgeted in the national plans were actually realised, with a particularly poor record in agriculture." ("Finance and Development: The Case of Botswana," *Journal of Modern African Studies,* 20, 1, 1982, p. 79).

6. Colclough and McCarthy, *op. cit.,* pp. 55–62, 76–84. For a detailed account of the role of foreign aid in Botswana, especially by the British, see D. Jones *Aid and Development in Southern Africa: British Aid to Botswana, Lesotho, and Swaziland,* London: Croom Helm, 1977. For a critical discussion of Canadian aid to the massive Selebi-Phikwe mining endeavour see R. Carty and V. Smith *Perpetuating Poverty: The Political Economy of Canadian Foreign Aid,* Toronto: Between the Lines, 1981.

7. Beef processing accounted for about 80 percent of agricultural output, and was Botswana's largest foreign currency earner until 1977. For a detailed analysis of commercial beef production, see P. Spray, "Botswana as a Beef Exporter", Working Paper No. 37, National Institute of Development and Cultural Research (N.I.R.), Gaborone: University College of Botswana, July, 1981.

8. G. Dahl has demonstrated the differential impact of drought according to the size and composition of herds in "Production in Pastoral Systems," in J. Galaty et al (eds.) *The Future of Pastoral Peoples,* Ottawa: International Development Research Centre, 1981, p. 203. Also see J. Soloway, *People, Cattle, and Drought in Western Kweneng District,* Gaborone: Ministry of Agriculture, 1980, pp. 44–45.

9. The term 'customary law,' insofar as it is used to designate a fixed set of 'traditional' rules and norms, is more of a colonial reification than an accurate characterization of actual Tswana legal precepts and practices. I. Shapera, in writing *A Handbook of Tswana Law and Custom,* (London: International African Institute, 1955) as an explicit aid to British colonial administration, was careful to record wide variation among various tribal groupings and change over time. See J.M. Walker, "Malete Contract Law," *Botswana Notes and Records,* vol. 1, 1968, p. 65. 'Tribal law' (indeed any legal system) is best conceived as a dialectic between rules and social practices in a process of constant transformation. See J.L. Comaroff and S. Roberts, *Rules and Processes: The Cultural Logic of Dispute in an African Context.* Chicago: University of Chicago Press, 1981.

10. A dual judiciary system comprising customary and statute law was retained after Independence, albeit with some modification. Tribal authorities presiding over customary courts hear tribal disputes and minor criminal cases, while more serious criminal cases and appeals revert to a magistrates court.

11. The proposal included ranching development in the Western State Lands, a system of growing out and finishing ranches for cattle produced by 'traditional' farmers, assistance to Karakul sheep farmers in the extreme southwest at Bokspits, and a marketing facility for the stockholders of the northwest.

12. Right and title to Tribal Land and water are vested in the Land Boards "in trust for the benefit and advantage of tribesmen of that area and for the purpose of promoting the economic and social development of all the peoples of Botswana" (Tribal Land Act [Cap. 32:02]. *Laws of Botswana.* 1968, amended 1970).

13. C. Colclough and S. McCarthy (1980:236) estimate that some three thousand boreholes were drilled in the ten years following Independence, representing "the single largest productive investment related to the agricultural sector during the period—apart from the natural growth of the cattle herd."

14. The policy is, however, cast in economic terms: "control over private boreholes has given a minority of wealthy individuals what in effect amounts to exclusive use of particular areas of grazing at no cost" (Republic of Botswana, *White Paper No. 1: Rural Development in Botswana,* Gaborone: Government Printer, 1972, p. 7). A close reading of the document reveals that these large cattle owners had little cause to worry as they were to be the prime beneficiaries of Government policy (see below).

15. I am following J. Rousseau's elucidation of the estate-system concept in the analysis of systems of stratification: "An estate system . . . is a form of social stratification in which the strata are jurally defined, and where strata present a significant homology with the system of relations of production. The ideology of the system legitimizes inequality and contributes to the secure position of the dominant estate(s). Estates form part of the political structure. Unlike castes, estates are categories, not groups." J. Rousseau, "On Estates and Castes," *Dialectical Anthropology,* 3(1978), p. 87.

16. The last remnants of the pre-colonial system are now giving way to the 'rationale' of free-market agriculture enterprise; poor households with few or no cattle that typically are short of labour are moving permanently to lands where they can supervise livestock and therefore plough more efficiently. Unable to compete with more highly capitalized producers, and unable to bear the rising costs of transport and marketing, they are compelled to consume their produce directly at the lands, or not to farm at all. See R. Silitschena in Botswana Notes and Records No. 10, "Notes on Some Characteristics of the Population that has Migrated permanently to the Lands in Kweneng District."

References

Carty, R. and V. Smith 1981 *Perpetuating Poverty: The Political Economy of Canadian Foreign Aid.* Toronto: Between the Lines.

Chambers, R. and D. Feldman 1973 *Report on Rural Development.* Gaborone: Government Printer.

Cliffe, L. and R. Moorsom 1979 "Rural Class Formation and Ecological Collapse in Botswana." *Review of African Political Economy.* Vol. 15/16.

Colclough, C. and S. McCarthy 1980 *The Political Economy of Botswana: A Study in Growth and Distribution.* Oxford: Oxford University Press.

Comaroff, J.L. and S. Roberts 1981 *Rules and Processes: The Cultural Logic of Dispute in an African Context.* Chicago: University of Chicago Press.

Dahl, G. 1981 "Production in Pastoral Systems," in J. Galaty, D. Aronson, P.C. Salzman, and A. Chouinard (eds.). *The Future of Pastoral Peoples.* Ottawa: International Development Research Centre.

Government of Botswana 1970 *Our National Development Plan.* Gaborone: Ministry of Finance and Development Planning.

Hart, J.K. 1982 "On Commoditization," in E.N. Goody (ed.), *From Craft to Industry: The Ethnography of Proto Industrial Cloth Production.* Cambridge: Cambridge University Press.

Hartland-Thunberg, P. 1977 *Botswana: An African Growth Economy.* Boulder, Colorado: Westview Press.

Jones, D. 1977 *Aid and Development in Southern Africa: British Aid to Botswana, Lesotho, and Swaziland.* London: Croom Helm.

1980 "Botswana: Economy," in *Africa South of the Sahara 1980-81.* London: Europa Press.

Khama, S. 1971 "Traditional Attitudes to Land and Management of Property," in R. Barrett et al. (eds.) *Proceedings of the Conference on Sustained Production from Semi-Arid Areas.* Special Edition No. 1, *Botswana Notes and Records.*

Konzcacki, Z.A. 1978 *The Economics of Pastoralism: A Case Study of Sub-Saharan Africa*. London: Frank Cass and Co.

Makgatla, N.S. 1982 "Finance and Development: The Case of Botswana," *Journal of Modern African Studies*. Vol. 20, No. 1.

Massey, D. 1980 "The Development of a Labour Reserve: The Impact of Colonial Rule on Botswana," *Working Paper No. 34*. African Studies Center, Boston University.

Odell, M.L. and M.J. Odell 1980 "The Evolution of a Strategy for Livestock Development in the Communal Areas of Botswana," *Pastoral Network Paper 10-B*. London: Overseas Development Institute.

Parson, J. 1981 "Cattle, Class, and the State in Rural Botswana," *The Journal of Southern African Studies*. April.

Parsons, N. 1977 "The Economic History of Khama's Country in Botswana, 1844–1930," in R. Palmer and N. Parsons (eds.) *The Roots of Rural Poverty in Central and Southern Africa*. Berkeley: University of California Press.

Picard, L.A. 1979 "Rural Development in Botswana: Administrative Structures and Public Policy," *The Journal of Development Studies*. Vol. 13.

1981 "Independent Botswana: The District Administration and Political Control," *Journal of African Studies*. Vol. 8, No. 3.

Roe, E. 1980 "Development of Livestock, Agriculture and Water Supplies in Eastern Botswana before Independence: A Short History and Political Analysis," *Occasional Papers*. No. 10. Ithaca: Rural Development Committee, Cornell University.

Rousseau, J. 1978 "On Estates and Castes," *Dialectical Anthropology*. Vol. 3.

Sandford, S. 1981 "Keeping an Eye on TGLP," *Working Paper No. 31*. National Institute of Research, University College of Botswana at Gaborone.

Schapera, I. 1940 "The Political Organization of the Ngwato of Bechuanaland Protectorate," in M. Fortes and E.E. Evans-Pritchard (eds.) *African Political Systems*. London: Oxford University Press.

1943 *Native Land Tenure in the Bechuanaland Protectorate*. South Africa: Lovedale Press.

1953 *The Tswana*. London: International African Institute.

1955 *A Handbook of Tswana Law and Custom*. London: Oxford University Press.

Soloway, J. 1980 *People, Cattle, and Drought in Western Kweneng District*. Gaborone: Ministry of Agriculture.

Spray, P. 1981 "Botswana as a Beef Exporter," *Working Paper No. 37*. National Institute of Development and Cultural Research. Gaborone: University College of Botswana.

Temane, B.K. 1977 "The Case of Botswana." Paper presented to seminar on Land Tenure. Madison, Wisconsin: Land Tenure Center.

Walker, J.M. 1968 "Malete Contract Law," *Botswana Notes and Records*. Vol. 1.

INDEX

Abu Gemai (Sudan), 89
Abyei People's Development Organization, 89–92. *See also* Abyei Rural Development Project
Abyei Rural Development Project, 4, 38
  controversies and conflicts, 85–88, 100
  major participants, 86–87
  ox plow crisis, 92–94
  political origins, 88–89
  village cooperatives, 94–99
Accelerated Mahaveli Development Programme, 65. *See also* Mahaveli Dam Project
Adleman, Irma, 77
AEA. *See* Association of Amazon Entrepreneurs
Afars, 92
Africa, 7
  class relations, 85, 91, 120, 124
  colonial period, 31–32
  local development projects, 2, 85, 94–95, 99–101
  pastoralists, 16, 31, 36, 46
  See also Eastern Africa; *names of specific countries*
Agrarian systems and agricultural communities, 105–110, 125
  commercialization failures, 53–55
  See also Peasantry and peasants
Ahluwalia, Montek S., 17
"AID to Traditional Agriculture," 89
Altamira (Brazil), 144
Amazon (Brazil), 143, 146
  colonization, 138–140, 151
  migration processes, 137–140, 148
  private enterprise initiatives, 137–139, 148–149
  state development strategy, 3, 136–141, 150
  See also Brazil
American AID. *See* United States Agency for International Development
Ancy, G., 127
Andhra Pradesh (India), 19
Animal husbandry, 50
Araguaia River, 141, 144
Arid-semi-arid-land program (ASAL), 38
Ariyaratne, A. T., 69, 73, 78–79
Articulation, 120, 127–129, 176
Arusha (Tanzania), 41
ASAL. *See* Arid-semi-arid-land program
Asia, 7, 10, 27, 31, 64. *See also names of specific countries*

Association of Amazon Entrepreneurs (AEA), 137, 139, 149
Autorité des Aménagements des Vallées des Volta (AVV), 2, 119–124
AVV. *See* Autorité des Aménagements des Vallées des Volta

Baggara Arabs, 37, 91
Baker, Randall, 44
Bandaranaike, Sirimavo, 62
Bandyopadhyay, Suraj, 20
Banfora (Upper Volta), 126
Bank of Amazonas, 2, 137
Bara, 86
Basic Christian Communities, 3
Baxter, P.T.W., 34
BDP. *See* Botswana Democratic Party
Bechuanaland Protectorate, 158, 161–163, 170–175. *See also* Botswana
Bengal (India), 109, 113
Bernstein, H., 128
Béteille, André, 19, 113
Bhalla, G. S., 17
Bihar (India), 18, 109
Blackfly control, 122
Blue Nile (Sudan), 38, 89
Blue Nile project, 89
Bobo Dioulasso (Upper Volta), 126
Boers, 170
Boer War, 171
Boran, 34
Borana, 40
Borehole technology, 165, 174, 176
Botswana
  class formation and relations, 157, 161, 166–167, 170, 175–177
  colonial period, 158–162, 170–176
  drought, 158, 160–162, 165, 171
  economy, 159–160
  livestock production, 6, 155–156, 159–161, 167–168
  pastoralists, 39–40
  state development strategy, 6, 8, 155–162, 165–170, 175–177
  tribal concerns, 6, 156, 160–165, 167–168
  water resources, 161–162, 165, 174
Botswana Commerical Farming Areas, 168
Botswana Communal Grazing Areas, 168
Botswana Democratic Party (BDP), 160, 162–165, 174
Botswana Grazing Land Policy (1975), 166

ecological zones, 119, 125–126
migration processes, 124, 126–127
simple reproduction "squeeze," 128–129
state development role, 1–2, 5, 8–9, 128–129
Upward divergence, defined, 17
USAID. *See* United States Agency for
    International Development
Uttar Pradesh (India), 17–18, 109–110

Volta River, 120–122
Von Eschen, Donald, 17, 20

Waller, R., 47
Wallerstein, I., 123
Washington AID. *See* United States Agency for
    International Development
Water resources, 34, 47, 161–162, 165, 174,
    176. *See also* India, irrigation frontiers

West Africa, 9, 36, 120. *See also* Africa
West Bengal (India), 20, 112–113
Wet cultivation technological regimes, 14–26,
    109–116
Widstrand, C., 44–45
Witwatersrand gold mines, 172
Wolpe, H., 120
World Bank, 3, 25
    basic needs approach, 45
    Botswana program, 159, 164
    eastern Africa program, 52–53
    Sarvodaya program, 72
    Sri Lanka program, 65, 67
World Health Organization, 122

Xinguara (Brazil), 143–144, 148
Xingu River, 141, 144, 149